Every Child, Every Classroom, Every Day

School Leaders Who Are Making Equity a Reality

EDITED BY

ROBERT S. PETERKIN

DEBORAH JEWELL-SHERMAN

LAURA KELLEY

LESLIE BOOZER

JOSSEY-BASS
A Wiley Imprint
www.josseybass.com

Published by Jossey-Bass

A Wiley Imprint
989 Market Street, San Francisco, CA 94103–1741—www.josseybass.com

Jossey-Bass books and products are available through most bookstores. To contact Jossey-Bass directly call our Customer Care Department within the U.S. at 800-956-7739, outside the U.S. at 317-572-3986, or fax 317-572-4002.

Jossey-Bass also publishes its books in a variety of electronic formats. Some content that appears in print may not be available in electronic books.

Library of Congress Cataloging-in-Publication Data
Every child, every classroom, every day: school leaders who are making equity a reality / Robert Peterkin ... [et al.].
p. cm.
Includes bibliographical references and index.
ISBN 978-0-470-65176-6 (hardback); ISBN 978-1-118-03701-0 (ebk.);
ISBN 978-1-118-03702-7 (ebk.); ISBN 978-1-118-03703-4 (ebk.)
1. School superintendents—United States. 2. School management and organization—United States. 3. Educational leadership—United States. I. Peterkin, Robert, 1945-
LB2831.72.E94 2011
371.2′011—dc22

2010047346

Printed in the United States of America
FIRST EDITION
HB Printing 10 9 8 7 6 5 4 3 2 1

This book is dedicated to the public schoolchildren of the nation. Every child deserves committed, effective, and caring teachers and school leaders in every classroom, every day.

At first people refuse to believe that a strange new thing can be done. Then they begin to hope it can be done. Then they see it can be done. Then it is done and all the world wonders why it was not done centuries ago.

—Frances Eliza Hodgson Burnett, 1829–1924
American author and playwright

ABOUT THE AASA, *EDUCATION WEEK*, AND EDUCATION WEEK PRESS

The American Association of School Administrators (AASA), founded in 1865, is the professional organization for more than thirteen thousand educational leaders across the United States and throughout the world. AASA's mission is to support and develop effective school system leaders who are dedicated to the highest quality public education for all children. For more information, please visit www.aasa.org.

Education Week is the nation's premier independent news source for K–12 education. Commonly referred to as "American Education's Newspaper of Record," the nonprofit newspaper has kept educators and policymakers abreast of important developments in schools for three decades. *Education Week* boasts a staff of some twenty-five reporters, editors, and contributing writers, each and every one an expert in the complicated world of covering education. Increasingly, *Education Week* is focusing on coverage that seeks to help policymakers and practitioners identify "what works," promising strategies, and model programs.

Education Week Press is one arm of Editorial Projects in Education (EPE), an independent, nonprofit corporation dedicated to elevating the level of discourse on U.S. K–12 education and best known as the publisher of *Education Week*. EPE is also the home of Education Week Teacher, the *Teacher PD Sourcebook*, TopSchoolJobs.org, *Digital Directions*, and the EPE Research Center, which partners with *Education Week* to produce the highly acclaimed *Quality Counts*, *Technology Counts*, and *Diplomas Count* reports. EPE's Web site, edweek.org, is an award-winning source of up-to the-minute news, information, and resources for educators, as well as in-depth research on issues pre-K–12. EPE also hosts Education Week Leadership Forums, webinars, and other live and virtual events.

CONTENTS

CD CONTENTS

Teaching Notes and Exhibits
Created by Rebecca A. Thessin

PREFACE

The Superintendent of Learning: A New Way of Leading School Systems

Paul D. Houston

The role of urban superintendent has changed over time, and has become one of great complexity and stress. The role now sometimes involves needing to do the impossible and to do it quickly, as the tenure of urban superintendents has shortened to an average of about three years. Jonathan Kozol, who has written eloquently on the plight of poor children, once commented that the urban superintendent's role was one of "mediating injustice." In essence it became a job of educational triage in a volatile and pressured environment. It is no wonder it has become increasingly difficult to find adequate numbers of highly qualified leaders for this position. By the late 1980s most city systems were made up of primarily poor and minority students, yet most urban superintendents were still white males. There was a need for more minority leaders and better leaders of any ethnicity to take the helm of urban schools.

It was under this set of conditions that the Harvard Graduate School of Education began the Urban Superintendents Program (USP) in 1990. This program was designed to prepare leaders who could survive and thrive in these difficult settings. USP placed particular emphasis on finding more women and minority leaders who would receive the benefits of a Harvard doctoral program and the credentials of such an experience so they could step into the void.

I have served as an advisor to the program for its entire twenty-year existence. I was an urban superintendent myself at the beginning of the program, as were the other members of the advisory committee. Much of our emphasis was on helping Harvard give the students the experience we felt we had not had to prepare us for this most difficult challenge. We made certain that they emerged not just with the theoretical framework to make a difference but also with the practical skills necessary to make change happen. The key was blending theory with practice. Most superintendent preparation programs tended to lean heavily toward one or the other. The Urban Superintendents Program combined and balanced them. For example, most of us had to learn how to deal with the media as a part of our "on-the-job" training. That is a pretty high-stakes proposition because in a volatile and highly visible environment, a small misstep with the media could spell career disaster. So media training became a part of the program. Students learned the theories underlying good public communications and were given practice in applying these.

But as with any group of highly experienced professionals, what we knew from our own experience might obscure what we might know about what was just around the corner. And none of us saw what was about to happen to public education in the next twenty years. It was Harvard's ability to navigate this white water of change that allowed the program to flourish.

First and foremost, the nation's expectations for public education were about to shift dramatically. We had been operating in a system that was focused on equal access to education. Most of the history of the last half of the twentieth century was about making schools accessible to all. From *Brown* v. *Board of Education* to Title IX, the role of schools had been to provide a place at the learning table for everyone. And by the 1990s that had largely been achieved. Anyone who wanted an education had access to it. But there was growing recognition that although there were seats at the table, not all plates held the same high-quality food. Further and even more important, it was no longer enough to simply offer a place to learn; everyone needed to learn at high levels. We had moved from an expectation of "universal access" to one of "universal proficiency and universal outcomes." As the title of this book indicates, it was an expectation for every child, every classroom, and every day. This called for a very different kind of education and a different kind of leader.

The fundamental problem leaders face is that the current system is perfectly designed to yield the results we are getting. If we are unhappy with the results, which almost everyone is, then it calls for a very different kind of design—and that becomes the leadership challenge for the twenty-first century. Urban leaders have to be able to face the challenges of a lack of resources; the intractable problems of race and poverty; a chaotic governance structure; and the multiple pulls of teachers, parents, and community, all while finding brand-new ways of educating all children to high levels of performance. That became the work of the Urban Superintendents Program.

The role of superintendent has historically been one in which you could be successful if you were good at dealing with what I call the "Killer B's." These were such things as buildings, budgets, buses, books, bonds, and boards. Today you have to be master of the "C's," collaboration, communication, community building, and, most important, curriculum improvement. A major focus of USP has been on teaching and learning, which is the core of the last C. The superintendent of early days had lots of inherent authority. Today, although accountability is centered on the superintendent, her authority is dispersed across the district. This calls for a leader who can bring people together, convince them of what is needed, and create the conditions to make it happen. But the bottom line of the work has to be the student and what happens to the student in the classroom.

When I became a superintendent, I entered the position from the role of assistant superintendent for curriculum and instruction. That was a rather unusual path. Superintendents in the 1970s were considered managers, and their expertise was more business-oriented. What happened in the classroom was someone else's business. It is now pretty clear that if you are to make a difference in the life of each child every day, as the leader of the system you have to be knowledgeable about and driven by what happens in the classroom. Leaders today have to be centered on teaching and learning.

One of the things I have admired about USP is its emphasis on creating a passion for the work and making certain that the leaders who emerge from the program select others who share that passion. Again, when I came up as superintendent I was expected to be competent, but not passionate about the work. In the context of today's environment, however, if you are not passionate or driven by that passion to create more successful learning environments for children, you will not make the difference that is so necessary in urban schools. This pursuit of passion and excellence is at the core of the work of urban school leaders. The focus of the work of USP is to help channel that passion into productive work for children. But passion is not enough. You also need the various skills required of a leader. It is like driving a car: you have to know the rules of the road, the basics of driving, and so on, but if you don't have fuel in the car and a sense of destination, the driving skills are useless. A commitment to equitable learning excellence and a passion to see students find their potential are the fuel for a good urban superintendent.

The emergence of No Child Left Behind (NCLB) in 2001 and the whole "accountability" movement that surrounds it have changed the superintendency as well. Today it is all about results, and much of those center on test scores. Leaders today are required to be data driven and to understand how students are assessed. The thing that separates the good leaders from the others is their understanding of how to calibrate this within the broader issues of teaching and learning. Adequate superintendents make certain that their districts are focused on assessment. Great ones make certain that their districts are focused on learning excellence, of which assessment is one part. President George W. Bush, who pushed for NCLB and saw it into law, was fond of talking about the "soft bigotry of low expectations" to describe the system that didn't expect enough from low-income children. Worrying about this implied bigotry of low expectations is indeed important. It is key that all students are expected to learn at high levels. However, it is also true that great superintendents know there is a "hard" bigotry to high expectations without adequate resources. They will push not just for higher test scores but also for creating the conditions and generating the resources that will allow good learning to take place, producing improved outcomes for children.

Superintendents today also face external competition for students. Some of this comes in the form of vouchers in a few cities where parents can take their money and send their children to private schools. Other types of competition come from the dramatic growth of charter schools and homeschooling. Despite the inherent differences in the various models, urban superintendents must find ways of meeting and exceeding their competition.

Today the most pervasive reform idea has been the competition created by charter schools. These can be public or private schools that operate outside the school system. They are growing in number nationally, and although some are quite good and stand as models for improvement, others are opportunistic and merely siphon off precious resources to schools outside the system. Urban leaders face a double-edged sword with charters. On the one side, they must contend with the unfavorable comparisons made between the good charters and the products of public education. On the other, they face getting students back from ineffective or corrupt charters at which the children have not been given adequate learning opportunities, or at which the state aid has been already siphoned off and is unavailable to educate these returning children. This competitive environment is a new challenge for school leaders and was hardly on the horizon in the late 1980s when USP came into existence.

There is another kind of "competition" that has direct relevance to urban leaders, and that is the competition for the job as a significant number of urban districts have opted for "nontraditional" leaders. This was almost unknown at the start of USP, but today New York, Chicago, Los Angeles, San Diego, New Orleans, Philadelphia, Seattle, Washington DC, and many others have or have had nontraditional superintendents. In fact, the secretaries of education in two of these states were former superintendents who had gotten into that role via nontraditional paths. The trend started in the early 1990s with the appointment of John Stanford as superintendent of the Seattle schools. Stanford had been an army general and a city manager prior to becoming a superintendent. He proved to be effective, particularly as a leader of community involvement, and many boards started asking themselves, "Where can WE get a general?"

Today one of the most visible superintendent preparation programs is run by the Broad Foundation and focuses on recruiting nontraditional leaders into the superintendency. Meanwhile, the jury is still out on this as a model for creating great leaders. Some of the nontraditional leaders, like Stanford, have been quite successful. Others have not. Washington DC also had a general, who only lasted about eighteen months, proving that not every general makes a good superintendent. This trend toward nontraditional superintendents was driven in part by the dissatisfaction with current leaders and the belief that someone else could surely do it better. Other motivation has come from the shallowness of the candidate pool facing urban boards, with the inclusion of nontraditional candidates offering different prospects.

The real issue here is not one of traditional or nontraditional experience. Instead, the real issue boils down to leadership and the dangers of amateur leadership. A superintendent's lack of experience and perspective on the issues of teaching and learning is particularly problematic at a time when an entire nation places a premium on the classroom. The difference between professionals and amateurs is that amateurs lack an appreciation for the complexity of the work. It is true that many traditional superintendents come to the role with a minimum of managerial experience, but it is also true that nontraditional superintendents often come with a lack of appreciation for the political quagmire that is public education, and with a very superficial understanding of what really goes on in a classroom. I once kidded John Stanford that he had ruined the superintendency because now everyone was going to want a general. He laughed and said if he had been a successful superintendent it wasn't because he was a general, it was in spite of it. He was an amateur who had an appreciation for the professional. In fact, he hired Arlene Ackerman as his chief academic officer precisely because she knew instruction and he didn't, and he empowered her to do her job. (Arlene, a graduate of USP, went on to successful superintendencies in Washington DC, San Francisco, and Philadelphia.) Where this kind of nontraditional superintendent will ultimately end up is unknown. What is clear is that the advent of the nontraditional superintendent has changed the face of the urban superintendency. The irony of USP is that its intense focus on teaching and learning and its support of understanding the political landscape make it a nontraditional preparation program. Most traditional preparation programs lack this intensity, and most nontraditional candidates lack the experience and training required for today's emphasis on teaching and learning.

The style and philosophy of the superintendent of the future will be very different from those of the past. I have suggested that we need to stop thinking of the "superintendent of schools" and begin thinking of the "superintendent of learning." With the growing ubiquity of technology and with the multiple pressures on the role of superintendent, the superintendency really will not be about a place called "school" or a system of schools—it will be about seeing that children learn, regardless of the conditions or the setting. This will require a superintendent who can create connections and relate to the community in new and more creative ways. It will not be about "protecting" the system, it will be about defending the faith—the essence of what learning is about. Superintendents will have to be the advocates for children in the broader world. They have the gift of perspective, and this perspective is crucial in helping others see what is at stake.

We will need leaders who are ethical and capable of seeing the broad view. They will not have much need of the skills of a CEO, because in education one person does not have that kind of power. Superintendents will have to be able to convene the players and persuade them to do what is right for children. That means it will not be so much of a job as a calling. Leaders will need the zeal of missionaries, the flexibility to adjust in changing environments, and the will to see it happen. The superintendents described in this book not only are trailblazing new means in their pursuit of equity for all children but also are effectively changing the landscape of what is expected of urban school systems today. Looking through the lens of the leadership framework to which the leaders in this book subscribe, and bearing in mind their skills and expertise, passion, and commitment to children, we can actually see the personal and strategic aspects of the superintendency in the context of today's developing age of accountability and demands of global economy.

ACKNOWLEDGMENTS

We recognize that being an urban superintendent is one of the hardest jobs in America today. Despite the tremendous pressures on their time, Arlene Ackerman, Andrés Alonso, Meria Joel Carstarphen, Rudy Crew, Maria Goodloe-Johnson, Beverly Hall, Deborah Jewell-Sherman, and Chris Steinhauser generously allowed us access into their school districts and shared their practice—the triumphs and the challenges. We are deeply indebted to the students, families, teachers, administrators, and board members in their districts for letting us study and write about their work as they strive to improve student achievement for all.

This book would not have been possible without the guidance and support of the Urban Superintendents Program (USP) Advisory Panel and mentor superintendents, including the many who served as book contributors and subjects of the case studies. Although the individuals who have been a part of the USP network are too many to name, we thank each of them for their endless support, mentorship, and commitment to excellence in education. Their generosity of thought and feedback, from the proposal to the final stages of the book, has increased the value of the lessons shared between its covers.

Special thanks to Linda Wing, USP's codirector for fourteen years. Linda's commitment to the education of the "head, hands, and heart" of every child, every classroom, every day gave focus to USP's mission for social justice and equity. Her insistence on rigor in the development of USP's leadership approach is found in each of the cases in this book.

USP's sponsors enabled the directors of the program to develop this new approach to leadership preparation. With assistance from the Stevens Trust, Ford Foundation, Pew Trust, GE Foundation, and Coca-Cola Foundation, USP was able to demonstrate a commitment to the ideals and reality of diverse leadership in support of educational equality for all children. Without their assistance, neither the program nor this book would exist.

We also thank the USP support and instructional staff members for providing the necessary assistance for the program and for the book project, including working night and day, weekends, and vacations. They are Janice Barclay, Lisa Betty, Jeannette Binjour-Lee, James Lucey, Eileen McGowan, and Amanda Scobie. In addition to this dedicated group, we thank the professors of USP students at the Harvard Graduate School of Education (HGSE), many of whom introduce the case studies. They have taught USPers everything from finance to politics to instruction, developing them into practitioner-scholars with the skills to improve educational outcomes for students. Their support in class and beyond has helped prepare a generation of school leaders who are serving the best interests of all children. A special thanks to our vision coach extraordinaire, Holly Weeks—without her guidance and attention, the proposal for this book would never have been completed. She taught us to see beyond the many moving parts and envision the whole.

We thank the numerous HGSE staff and the doctoral and master's students who gave us support along the way, particularly Ashton Wheeler Clemmons, Tara Czupryk, Mitalene Fletcher, Amy Fowler, Steven Harris, Nithin Iyengar, Stephen Hyde, Julianna Kershen, Richard Murnane, John Roberts, Kath Smith, and Joseph Zolner. We owe special gratitude to Rebecca Thessin, our incredible exhibit creator. Her countless hours tracking down data and creating visuals for our book made our cases more accessible and understandable, and her careful eye and thorough research put finishing touches on all of them.

Finally, we'd like to thank our families and close friends for their love and support throughout our travels and hours spent writing, editing, and revising. Special thanks to Louise Peterkin, Cornelius Sherman, Curtis Jewell, Donna Bryan, Earl and Elaine Kelley, Kenneth Kelley, Paige Stratton, Lesley Edmond, Dennis and Ella Anne Boozer, Andrea Boozer, Susan and Doug Daniel, Christine Altomari, and Ayesha Brooks. They are the reason we are able to give our all to students, to districts, and to teaching and learning.

CHAPTER 1

The Urban Superintendents Program Leadership Framework

Larry Leverett

Quite a few years ago I came across an alarmingly true-to-life fable recounting how generations of "wise men and women" talked, debated, argued, and, ultimately, could not agree on how to solve the problems confronting the education of their children (Bushkin, 1969). One day the "wise men and women" faced their failure as they looked upon countless children grown up in a system of mis-education—their faces showing anger, frustration, and hopelessness. The failure of the not so "wise men and women" to act boldly resulted in tragic suffering across their land, in communities of every size and all demographics.

Unlike the "wise men and women" of yesteryear, we have the tools and knowledge needed to dramatically change schools so that all of our children can be guaranteed the opportunity to succeed in school and life. The Urban Superintendents Program (USP) Leadership Framework is among the tools available to equip the "wiser men and women" of our time with a comprehensive model for systemic improvement of outcomes for all learners. It is a tool that is action- and solution-oriented, elegant in its thoroughness, and strategic in design; a tool that informs comprehensive action for approaching the complex challenges of excellence and equity.

There have been many frameworks developed to inform the field of urban education over the past several decades. Many of them are well researched and thoughtfully developed and have been used with varying degrees of success. There is no shortage of frameworks for policymakers and practitioners to adopt and adapt to guide their journey toward eliminating the pernicious achievement gaps that exist in urban, suburban, and rural schools. *Every Child, Every Classroom, Every Day* provides practitioners in varied roles with a leadership framework and authentic examples of superintendents who are acting boldly to demonstrate that schools can effectively improve outcomes for all students—regardless of race or socioeconomic status. The uniqueness of the USP Leadership Framework is its voluntary ownership by a community of men and women who have shaped the framework's core values and principles, and who have embraced the framework components to guide their whole-system change so as to ensure equity and excellence for every student in their charge.

The USP Leadership Framework, as an interdependent, nested construct, provides a comprehensive approach for leading and managing system-wide efforts to improve academic outcomes; foster collaboration across all stakeholders; pursue aggressive actions to plan, implement, and sustain an aligned, coherent focus on the improvement of the instructional core; and support accountability systems that are reciprocal and consistently applied across the entire school district organization. The framework itself is the result of collaborative learning and research over the past twenty years that has engaged superintendents, policymakers, practitioners, researchers, reformers, and doctoral students. It is informed by theory, applied research, evidence-based best practices, and the literature on leadership and management.

To illustrate the framework in practice, this book includes descriptive case studies of superintendents and school districts that have positively influenced teaching and learning, leadership and management, collaborative efforts, resource allocation, politics, state and federal accountability mandates, and the supports to address school and nonschool factors affecting student performance. The case studies of superintendents and the portraits of their demanding circumstances detail approaches to overcoming challenges that have application from the boardroom to the classroom. The school districts featured in *Every Child, Every Classroom, Every Day* exemplify the context-specific application of the USP Leadership Framework as a resource for giving direction in the areas of leadership, equity, instruction, collaboration, governance, resource allocation, and accountability.

The book is not necessarily intended to be read from cover to cover. You will, however, gain a more nuanced understanding of the various components of leadership and their interconnectedness by reading the book in its entirety. The book is designed to be a resource for superintendents, principals, central office staff, board members, aspirant leaders, and others to examine the application of the components of the USP Leadership Framework to their work. For example, sitting superintendents making decisions about reform can read the book with their senior leadership teams to learn from their contemporaries, examine and push their own work forward, and devise new plans for improvement. A principal with a handful of high-quality, effective teachers determined to scale up the intermittent success in his school can learn how collaborative leadership focused on instruction could enhance overall teaching and learning. Teachers committed to increasing family engagement in their school can examine the leadership and lessons learned from superintendents' communication and community engagement plans.

The above are only a few of the ways the book can be used. The intent of the contributors is to provide useful information that illuminates how transformation-oriented school districts and leaders have applied the framework as a means to tackle a variety of issues and challenges. By focusing on real work and authentic circumstances, this book provides access to not only the tactical and strategic thinking behind the actions of effective school district leaders but also the high-leverage strategies they selected to improve learner outcomes and increase effectiveness of district operations. The USP Leadership Framework represents a touchstone for readers interested in rethinking the comprehensiveness of their own district transformation efforts.

Every Child, Every Classroom, Every Day offers readers detailed explorations of superintendents who are operating within a belief system that is based on high levels of student achievement in challenging content. The rich portraits center on superintendents in districts of varying sizes, demographics, geographic regions, governance structures, and levels of financial support. Equity, instructional focus, politics, resource allocation, accountability, and community engagement are common themes that are reiterated across the district portraits. Each case study is preceded by the perspective of an expert with extensive background in the USP Leadership Framework components highlighted in the case study. The cases transparently present the unique challenges, issues, and opportunities superintendents face. You will quickly understand that there is no "one-size-fits all" strategic approach that can be easily transplanted from one place to another. Context does matter, and responses to context are important to consider in designing your district's change strategy. Each case study is thus followed by a reflection from a practicing leader, usually a sitting superintendent, who discusses how the work looks different in his or her context. Regardless of circumstances, an unequivocal commitment to the vision of excellence and equity across a community's entire student body is nonnegotiable. These core beliefs are embedded throughout the USP Leadership Framework.

As you engage with the rich teaching cases of superintendents and school districts featured in this book, you inevitably will examine your own practice, gaining deeper insights that will challenge you to determine your role in the improvement of district effectiveness. The emphasis of the book is on the urban superintendency; however, we believe that the cases presented have relevance to superintendents in all types of districts, as well as school board members, central office staff, school-level staff and administrators, or graduate students preparing for leadership roles at the school or district level. The USP Leadership Framework is a useful construct whether you are at the emerging, early, or mid-career stage, or engaged in the entry or exit phase of a superintendency. In a field that suffers from whiplash-like exposure to ideas, solutions, fads, and regulations, the USP Leadership Framework will persist through the actions of leaders at different career stages who passionately embrace the framework's values and principles and adapt it to their own theories of change (Institute for Research and Reform in Education and Aspen Institute Roundtable for Comprehensive Community Initiatives, 2000).

FRAMEWORK OVERVIEW

The instructional core is the heart of the USP Leadership Framework. As Richard Elmore and others have shouted from the rooftops of public education and in their book, *Instructional Rounds in Education* (City, Elmore, Fiarman, & Teitel, 2009), changes in the effectiveness of the instructional core are the primary lever for increasing student learning and performance. The USP Leadership Framework, with the instructional core as the central focus, informs the development of comprehensive, system-level improvement designs that exist to support improvements at the student and classroom levels. Further, the framework design includes the engagement of a wide cross-section of the school, local community, and leaders at the state and federal levels, all of whom are important to efforts to influence the instructional core. Too often we get bogged down in the politics, the conflicts, and the complexity of leading school districts, and we become detached from the classroom as a central focus of the system's work. Until superintendents and other district leaders accept the instructional core as the central focus of everyone's work, little will change, and the children will continue to wait.

The four core values of the USP Leadership Framework presented in Figure 1.1 are anchored in the belief that the instructional core must be

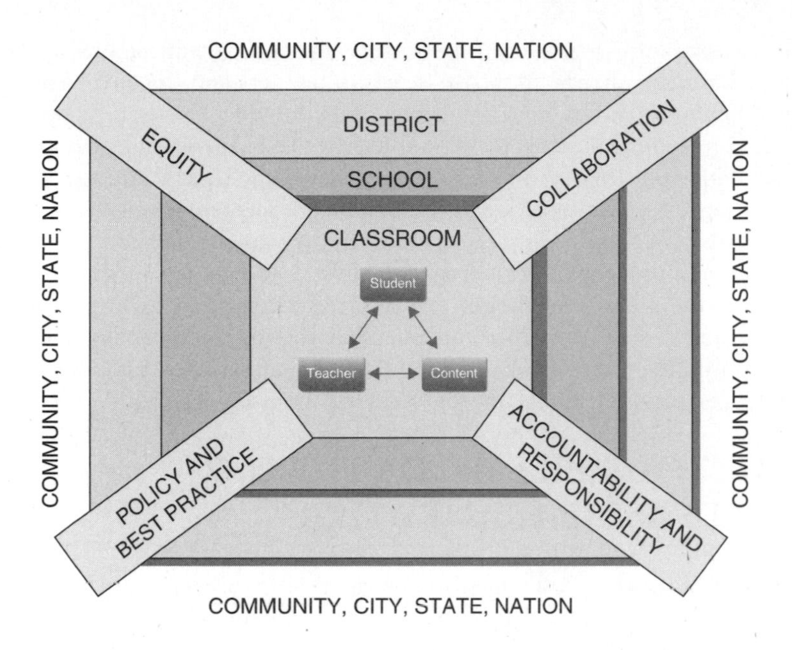

FIGURE 1.1 Urban Superintendents Program Leadership Framework

the central focus for all adults who make decisions that influence the interactions of teachers and students around academic content. School district superintendents must have sound knowledge of the instructional core to lead the system from having isolated classrooms or schools providing effective instruction to system-wide consistency in every classroom for every child. Every decision at the classroom, school, district, community, city, state, or national level must be measured on the value-added scale to enhance the quality of the instructional core and the meaningful engagement of students in schoolwork that will prepare them for positive adult roles. All other efforts amount to little more than window dressing that will have little impact on student dispositions and their acquisition of knowledge and skills.

Focusing whole-system change on the improvement of instructional effectiveness requires that superintendents have an intimate understanding of the instructional core, which comes from deep and consistent observation of teaching and learning. Superintendents need to be engaging with teachers, school-level leaders, board members, and central office staff in conversations that lead to observation and analysis based on an understanding of what constitutes high-quality classroom instruction. As a colleague recently said to me, "You can't lead changes to improve instruction if you don't know how good instruction looks in real classrooms." Without this knowledge, the superintendent and others have limited awareness of the real needs of teachers and students. When instruction is truly at the core, effective superintendents have their sights fixed on alignment across the school district. The superintendent is in the unique position to lead, direct, and manage the change process, and knowing the centrality of the instructional core must increasingly become the basis for accountability for all adults in the school system.

If the improvement of student performance and success in schools and communities is the desired end result of improvement efforts at all organizational levels, then equity, collaboration, accountability, and responsibility; responsive policy; and the deployment of best leadership practices for instructional improvement are necessary means.

THE FOUR PILLARS OF THE USP LEADERSHIP FRAMEWORK

In the USP Leadership Framework, there are four core values and guiding principles—equity, collaboration, accountability, and policy and best practices—that direct every action a superintendent takes and underpin decision making at every level in the district to support the instructional core. Customarily, achievement-oriented leaders might follow three of the four core values and guiding principles, encouraging collaboration both to use best instructional practices and to hold people accountable for the achievement of some of the district's students. But the radical reformers committed to the USP Leadership Framework are also profoundly committed to ensuring equity—for every child, in every classroom, every day. In fact, superintendents committed to this framework pursue equity for all by tearing down silos, infusing best practices, and holding everyone accountable for each and every child's achievement, at times even influencing state and national policy.

Equity

Equity is the heart and soul of the USP Leadership Framework. True equity ensures that all learners, regardless of race, ethnicity, language proficiency, or socioeconomic status, have access to opportunities to be engaged in high-quality instruction and learning environments that prepare them to meet or exceed academic performance expectations. Equitable schools support students' development for full participation in society in family, community, and work settings; and they eliminate barriers to achieving equitable outcomes for all learners. Academic excellence and equity are twin goals within this framework. You can't have one without the other. The pursuit of equity requires the superintendent to be the anywhere-anytime advocate for the equity agenda in the school district and communities. There is no school district role that is better positioned to robustly communicate the equity vision than that of the superintendent.

Each superintendent included in this book models the beliefs and values that are fundamental to the USP Leadership Framework. Collectively they are unified in their belief in the ability of all students to be successful in rigorous academic programs, and they are intolerant of the excuses and alibis that have been used to explain the failure of a district to successfully educate each and every child. The superintendents featured in the case studies have taken on the status quo and used their positions as the bully pulpit from which to persistently place the equity vision before all stakeholders. The case studies in this book illustrate strategies superintendents have used to make equity everybody's business. Whether instructional or noninstructional, no school district employees are exempt from aligning their functions and operations with the equity vision the superintendent advocates.

Atlanta Public Schools superintendent Beverly Hall adopted the balanced scorecard as a system tool to demonstrate transparency in the district's efforts to reduce dropout rates and improve college readiness and success. Every department within Atlanta Public Schools is accountable for specific functions that are constantly monitored and reported to the board and public. Arlene Ackerman, superintendent of the School District of Philadelphia, used school visits on her first day in the district to immediately send her equity message to the community, contrasting well-resourced schools endowed with science labs, adequately stocked libraries, and rigorous instructional programs with other schools that had bathrooms with no doors on stalls, textbook shortages, peeling paint, and other indicators of inadequate conditions and opportunities for students and their teachers. Within just six months she instituted changes in resource allocation and plans to develop a weighted funding formula to further provide differential systems of support for students and their families based on student needs.

Chris Steinhauser, Long Beach Unified School District superintendent, made it clear that it was unacceptable to continue differential access to advanced placement courses that excluded nearly 80 percent of his student population from full participation in rigorous coursework at the high school level. Christine Johns, superintendent in suburban Utica Community Schools in Michigan, collaborated with less-affluent urban districts to provide access for students who were disproportionately denied the quality of education offered in her school system. Every case study and superintendent reflection presented in this book includes discussion of equity approaches used by superintendents to scale up solutions of excellence across, and sometimes even beyond, their school districts.

Collaboration

The belief that superintendents, school boards, district and school administrators, unions, and politicians acting independently of each other can mobilize the moral, political, and organizational will to achieve equity and excellence for all students is uninformed. The archaic, systemic arrangement of all too often adversarial roles acts to hinder, rather than facilitate, the change needed to accomplish important outcomes for our students.

Context matters immensely in shaping the approach to collaboration that will best address the political and governance structures, organizational culture, relationships, collective bargaining history, and influences of race and social class membership in any given place. Each case study includes a discussion of a broad spectrum of strategies to engage important stakeholders in the reform process. Each superintendent shares the context-responsive approach to build support for equity and excellence for all students. In every district discussion, the focus of collaboration is to address conditions that can influence the system's ability to guarantee opportunities for all learners. Inevitably you will also be exposed to the issues and challenges of working through thorny human resource decisions, tough labor negotiations, accountability for implementation of programs and activities identified to improve student performance, and controversial efforts to link compensation to student performance. Collaboration is desirable, but the best interests of students must always dominate the purpose of these efforts. Collaboration on power sharing for adult interests only is not a model that is likely to change access to equity and excellence for our children. Collaboration anchored in a mutual commitment to prepare students for success in their lives must be the chief goal of a partnership across stakeholders and their interests.

Accountability and Responsibility

A commitment to equity requires well-defined accountability strategies in which individuals and district units at all levels are clear about performance targets and responsibilities. The design of accountability strategies must be driven by the system-wide instructional focus and must act to communicate the improvement of student performance as everyone's job, including both instructional and noninstructional personnel. We must move the focus of accountability from federal and state mandates to internally driven accountability systems that have credibility among the people who are expected to meet goals and targets. Contributor Richard Elmore maintains that external accountability must be preceded by internal accountability, which he defines as occurring "when school personnel must share a coherent, explicit set of norms and expectations about what a good school looks like before they can use signals from the outside to improve student learning" (Elmore, 2002, paragraph 12). The reality for many school superintendents is that the further away the source of accountability is from the school, the more irrelevant it is in the classroom. Building commitment to internal accountability is enhanced by active engagement between the school-sites and central office, continuous monitoring of performance, and communications of expectations and results. The superintendents featured in this book have developed context-specific approaches to internal accountability that align with external accountability pressures. In each of the district stories presented here, school leaders have implemented reforms in which expectations, expressed as internal accountability systems, are aligned well with external state and federal requirements.

Policy and Best Practices

More and more educational policies emerging at the state and federal levels are directly affecting school districts, schools, and classrooms. Districts and schools have the hard job of managing the tentacles of external policies to reduce the diffusion of focus on instructional improvement. The case studies of Chris Steinhauser in Long Beach; Rudy Crew in New York and Miami-Dade; and Deborah Jewell-Sherman in Richmond, Virginia, are examples of how superintendents can maintain a laser-like focus on the instructional core while serving the external policy and accountability expectations. Public schools will always live in an external policy context that makes it difficult for district and school leaders to meet such requirements while developing and sustaining a tightly coupled local policy approach that protects the focus on the instructional core.

Finally, *Every Child, Every Classroom, Every Day* contains many examples of best practice strategies and activities that are getting results as measured by student achievement indicators. Elmore's reciprocal accountability at the policy and operational levels is a must to ensure the consistent presence of best practices across all classrooms. The absence of pressure to expect consistent implementation of instructional strategies for which there is strong evidence of a positive impact on student learning is unacceptable. Likewise, it is unacceptable to fail to provide a level of support commensurate with the expected changes of practice.

"All pressure + no support = no change. All support + no pressure = no change." Reciprocal accountability to align the commitments and expectations of the school, district, and board is essential to eliminate alibis and excuses, which prevent every classroom from being a learning environment in which best practices are consistently present for all learners.

OVERVIEW OF *EVERY CHILD, EVERY CLASSROOM, EVERY DAY*

When the editors went about designing the book, they brainstormed the major facets of the work of urban school leaders. Although the superintendency is much too nuanced to be distilled into a few large pieces, they wanted to highlight key areas of the work. Rather than write theoretical pieces, they decided that teaching cases would better illustrate the multifaceted nature of the work. Each case study site was chosen to illustrate particular approaches and practices. For instance, even though Beverly Hall is known for raising student achievement, adopting sound business practices, and working with state and local governments to support her education initiatives, the editors chose to highlight the community engagement portion of her work in Chapter Eight. Naturally, the teaching case only provides you with a glimpse into this complex work and is not intended to tell the entire story. You instead are encouraged to be an active participant, a member of Hall's cabinet. How would you advise her to push forward? What would you change? Then, step out of the scenario and envision how you could take the lessons she has learned and apply them to your personal situation.

By using the case study method, this book gives you the rare opportunity to devise solutions to situations that are steeped in both theory and practice. We hope that you will take the opportunity to discuss each case with your colleagues and fashion an approach that works not only with the facts of the case but also in your context. To assist you on this journey, below is a description of each of the following chapters.

Chapters Two and Eleven offer insight into considerations and strategies of a superintendent's entry and exit, respectively, two important periods in the tenure of a school superintendent. The discussion of entry in Chapter Two examines the challenges facing leaders entering districts in various ways—through promotion from within and from outside; in low-performing districts that are in chaos; and in districts that are high-performing for most but with clear evidence of failure when it comes to students of color, poor students, English language learners, and students with special needs. The entry strategies presented in this chapter range from formalized approaches involving high-powered transition teams and external audits of instruction and operations to more internally driven stakeholder engagement designs that place the superintendent in a listening and learning role. Chapter Eleven focuses on the critical importance of planning for exit, discussing the implications of the various motivations for superintendents to leave school districts, including planned retirement, new job opportunities, political dynamics, or personal reasons.

Holly Weeks begins Chapter Three, Communicating the Vision, with a commentary about a superintendent's core truths and the tools with which she conveys her message for change. The case study shares the experience of Meria Joel Carstarphen, former superintendent of St. Paul Public Schools in Minnesota, who worked to debunk myths about long-ignored major achievement gaps. Superintendent Brian Osborne reflects on his experience of communicating his vision as a contrast to Carstarphen's experience. He offers his perspective on communicating the vision in a more affluent suburban district in which equity for all students and closing performance gaps were not part of the community's conversation or vision prior to his arrival.

In Chapter Four, Strategic Planning, Janice Jackson frames the importance of a unified planning strategy to align the efforts of the many stakeholders who move the school district toward improved student achievement. The case study depicts how Seattle Public Schools superintendent Maria Goodloe-Johnson employed a diverse set of systematic data collection strategies and analyses, used performance management strategies, and commissioned numerous audits examining different aspects of the school system—from operations to curriculum and instruction. The data informed a comprehensive approach to developing the "Excellence for All" plan to accomplish five major system goals. Maree Sneed, a former teacher and school district administrator and current outside counsel to urban districts across the country, shares her perspective as an educator and an attorney about how districts can plan and prepare for change to address instructional, legal, and managerial challenges through deliberate, thoughtful, strategic planning processes.

Chapter Five, Instructional Improvement, examines the imperative for superintendents to provide aggressive leadership that is deliberately and intensely focused on the improvement of instruction for all students. Richard Elmore has deep and extensive knowledge of research, policies, and practices, with much of his own research concentrated on the instructional core—specifically, "the essential interaction between teacher, student, and content that creates the basis of learning" (Blanding, 2009, paragraph 1). The efforts of Deborah Jewell-Sherman in Richmond Public Schools tell the story of radically transforming a low-performing district into one that fostered unprecedented improvements in performance for students historically undereducated in failing schools. Rudy Crew, former chancellor of the 1.1 million students overseen by the New York City Department of Education, provides the reflection on Jewell-Sherman's work. Crew is nationally known for leading some of the nation's largest school districts and for forcefully addressing the problem of underperforming schools by providing differentiated supports in the New York City and Miami-Dade school systems.

Chapter Six, School Boards and Unions, presents the work of Andrés Alonso, chief executive officer of the Baltimore City Public Schools. Susan Moore Johnson opens the chapter by providing expert commentary on organizational change, unions, administrative practice, and management approaches needed to drive higher levels of student performance. Then the case study of Alonso illustrates the complexity of collaborating with governance and the collective bargaining units in school districts of every type and size. The case study highlights his leadership decisions and partnerships with the board of education, city and state governance officials, and the unions. Joshua Starr, superintendent of schools in Stamford, Connecticut, reflects on his efforts to manage the delicate balancing of his governance relationships with a highly politicized, nine-member elected school board, as well as with the board of finance and board of representatives.

Chapter Seven, Realigning Resources, discusses the disciplined alignment of the financial resources of the district to the superintendent's vision for instructional improvement. James Honan explores the work of financial management and aligning resources with organizational mission, two areas of critical importance to the success of the superintendent. In this chapter's case study, Arlene Ackerman, leading the School District of Philadelphia, demonstrates her financial acumen and ability to align resources with a vision of equity for all students. The case study captures Ackerman's short- and long-term strategies for addressing an inherited deficit while establishing a tactical focus for the re-allocation of dollars to follow the needs of students. The reflection by Christine Johns, superintendent of Utica Community Schools, portrays the financial and equity issues in an urban-suburban district eight miles north of Detroit. Utica has a reputation of being a high-performing school district, but not for all students, and Johns outlines the challenges her district faced during the recent economic downturn.

Introducing Chapter Eight, Community Engagement, is Karen Mapp, who calls for school systems to reframe the relationship with parents and communities in urban school districts to assemble an array of resources for raising levels of student performance. The case study of Beverly Hall in Atlanta Public Schools tells the story of the positive benefits of superintendent-led community engagement initiatives to mobilize the school system and its diverse stakeholders around a collective responsibility to improve student achievement. Her community engagements included insiders and outsiders, parents, and CEOs; the mayor and governor; community-based organizations; and a host of social and civic groups. Superintendent of the Boston Public Schools Carol Johnson and her assistant superintendent of family and student engagement Michele Brooks collaborated to share their leadership work of building relationships across diverse cultures and populations, a process used to reconnect the entire community in new and active ways.

Scaling up instructional reforms to ensure that every child has equitable access to opportunities to be successful in a high-quality instructional program is a challenging and elusive goal for superintendents. In Chapter Nine, Scaling Up, scholar and practitioner Robert S. Peterkin maintains that bringing best practices to scale to achieve equity and excellence for every child is the moral responsibility entrusted to the school superintendent. He provides his perspective on the essential components of efforts to scale up high-quality instruction for every child, in every classroom, every day. The case examined in Chapter Nine details how Rudy Crew, a powerful and passionate educational leader, implemented his many-sided approach to leading for learning. His strategy ranged from dismantling corruption to litigation for fiscal adequacy to assumption of personal responsibility for the organizational leadership of the Chancellor's District, which included the most persistently failing schools in New York. Amalia Cudeiro, superintendent of the Bellevue School District in Washington, provides the reflection on scaling up as she describes her efforts to reorganize the smaller district of Bellevue schools to meet persistent performance gaps among students.

Chapter Ten, Sustaining Improvement over Time, focuses on work in the Long Beach Unified School District in California. The twenty years of stable leadership by Carl Cohn and his chosen successor, Chris Steinhauser, present a unique perspective on sustainability. Cohn introduces the chapter, sharing his intimate knowledge of the Long Beach district and the extreme difficulty of replicating its success in San Diego, another testament to the importance of context. Since 2002 Steinhauser has demonstrated his commitment to ensuring every child in Long Beach has access to high-quality instruction and postsecondary opportunities, continuing to improve educational outcomes for all. Pascal Forgione, the ten-year superintendent of the Austin Independent School District in Texas, reflects on Steinhauser's case using his insights into the challenge of sustainability. Sharing successes and proactive strategies for longevity, Forgione compares and contrasts his leadership decision making with that of Cohn and Steinhauser in Long Beach.

The people presented in the cases in *Every Child, Every Classroom, Every Day* might be considered "heroes" with special gifts and talents that are not transferable to the other superintendents who work hard to create the conditions of excellence and equity in their school districts. Actually, I think the featured superintendents are heroic in their courage, core beliefs, and passion to ensure that all students under their charge receive access to high-quality instruction that engages them and spurs their academic growth, but that is not the whole story. The real story rests in their use of proven, research-based strategies that keep the improvement of the instructional core as the preeminent focus of their labor as superintendents. In their body of work, equity; accountability and responsibility; collaboration; and the adaptations of evidenced best practices in leadership, management, instruction, and collaboration at all levels are what become the transferable knowledge represented in the USP Leadership Framework.

Most important, these superintendents engage in the work of leading school districts and communities with a belief in the ability of ALL children to be successful if provided with the right supports and consistent access to high-quality instruction. They bear out the wisdom of Ronald Edmonds, founder of the Effective Schools Movement: "We can, whenever and wherever we choose, successfully teach all children whose schooling is of interest to us" (Edmonds, 1979, p. 23). We know what needs to happen, and we have a growing number of schools and school districts that are achieving success. Karin Chenoweth, in her book *"It's Being Done": Academic Success in Unexpected Schools* (2007), and Katy Haycock and her colleagues at the Education Trust (http://www.edtrust.org/) make the case that many schools and districts are doing what needs to be done. We hope that the knowledge, wisdom, and experiences of the scholars, practitioners, and advocates included in this book supply you with a framework that assists you as you search for policies, practices, theories, and exemplars to guide your work on behalf of the children in your school district. Children have waited too long for action, and we can no longer tolerate the cumulative losses that distribute pain and suffering across our society.

Finally, it is important to remember that the case studies written in this book are intended to be teaching cases, offering lessons of, and insight into, urban school leadership. By providing a window into the worlds of urban superintendents and the thinking behind their decisions, we hope that current and aspiring school leaders will take away ideas and lessons that will inform their own practice. These cases are not intended to serve as endorsements, sources of primary data, or illustrations of effective or ineffective handling of administrative situations. Instead, they are intended to place you in the "head, heart, and hands" of the urban superintendency.

REFERENCES

Blanding, M. (2009). *Treating the "instructional core": Education rounds.* Retrieved April 30, 2009, from www.gse.harvard.edu/blog/uk/2009/05/treating-the-instructional-core-education-rounds.html.

Bushkin, M. (1969, May–June). A fable for our modern wise men. *Newsday*, pp. 8–9.

Chenoweth, K. (2007). *"It's being done": Academic success in unexpected schools.* Cambridge, MA: Harvard Education Press.

City, E., Elmore, R. F., Fiarman, S. E., & Teitel, L. (2009). *Instructional rounds in education: A network approach to improving teaching and learning*. Cambridge, MA: Harvard Education Press.

Edmonds, R. (1979). Effective schools for the urban poor. *Educational Leadership, 37*(1), 15–24

Elmore, R. F. (2002, Spring). Unwarranted intrusion. *Education Next*, *2*(1). Retrieved from http://educationnext.org/unwarranted-intrusion/

Institute for Research and Reform in Education and Aspen Institute Roundtable for Comprehensive Community Initiatives (2000). *The theory of change user's guide for planning and evaluation.* Draft copy.

CHAPTER 2

A Superintendent's Entry

Leslie Boozer

We all remember our first day as a new classroom teacher, fraught with nerves as we look into a sea of eager, sometimes skeptical, faces waiting for us to give direction. Within the first few weeks, some begin testing us to see how easily persuaded we can be—trying to determine our triggers, weaknesses, and routines. In every classroom, there are those who are willing to work hard and please, those who are indifferent to our presence, and those who test us early and often. Not surprisingly, entering a new superintendency is remarkably similar—only the classroom is much larger, and the stakes are even higher.

Bringing high-quality teaching and learning to scale in any school district requires an enormous amount of planning, concentrated effort, and a degree of continuity. In a typical district, the administrative and teaching staff is accustomed to seeing superintendents come and go; the mean tenure for district leaders remaining between five and six years (Glass & Franceschini, 2007). For urban superintendents, the average is even less, a mere three-and-a-half years (Council of the Great City Schools, 2008). With limited time to enact change, planning for entry as a new superintendent is a necessity.

To ascertain the best approach for a new leader's entry, we interviewed over thirty former and current superintendents to learn from their experiences entering new school districts. We also interviewed over seventy-five school board members, union leaders, and central office and school personnel to gain their perspective on a superintendent's entry. From these conversations we learned that how you enter a new position, whether you are a first-time superintendent or a seasoned leader, can determine your success or failure. From the first day in office, superintendents face tough challenges, such as state and local budget crises; divided school boards; mayors fighting for control of their schools; hostile union-management relations; and, most important, significant achievement and opportunity gaps. Superintendents and stakeholders agree—if you fail to plan, you plan to fail.

I GOT THE JOB!—NOW WHAT?

After winning over the search consultants, the board, and often the community, you are chosen for the job. However, in the typical case, proving yourself worthy of leadership has only just begun. It is now time to engage with all district stakeholders, learn more about your new district, and start planning your transition from candidate to superintendent.

"I hope he's different from the last one," Victoria, a frustrated central office employee, noted as she saw the new superintendent walk into the elevator to head up to his office.

Her colleague Peter glanced over and nodded. "They always start off saying how they are going to 'change things,' but no one takes a second to actually ask us what is working. I know our district has a way to go, but come on—I know a lot about what works here and what doesn't."

Victoria replied, "You're right. Sometimes they say they'll listen and work with district insiders, but look what happened last time. The superintendent had a solid plan, but she never seemed to work with those of us who were here before she came. Now we're still here, and she's gone."

"Yeah, and district politics seemed to usurp instruction. All that was in the press was how our superintendent and board couldn't stand each other. No one talked about how schools in my area made significant progress—test scores, parent involvement, and community pride all went up. I'd like to hear some good news reported for a change!" Peter exclaimed.

Upstairs the new superintendent, an experienced Latino male, looks out his window at the news van parked below. His entry is big news in the city, particularly because the board fired his predecessor. She had butted heads with the board chair over how the district was going to close the achievement gap. The district employees were left feeling divided and abused. He realizes he must build on the work of his predecessor that resulted in increased student achievement, while "healing" the district and determining what kind of culture he wishes to construct during his tenure.

ENTRY PLANNING: IT'S ALL ABOUT THE DATA

Virtually every superintendent we talked with, whether on her fourth superintendency or her first, stressed the importance of planning, and over 80 percent had developed a formal, strategic entry plan. Many turn to Barry Jentz and Joan Wofford's 2008 guide, *The EntryPlan Approach: How to Begin a Leadership Position Successfully*. The book recommends a collaborative process wherein a new leader works with key groups to draft, revise, and publish a plan that will guide the leader's early actions. As one superintendent described,

> This process gave me a clear map about what I would do in the first one hundred days and next steps after I finished. I was on a "listening and learning" tour, with no commitment to change until after I understood the district landscape.

According to Jentz and Wofford, it is important to start discussing your entry approach from your first interview. This will not only impress your new boss but also start laying the groundwork with the people who will be involved in the process, including the board, the administrative team, teachers, parents, students, and community members.

Don't hit the ground running. Instead, Jentz and Murphy (2005) recommend that as a new superintendent you hit the ground listening and learning. Your time will be engulfed with meeting parents; attending political engagements; and building rapport with your board, administrators, teachers, and students. You will be tempted to start offering solutions to long-standing district woes, particularly those that are obvious or inequitable. However, you cannot lead the system until you have had time to understand it. As one experienced superintendent noted, "You can't possibly know what is really going on until you are in it. You might think you know—but trust me, you don't."

Having a clearly defined entry strategy is a precondition to effective listening and learning. In the Seattle case study in Chapter Four, you'll learn how Maria Goodloe-Johnson embarked on a "listening and learning" campaign, which included a series of school bus tours with her board members and laid the foundation for her strategic plan. Each tour ended at a local community school, where she met with parents, teachers, students, and community members. She used this time to hear what she described as "the good, the bad, and the ugly" from these key stakeholders. As a district outsider, she felt that hearing this information firsthand was critical to her superintendency. It not only gave her a historical perspective but also allowed her to actively engage with the community by hearing their fears, hopes, and dreams for Seattle schools.

Afterward, Goodloe-Johnson began collecting volumes of data. Like Deborah Jewell-Sherman in the Richmond case study in Chapter Five, she turned to outside experts, such as the Council of the Great City Schools, to conduct audits of various district systems on topics ranging from English language learner instruction to capital projects and transportation. Several superintendents echoed this strategy, with one noting, "As superintendent, you have to know where you are to figure out the steps to take you where you want to go." With scarce resources, superintendents must think strategically about the use of time, personnel, and finances in order to optimize learning and reduce distractions. They often find having an external group assist with this process gives validity to the findings and reduces political backlash.

Although collecting data is critical to making future decisions, superintendents are remiss if they halt district progress during this time. Even while you are planning, the district needs to run efficiently and effectively. Schools open, crises strike, and employees must be managed throughout your planning process. We found that, in addition to handling day-to-day business, almost all of our superintendents enacted a major reform or initiative within the first six months of their tenures. Even though about half felt they acted too quickly, they still acknowledged that some situations require immediate action. With this constant tension between taking the time to obtain buy-in and the need to act with urgency, experienced superintendents argue that you must take full advantage of the interview process to deeply study your prospective district; converse with multiple stakeholders; discuss your personal core values and priorities; and develop relationships with board members, union leaders, and district administrators before accepting the position. Armed with this knowledge, new superintendents can make the most informed decisions possible when facing difficult time constraints.

BUT OUR LAST SUPERINTENDENT . . .

District leaders repeatedly tell us that one of the greatest obstacles upon entry is signaling change and distinguishing yourself from your predecessor. Whether they are long-standing district insiders or outsiders brought in to initiate change, superintendents struggle to find the balance between setting their own agendas and recognizing strengths from the previous administration. Entry is not just your opportunity to learn the context; it is also your chance to share who you are—your vision, core values, and beliefs.

Several superintendents suggested interviewing key individuals, including those outside the positional power structure, to better understand the district context. One of the reasons we strongly encourage this technique is that it also provides you with an opportunity to share your personal agenda. For example, one superintendent asked the following three questions to approximately fifty central office staff members, community leaders, principals, and board members: (1) What do you do well that you are proud of? (2) Why do you think there's an achievement gap? and (3) What would you do if you were me? The superintendent employed the first question as a warm-up. The second question yielded the most intriguing answers because it gave him a sense of what people were all about, particularly their values and beliefs. His third question generated everything from the comical to routine suggestions. Although he heard much of the expected, he used these questions to start the conversation on equity, which later resulted in dismantling the tracking system in his district.

TO WHOM DO YOU TURN FOR ADVICE WHEN YOU ARE THE BOSS?

Superintendents work mostly in isolation. But when you are new to a context, it is hard to determine on your own where to focus your attention first. By using a team approach, you can quickly examine multiple aspects of the school district, talk with more stakeholders than when working alone, and have assistance with devising your entry plan. Jentz and Wofford (2008) describe this planning process as iterative and best completed using an interpretive community of practitioners and community leaders to assist with revisions. It is important that this community of stakeholders include those individuals who are key to your success. Many of our superintendents discussed the need to identify and include the "power brokers" in the district, those who will influence others, particularly during controversial action.

A thirty-something African American woman is about to enter her first superintendency. She is determined to establish her intent to lead all students—regardless of race, class, or gender—in a district previously only run by white men. She is worried about alienating key stakeholders if she criticizes the system and its long-standing inequities. If this isn't hard enough, she also realizes that she must focus the district on the real work of schools: teaching and learning. However, she has never been a principal, and she wonders if they will value her opinion.

To ease her transition, she wants to quickly gather all the data she can, but she doesn't have the money and time necessary for extensive audits. With the support of her local education foundation, she decides to work with a transition team of district insiders and national education experts. Together they will help her create a plan for her first ninety days and then her first year.

In Harvard's Urban Superintendents Program (USP), members of the first cohort onward have turned to transition teams to ease their entry. E. Wayne Harris, former superintendent of Roanoke, Virginia, described this process as one of using "a panel of experts" to help understand the context and craft the superintendent's entry plan. When he entered the superintendency he had four former superintendents and a data analyst partner with him to identify strengths and challenges and to create his entry plan before he presented it to his board. Many superintendents have expanded on this process by convening a hybrid team of outside experts coupled with local insiders, often chosen through a vetting process with the school board, foundation executives, and political figures.

In our experience, this process combines best business practices with best education practices. The team can help a new superintendent adopt a zero-based budgeting process as well as determine what curriculum initiatives have been most effective. More important, it allows the superintendent to move quickly. As you'll read in the case study of Arlene Ackerman's entry into the School District of Philadelphia in Chapter Seven, her transition team provided evidence that gave her leverage to initiate multiple reform strategies, including the holistic Empowerment School Model, within the first six months of her tenure.

As another option, some superintendents obtain the services of an onboarding or executive coach. Although some organizations, such as the Broad Foundation and many state associations for superintendents, ask retired superintendents to provide guidance, others are beginning to look to their local contexts to find coaches. A coach can also be a local political insider who quickly enables the superintendent to navigate through the political and cultural aspects of a city. (Who do you talk to in the first week? In the first month?) As one urban superintendent described,

> Every community is different. They want to be treated differently, and if somebody's not guiding you, you're going to step on political and social network landmines. I was fortunate to have somebody who has lived there all her life and is a relationships person. She helped me identify the people I needed to meet with right away, and who are the people who can wait. You come in, you have hundreds of people waiting to see you and talk to you. I didn't have to fight some of the political battles, because I got to know those folks early on.

Even with the above benefits, many superintendents do not recommend having a transition team or hiring an onboarding coach. The members of the team are often seen as your ambassadors, allowing you to get your message out tenfold. But there are drawbacks. As the new leader, you are being examined with an intense focus similar to the one you are using to inspect the district. The media and district personnel will closely scrutinize your team and their actions. How much money are you spending, and where is it coming from? Who is invited to participate? How long are you taking to produce results? Even if your team of experts volunteer their time or your coach is paid for by a foundation, you should wisely consider how best to employ their skills and knowledge and carefully craft how this use is portrayed by the media. This reinforces the importance of discussing the use of an entry process with your new school board and keeping them duly informed during the data collection period.

MAKING PURPOSEFUL CHANGE

It is important to get to know your district, and for the stakeholders to get to know you, as quickly as possible because although change is never easy, it is best to start early. Experts, including Jentz and Wofford (2008), argue that entry is the best time to enact significant reform measures aimed at raising student achievement. You are in the "honeymoon phase," a time period when goodwill abounds and change can be undertaken with as little confrontation as possible because stakeholders trust that you can make a difference (King & Blumer, 2000). After all, the school board has reached consensus and selected you as their change agent.

A first-time superintendent has just finished enacting his entry plan in a suburban school district. The district has a reputation for providing a high-quality education for its largely middle-class, white population. After examining the data collected from new formative and summative assessments, the superintendent realizes that although the district as a whole performs well, the new immigrant student population, as well as students of color, are not all performing on grade level. As he prepares his first State of the District address for the community and teaching staff, he knows he must balance praise for the district's achievements with pushing the staff, board, and community to realize that federal mandates require *all* students to excel. Changes in the seemingly solid instruction are necessary to meet the needs of all students. In particular, he has to get the three newly elected board members (of his five-member board) behind him. He wonders, Do I still have enough goodwill left to have this conversation?

From our work we learned that superintendents are split when it comes to discussing whether or not they had a "honeymoon" in their districts, generally described as a period of goodwill lasting approximately one year. Many superintendents argue that their honeymoon period lasted much longer than their first year, with one noting a ten-year honeymoon under an appointed board. Meanwhile, others claim they never had a honeymoon, or that it lasted significantly less than six months. More seem to agree that increasing pressures result in decreased opportunity for reform. Linda Wing, former codirector of USP, aptly described this phenomenon: "There is no more honeymoon period. In this age of high stakes and high standards, people are impatient for results" (as quoted in Harrington-Lueker, 2002).

It may seem obvious that in this era of accountability the honeymoon period is becoming shorter, or even nonexistent. Many of our superintendents stress that the honeymoon is over before their first day on the job, and they warn that a thoughtful contract could be your best protection. In the case study in Chapter Six, Baltimore chief executive officer Andrés Alonso knew one of the most challenging aspects of his job would be working with his board, and he wanted to clarify their roles and responsibilities. Therefore, he negotiated unprecedented power into his contract, which gave him the authority to make critical management and educational decisions.

AFTER THE PLAN: A TIME FOR ACTION

Now that you've planned your entry, it is time to put your plan into action. Many superintendents suggest attacking the "low-hanging fruit," meaning the relatively quick changes that are symbolic of your priorities. For example, in Philadelphia Arlene Ackerman first took some basic actions like hanging doors on the bathroom stalls and extending customer service hours.

As Jentz and Wofford (2008) argue, action plans should be executed vigorously. Once plans are established, supported by the board, and vetted through district stakeholders, superintendents must charge ahead and passionately pursue their vision and goals. Superintendents repeatedly tell us that it is best to hit one out of the park early on. Meria Joel Carstarphen in St. Paul Public Schools, for example, aggressively campaigned to pass a referendum, which she knew would set the tone for her tenure (see Chapter Three).

However, even once you start to understand the context and implement the plan, experienced leaders recognize that you need a team to help you make systemic change. All leaders must learn that although it's tempting, it's not possible to have a hand in everything. Later in this book, in Chapter Eight, you'll read about the work of Beverly Hall as the leader of Atlanta Public Schools. Upon entry Hall realized that she needed to build a strong internal team, and she had to win the trust of the outside business community. Although she is an extraordinary leader, Hall learned that she had to pick and choose where to concentrate her energy during her entry and that any errors made in selecting members of her internal team had to be quickly corrected.

Regardless of how you allocate your time and energy, you must effectively communicate your vision for change if you want to be successful. Our first case study, which discusses Carstarphen's entry into to St. Paul, explores how one superintendent framed her entry by engaging in a dialogue to share her vision of raising achievement for all students. Just like Carstarphen, new leaders will face opportunities throughout their entries to make a difference for every child in their districts. We encourage prospective leaders to pursue those opportunities with passion. If entry is indeed the best time to enact change, it should be used to challenge the inequitable status quo; raise student achievement; remove barriers to success; implement best practices; hold adults accountable; and create a culture of equality, collaboration, and high expectations. Whether you oversee hundreds or hundreds of thousands of children, they deserve nothing less.

REFERENCES

Council of the Great City Schools. (2008). Urban school superintendents: Characteristics, tenure, and salary sixth survey and report. *Urban Indicator*. Retrieved April 5, 2010, from www.cgcs.org/Pubs/Urban_Indicator_08–09.pdf.

Glass, T. E., & Franceschini, L. A. (2007). *The state of the American school superintendency: A mid-decade study*. Arlington, VA: American Association of School Administrators.

Harrington-Lueker, D. (2002, October). Superintendent rookies. *School Administrator*. Retrieved September 14, 2008, from www.aasa.org/publications/saarticledetail.cfm?mnitemnumber=&tnitemnumber=1866&unitemnumber=&pf=1&snitemnumber.

Jentz, B., & Murphy, J. T. (2005, January). Embracing confusion: What leaders do when they don't know what to do. *Phi Delta Kappan, 86*, 358–366.

Jentz, B., & Wofford, J. (2008). *The EntryPlan approach: How to begin a leadership position successfully* (Education ed.). Newton, MA: Leadership and Learning.

King, M., & Blumer, I. (2000, January). A good start. *Phi Delta Kappan, 81*, 356–360.

CHAPTER 3

Communicating the Vision

Breathing Life into Your Vision

Holly Weeks

In its simplest expression, our vision is the shape we give to our core truths—our beliefs, values, passions, and experiences—so we can communicate them to others. Even the core truths that drive us start out scrambled inside us. A developed vision brings coherence to the connections between our values and beliefs, the knowledge and experiences that have brought us to our strongest convictions, and our commitments as urban superintendents. A coherent vision might be large and bold and ambitious, but it's also focused and actionable and has a plan. Such a vision has a rationale—it helps us think and act clearly and with direction, driving the work we have committed to doing. And when that vision is also well communicated and actively in play, it drives the work of a whole district. That's its full purpose.

While we work out our vision on our side, we must reach across to people on their side by communicating our vision in a clear, consistent, convincing, and compelling way in order to make our vision theirs, too. If we are going to win them over, we have to balance the ideas, values, and knowledge that are important to us with their interests, experiences, and concerns. The realization of our vision is not an end result as much as a constant reaching across and a constant moving balance—it is our vision come to life, lived out by children in our community.

REACHING ACROSS TO THE OTHER SIDE

Specifically, how do we put our vision across so it's clear, compelling, shared, and alive? What do we have that we can use, and how do we use it? We have our presence, our heads, our hearts, our voices, and our imaginations.

When people say in politics, "That was a completely character-driven campaign," by *character* they mean the sense of a leader that others take in, separate from his or her position or argument: the leader's *presence.* Our presence is shaped by our beliefs, values, experiences, and relationships, just as our vision is shaped by them, and we develop our presence the same way we develop our vision. A well-communicated presence is the single most compelling leadership trait; it won't make us leaders, but we can't be leaders without it.

We have our *heads* to help us communicate our vision clearly and coherently. Here we are strong. For example, we are masters of data, and we have *lots* of data. Our heads let us use data to recognize what's good in the district that we can applaud and build on, and where to call for new action. Our heads also let us judge how to be clear and bold about our own sense of purpose and what people can hold us to. Our heads let us balance the big picture of our vision with the details that make it concrete for others. But it is rarely the cerebral discussion of data that moves people to act.

For that we use our *hearts,* to reach across and communicate with the hearts of our listeners. It is our listeners we want to move, so it is sympathy with their emotions (hope, fear, anger, regret), and recognizing and respecting them, that are important, not stirring and broadcasting our own emotions. We use skill when we need to change the mood their emotions create in order to move people. For example, the ability to speak passionately about our vision for the district's children may be exactly what we need when we must ask people to act, but speaking passionately is a skill, one we sometimes must call up many times in a day, not a tremulous moment of spontaneous feeling on our side.

Then, in a literal sense, it's our *voices*—and how we say what we have to say—that do the heavy lifting in communicating our vision. Our voices' job is, always, to put across what we have to say to listeners in the way listeners hear best. To develop those voices we need an accurate idea of how listeners take in a message and what they respond to. If we want people to understand, accept, and act on complex, multifaceted issues, we must shape the issues concisely into points that are relevant to those people; link those points to a story, image, or metaphor to make them memorable; and talk them through tightly, colorfully, and vigorously in language that is simple, clear, and direct. With all that, every aspect of our vision must be elastic and repeatable: we can speak about it clearly and well for four minutes or forty minutes, and our listeners can understand it clearly and say it again to others.

And certainly connected to our heads and our hearts, but in this case particularly to our voices, our *imaginations* recognize the stories and images that are the most underrated ways to communicate with anyone. Humans are probably hardwired for stories and certainly hardwired for images. Either a story or an image can be simple, easy to identify with, emotionally positive, and as brief as a single phrase, like this small, powerful story: "These children were so eager to come to school that they were standing under their mothers' umbrellas when the doors opened." Or consider Meria Joel Carstarphen's perfectly simple, clear, powerful, and repeatable image in this chapter's case: "Closing the achievement gap, solidly and forever, for all groups of kids." We must not underestimate the power of any image or story, including our own—not only because people want to know what has driven us to our vision but also because we want them to know.

None of this is startling information, but we tend to weigh differently what we use to communicate, valuing our better or more comfortable characteristics more and the others less. That's a problem because of the enormous amount of work our vision will do over the course of our careers, often under pressure and against considerable odds. We need everything we have, fully developed, because, for all the attention given here to how we put across our vision, we must not mistake our listeners for passive receptors. A powerful vision will resonate with many people, and they are likely to get on board with it initially if in principle they accept it. But it is then, when a vision is accepted, that its life and work change, tribulations multiply, very difficult conversations take place, and everything is harder.

MOVING PEOPLE TO CHANGE

Part of the trouble starts on our side. Very often, when we are caught up in the importance and urgency, from our own vantage point, of the work to be done for children, we are prone to reject other people's more parochial priorities when they conflict with ours. But being so committed to our own vision, we put out of mind the fact that our vision developed from our own personally compelling values and experiences, not from universal agreement on the right and the good. Like us, however, our counterparts are focused not on someone else's stuff (not even ours) but primarily on their own compelling concerns and experiences. Then—moving outward from that first focus like ripples on a pond—they look to the concerns and experiences of those nearest to them, and then, still further from their central concerns, our counterparts focus on outlying social issues. We are quick to focus on what we want people to move *to*—very often seen by them as an outlying issue—and dismissive of those nearer concerns we want them to move *from*. That's when they push back.

When people hold beliefs, values, or views in common, they share a "commonplace" in the original sense of a word that has come to mean "obvious." The toughest conversations in a district happen when a superintendent's vision hits the ground and runs up hard against some group's commonplaces and near interests.

Yes, in principle we reached them through their heads with arguments in favor of good practices supported by research, and with reasoning laced with good data. How often have we heard, confidently spoken, "They can't argue with the numbers"? But it's easy to understand something and be indifferent to it—maybe our counterparts can't argue with the numbers, but they can ignore them.

And yes, in principle we reached their hearts with compelling pictures of collaboration or equally compelling stories about the harm wreaked by inequity. But it's easy to feel strongly about something without thinking it through, or wanting to think it through. Our counterparts may want equity, for example, but they may want even more the competitive advantage when vying for resources to go to their section of the community. Here are the points at which principle has taken a backseat to commonplace.

Even in these circumstances, however, if our vision has legs, we can use it to move the reluctant. The truth is that people can hold inconsistent, even contradictory, commonplaces simultaneously (although it's hard to talk about them at the same time). So by broadening a commonplace or reframing it, or by turning from one concern to another, or perhaps by changing the language in which a commonplace is discussed, we can move people even if they appear to be far from our position. The strategy here is to make a new, less contentious commonplace.

But, specifically, how? Usually not by force—although if we have the power to compel change and we understand and accept the consequences of doing so, we should use it now. Otherwise, we want to start with something our counterparts believe or want, and we need to anticipate their concerns. We will be familiar, of course, with what we ourselves believe, want, and are concerned about. It is by reaching across to their commonplaces and interests, in words of our choosing to shape the conflict both in language and in framework, that we can avoid the pitfall of presenting an argument that is fully persuasive to us but not remotely persuasive to them. In fact, it's a valuable skill—and a good idea—to set the bar very high: we're not ready to move the resistant from a commonplace we cannot share with them to one that we can, until we can put our counterparts' position even better than they did—and answer it. Instead of standing against it, we respect their premise without deferring to it, and we respect our own with equal or greater vigor. It is by actively respecting our counterparts' concerns that we are able to be forceful about our vision of change without simply escalating the conflict between two sides.

VISION IN PRACTICE

What does all of this development and use of vision look like in practice? In St. Paul, Minnesota, where the traditional values of smoothing over differences and maintaining polite agreement made conflicts initially hard to grapple with and later virtually impossible to discuss, Carstarphen worked through several conflicts in this way. Her community was divided, with some groups further apart than they were willing to acknowledge and some more closely aligned than they knew. She also had a communications staff with divergent priorities.

In regard to her staff, Carstarphen did have the power to require change, but she wanted an outcome she couldn't get under compulsion. Carstarphen talked clearly, frankly, and repeatedly about the work of improving outcomes for students until her staff began to see this central aspect of her vision as the first priority for all district staff, and so began to think of their own work differently. Even as they disagreed about methods, they talked about their differences in the context of their new commonplace—what they now considered to be the real work of the district. The changes Carstarphen saw in her communications staff's beliefs and expectations were the changes she was looking for across the district, and she now had an army of missionaries speaking with her to their divided community about their newly shared vision for St. Paul Public Schools.

After three years in the School District of South Orange and Maplewood (South Orange-Maplewood), Brian G. Osborne, communicating his vision of equity clearly and well, knew that he sometimes got lip service rather than action when the prospect of equity across all student groups bumped up against a commonplace favoring just a few. Osborne could see that pushing back against a stubborn, misguided commonplace would feel satisfyingly faithful to his vision but would undermine it in the long term. He is still patiently working, not to impose his convictions but to change the commonplace to one that serves the interests of the resistant group even better than their old one does.

If, from the beginning, we breathe life into our vision in order to move people, the ground will be laid to use it in difficult conversations ever after. We use what we have—our presence, our heads, hearts, imaginations, and voices—in the service of our vision, and our vision goes to work in a new way. What follows is the story of how one person tried to do it.

Meria Joel Carstarphen, St. Paul Public Schools: Where Imagination Meets Destination

Leslie Boozer and Laura Kelley

It was February 2006, and Meria Joel Carstarphen was the community's new choice for superintendent of St. Paul Public Schools (SPPS). Not all in the community, however, were behind her. As she completed the last four months of her term as the chief accountability officer in District of Columbia Public Schools, Carstarphen learned that the leadership of one of her most powerful new constituent groups, the St. Paul Chamber of Commerce, was visiting Washington DC in late March. But no one from the chamber had asked or made any arrangements to meet with their incoming superintendent. She feared something was wrong, and she began to wonder if they viewed her as just another bureaucrat who would be asking for resources to fulfill another set of empty promises. As Carstarphen looked around her office at pictures of past students, she began to feel the weight of her responsibility, realizing just how hard being superintendent was going to be. She hadn't even started, and St. Paul's business leadership wasn't giving her a chance to prove herself. Carstarphen questioned, "Can I convince them that things will be different under my leadership?"

Disappointed but not deterred, Carstarphen requested a meeting with the chamber at her office in Washington the next month. What she heard from them was disconcerting. The St. Paul businessmen and -women were frustrated with SPPS and the school board. They were angered by rumors that the district would be trying to float yet another tax referendum. They had no proof that she would deliver results, and they planned to campaign against the referendum as they had successfully done in the past. They shared their reasoning with her: they believed that the schools wouldn't properly use the money, and therefore that the business community would see no benefits from the money spent. After passing previous referenda they had wanted to know how the money was used to improve the schools, but their pleas resulted in vague statements that skirted the issues of accountability and results. Thus the chamber believed the referendum money would not be spent strategically, resulting in few benefits to the students or the community. The chamber members longed for direction, transparency, and accountability; they felt they had not had it before, and they didn't have any reason to believe they would get it now.

Carstarphen listened closely as they expressed their many concerns. She agreed with their frustration over not knowing how the money was spent, and emphatically expressed that under her leadership there would be transparency and accountability. Carstarphen carefully explained why the money was needed, and how she would demonstrate to the entire community where the funds were spent and how they were linked to student outcomes. Realizing she wouldn't have any of this in place when she began her superintendency, Carstarphen asked the chamber to have faith—faith in her ability, in her vision, and in her leadership. The chamber gave her the benefit of the doubt, and together they sketched out an informal agreement of what she promised to deliver.

After the chamber left, Carstarphen sat back at her desk and pondered what had just occurred. She was grateful for the chamber's initial support, but she knew this was only the beginning. If the district were to have the operating funds to undertake the work that was fundamental to realizing her vision for SPPS, the vision that was the basis of the commitment she had made to the schools and the community in accepting their superintendency, then it was critical that the referendum pass. She also recognized that if the chamber needed to hear her vision and personal promise for transparency, the rest of the community also needed to hear directly from her if they were to regain confidence in the system. She had spent years in other districts as a member of senior administration, fighting public mistrust of school district spending and decision making. But the situation in St. Paul was different. As superintendent, she would be selling her vision, and she would be ultimately responsible for its success.

THE CALL FOR SIMULTANEOUS ACTION

With a sense of urgency after her conversation with the chamber, Carstarphen organized a transition team to help her assess the new context of St. Paul. The team echoed concerns Carstarphen expressed about the persistent achievement gap. The state's achievement test, the Minnesota Comprehensive Assessment-II (MCA-II), revealed in 2006 that the percentage of white students proficient at each grade and subject was an average of 25 points higher than that of African American students, regardless of income status (see Exhibit 3.1 on the CD to view 2007–2009 MCA-II data). With core values centered on equity and accountability, and a focus on classroom instruction, Carstarphen was emphatic that raising achievement of all students had to be a top priority. However, she realized she did not have a network of people in place in St. Paul to make this happen. Moreover, she lacked strong political clout to change long-standing perceptions, and she did not have the money the district needed to institute new initiatives and strengthen existing ones.

"I had to decide what I needed to focus on first, second, and third. But multiple concerns needed to be addressed at once. I didn't have the luxury of time to waste," Carstarphen explained. She did, however, have a strong vision and the ability to communicate it so that other people understood it and wanted to buy into it. To get where she and the district needed to be, Carstarphen knew she had to do three things at once, and out of the usual order. The immediacy of the referendum meant she had to ask a community that didn't know her to trust her leadership enough to pass a substantial, multiyear referendum—$30 million each year—to fund the district's academic programs. At the same time as she lobbied voters, she had to craft a vision collaboratively with her board to give direction to their work and communicate that direction to the community. In addition to these two overwhelming tasks, before even beginning as superintendent of St. Paul Public Schools, Carstarphen would have to demonstrate to the community that student outcomes would be different under her leadership and declare how she would hold the adults in the system accountable for raising achievement across the board.

Carstarphen wondered if she could convince the community to give her, a little-known quantity, millions of dollars before she had fully developed a plan to account for and track the money. To add to the pressure, there was even more on the line in this first test: if Carstarphen couldn't persuade the voters now, she would have a hard time garnering support for future reforms. This test of the community's faith in her was likely to determine her success as a leader in St. Paul.

Making the difficult choice between priorities, Carstarphen decided she would build on the momentum she had gathered as the community's pick for superintendent and use the urgency of the referendum to craft the district vision, communicate her values and beliefs, and demonstrate her passion for educating all students. She saw that by offering to be held accountable for her results, she would be best positioned to define the problems she intended to take on and resolve.

She began formulating a plan to engage the community in a comprehensive public information campaign aimed at securing the tax money the district would need to make her vision a reality. By doing so, she also meant to convince the St. Paul Chamber of Commerce and the rest of the city that she was indeed the type of leader who embraced data-driven strategies, transparency, and the all-important accountability.

BRINGING A GLOBAL PERSPECTIVE TO THE MIDWEST

Meria Joel Carstarphen, a thirty-six-year-old African American woman native to Selma, Alabama, was the youngest of the five finalists in the running to lead St. Paul Public Schools. The board in St. Paul called her a "rising star," and Carstarphen described her career path to the superintendency as "accelerated but not hastened." The superintendency of SPPS would be her sixth job in less than a decade, which worried some members of the community about her willingness to stay in St. Paul on a long-term basis. Carstarphen, however, who had served as the chief accountability officer in District of Columbia Public Schools, executive director for comprehensive school improvement and accountability in Kingsport City Schools in Tennessee, and special assistant to the superintendent in Columbus City Schools in Ohio, declared the breadth of her senior leadership experience a distinct advantage and won the job.

Carstarphen had learned from family, friends, and teachers in Selma about her community's volatile voting rights campaign that marked such suffering in our nation's history. Her strong beliefs about education grew out of Selma's fight for basic freedoms: "Public education is the cornerstone of our democracy, and working in public education is the most important job in the world. It's what I'm supposed to do."

But first Carstarphen worked as a journalist and photographer for *National Geographic* magazine. While a reporter in Caracas, she volunteered to teach in shantytowns during her time off and grew acutely aware of the inequities children continue to face. She learned of a local church that supported a hardworking young student financially and emotionally, even providing for her college education in the United States. Seeing a narrative that pulled her interests together, Carstarphen reported the young girl's story, capturing the way her life was changed by the power of education. Carstarphen was inspired by the girl's transformation and the dedication of the adults who supported her, and she became a teacher in Spain and Venezuela, and back in her hometown of Selma.

Carstarphen's strengths as a leader in a community as diverse as St. Paul's came from her own education, her multicultural experiences, and her commitment to addressing inequalities in public schools. She had a strong and direct leadership style and did not apologize for her tough-talking approach to urgent problems in the schools she cared about so much. She was committed to, and held herself accountable for, high expectations for all children. Her confidence lay in her conviction that all children can learn and perform at the highest levels, without such artificial barriers as gender, race, language, or special education status setting limits on their success.

Her confidence both encouraged the SPPS board and motivated many of her staff and students. Known for setting the example for others in the system, Carstarphen took on the task of mentoring students in St. Paul Public Schools. In particular, she found solace working with students who had overcome great obstacles and instilled in them courage to pursue their educational dreams. "Dr. Carstarphen is not afraid to take charge—her integrity, honesty, and straightforward approach make her an inspiring role model," explained Carstarphen's mentee Air Yang, now enrolled at the University of Minnesota. When Yang's parents came to the United States, they were illiterate and struggled with navigating the public school system. Yang taught her brothers how to read, and they in turn taught her mother. Together, her family achieved success. Carstarphen would need to demonstrate similar resilience as she approached her work in St. Paul.

BACKGROUND AND CONTEXT

Despite facing seriously declining enrollment, St. Paul Public Schools served over forty-one thousand students as Carstarphen took the lead on July 31, 2006. St. Paul is Minnesota's capital city and second-largest school system, and its student body reflected the great diversity of its multicultural community, with total students speaking over seventy native languages at home. At that time the student population was almost 74 percent students of color: 30 percent African American, 29 percent Asian, 26 percent white, 13 percent Latino, and 2 percent American Indian. In addition, 69.5 percent of the district's students qualified for free or reduced-price lunch, 17 percent were considered special education students, and 43 percent were classified as English language learners (ELLs).

District data revealed that dramatic achievement gaps lay between African American students and their white and Asian counterparts, a fact frustratingly well known to the African American community but not entirely acknowledged by the larger St. Paul community. Fighting to put a face on the statistics, African American parent Rita Burch argued to the school board just how severely this achievement gap taxed the citizens of St. Paul. She brought her fifth-grade son Darien to a board meeting, telling members how the teacher's low expectations and failure to recognize her son's different learning style were destroying his self-esteem and quashing his desire to learn. "These are the kids you're losing," she argued (Belden, 2007b, paragraph19). She further explained her belief that St. Paul's persistent achievement gap "speaks to something I don't think people really want to be honest about.... I won't say racism, but I'll say lack of tolerance for people not like them (paragraph 10)." The district's test scores supported her declaration of inequity. The district's student achievement on the Minnesota Basic Skills Test (BST), which students must pass to graduate, demonstrated that stark differences remained among student subgroups (see Exhibit 3.2 on the CD).

Carstarphen entered St. Paul committed to closing the achievement gaps that existed in SPPS. For Carstarphen, this meant more than merely raising test scores. She repeatedly explained to the community that one of her primary goals was to make St. Paul a model for "closing the gap solidly and forever for all groups of kids." Armed with data, she committed herself to addressing and closing gaps in opportunity and access as well as achievement.

Even before Carstarphen entered as superintendent, there was a great divide in the St. Paul community between those who wanted to see—and had not seen—measurable results for their tax dollars and those who believed that extra funding would finally make a difference in their own children's education. This had led to checkered results in previous efforts to secure funding by referenda, some of which voters had declined. The community had most recently approved a referendum in 2002, giving the district an additional $17 million a year, but it was set to expire as Carstarphen entered.

With additional funds needed to maintain and improve instructional programs, the district in 2006 would either have to find financial support or cut core academic programs at each school. The potential loss of new referendum funding was not the only financial hardship facing the district. There was a further triple-threat challenge to continued progress: unpredictable state support from year to year, skyrocketing energy and health care costs, and unfunded state mandates. For example, no funding was being provided for at-risk pre-K children, and the state had just mandated new requirements in math and science for secondary students. The referendum funding, however, was the one challenge within the control of the St. Paul community.

The divergence in the community between public mistrust of school district spending and decision making, on the one hand, and the expectation that additional funding would improve their children's education, on the other, drew lines that were not easily discussed in St. Paul. The traditional values of smoothing over differences and maintaining polite agreement—appreciatively called "Minnesota nice"—made it easier to highlight the successes in the district and more difficult to speak of the spottiness of those successes. Given this tendency to avoid conflict, the divisions and tensions in the community increased as the data revealed the discrepancies in educational outcomes.

The previous SPPS superintendent had played a quiet role in the 2002 funding campaign, perhaps out of Minnesota nice, perhaps to avoid pointing out or exacerbating community differences. Instead she focused on personal relationships with the community. As she explained, "That's the small 'p' in public education. Families are giving you their children to educate. You have to let them get to know you" (Gewertz, 2006, paragraph 26). Even though she had developed a strong relationship with the board, business leaders, and city and state leaders, she chose not to say what the money would be used for or how it could be used effectively to fund academic programs. Her approach was unsettling to members of the St. Paul Chamber of Commerce, who saw personal relationships where they needed to see sound business practices, particularly transparency and accountability. Due to this rising discontent with the leadership, the chamber had actively campaigned against *all* referendum requests since 2000. Nevertheless, the community support was strong enough for the 2002 referendum to pass.

Carstarphen, relying on her straightforward, no-excuses approach, perhaps in conflict with the culture of Minnesota nice, realized that she had to use her vision to unite the community. Explaining her thinking, Carstarphen noted,

> I was clear about the fact that I was going to be focused on the achievement gap, and even from the time the board interviewed me for superintendent I communicated that it's about data for me. I made no bones about it and said, "That's what I want to do. Reform and recommendations are going to be based on two things: the data that we have and best-practice research."

Carstarphen's vision was ambitious, and she was staunchly committed to it. Going into the community in support of closing the achievement gap and requiring accountability meant talking directly about the very issues that St. Paul tended to sidestep in conversation. By diverging from the Minnesota nice tradition in her urgent and unapologetic way, Carstarphen risked striking St. Paul as blunt and off-putting from the start. Carstarphen's propensity to speak plainly and dig to the heart of difficult issues was new for St. Paul. As she explained, "I really listen and I really engage. I ask a lot of questions. I think for some people that gets misinterpreted" (Belden, 2007c, paragraph 3). But she would not be dissuaded. She believed the stakes were so high that it was a risk well worth taking. Now she needed the community to share her vision.

CRAFTING A VISION FOR ST. PAUL PUBLIC SCHOOLS

Every district needs a clear, concise vision to guide the work. Carstarphen knew this as she read through the district's expired strategic plan. She had asked longtime staffers about the district's vision statement, and everyone responded in a generic way, commenting that it was something around all students succeeding. Carstarphen knew the work ahead of them would require a more concrete and inspiring vision. "I need a vision that the community will unite in support of. A vision that speaks to the values of district leadership and desires of the community," Carstarphen thought to herself. Yet the district was already embattled in the campaign for the referendum. "Can I do both at the same time? I have to," she realized.

Vision Retreat

As the referendum campaign moved forward, Carstarphen started the process of creating a district vision statement that addressed the work and the goals to which she was committed. More important, she needed the board and the community to claim it as their own and commit with her to that work and those goals. Describing the importance of both, Carstarphen explained:

> The district vision cannot stem only from the superintendent. You need enough people in the system that believe in that vision so you can do the work that you need to do. As a district leader, you are constantly fighting an uphill battle, and oftentimes you will not win, especially when it comes to the political and financial battles. But when you are fighting for all children, there are two starting points you have to get right. First, you need the right match between you and the board. Second, it is critical to have a shared vision—one that both you and the board can believe in and stand behind as you fight the battles ahead.

Carstarphen began the process of creating the shared vision by holding what she coined a "vision retreat" with her board. Knowing the board members were new to the process, she wanted to give them ample time to focus solely on developing a strong vision statement. Drawing upon her teacher roots, Carstarphen assigned homework to the board. She asked them to complete two tasks prior to the retreat. First, they were to find vision statements for other organizations that resonated with them. For Carstarphen this served an important purpose: "I didn't care if they were school district visions or vision statements from Fortune 500 companies—I just wanted them to understand what a powerful vision statement looked like, how it spoke to them." The second task was for board members to prepare a list of school districts they respected and aspired to emulate. "Again, this task was all about recognizing common threads of excellence in school districts. I needed the board to think through what made a district great."

Before the retreat, Carstarphen and her staff compiled the vision statements of those districts and printed the statements on large charts that they posted around the meeting room. Unsure if she was the best person to lead this task, Carstarphen realized that the board was looking to her to set the tone, and she wanted to lead by example. Well versed in curriculum best practices, Carstarphen appealed to board members' diverse learning styles by leading them through a series of activities. She broke them into small groups and asked the board members to circle words they felt should be a part of the vision. After the process and a lengthy discussion, Carstarphen and her staff took all the feedback to the central office and put the work together to create multiple vision statements.

Although it was critical for the board to believe in the vision, it was also necessary for the entire central office to buy into the statement. The board continued to work through versions of the vision, and Carstarphen and her staff would send the versions out to the district personnel for feedback. After several iterations, the board approved a vision statement that portrayed all that SPPS desired (St. Paul Public Schools, 2008):

SPPS Vision Statement

Imagine every student

inspired, challenged, and cared for by exceptional educators

Imagine your family

welcomed, respected and valued by exceptional schools

Imagine our community

united, strengthened, and prepared for an exceptional future

Saint Paul Public Schools: Where Imagination Meets Destination

After this lengthy process, Carstarphen was proud of the "well-thought-out, poetic vision." The process of crafting the vision laid the foundation for the strategic planning work later in the year. As Carstarphen explained, "By going through the process of defining our core values, we were able to develop specific goals tied to outcome statements that would guide our work for the next five years" (see Exhibit 3.3 on the CD for the strategic plan framework).

Funding the Vision

The drafting of the vision progressed alongside Carstarphen's aggressive campaign to promote the referendum. Although many constituents were excited about the energetic, "fresh" young superintendent, mistrust over the district's previous spending and absence of reporting measures were endemic in St. Paul, and people were still wary of her decision to ask for more money. Overcoming that doubt depended heavily on Carstarphen's willingness and ability to communicate the district's new direction with its emphasis on accountability.

The simultaneous need both to craft a vision for the district compatible with her own vision for the children of St. Paul and to win conclusive support for the referendum had a silver lining. It pushed Carstarphen and her team to present a very clear message to the community that conveyed what it could expect should the funding be approved.

The campaign was designed to inform voters about the district's new major initiatives. First, the money would be used to emphasize commitment to what Carstarphen described as the "bookends" of education—early childhood and kindergarten programs coupled with high school initiatives. Starting with the youngest students of SPPS, the additional funds would provide all-day kindergarten to all students at no cost. Also, at-risk four-year-olds could attend the new kindergarten programs. For the high schools, the money would be used to stabilize class size and provide technology upgrades. Carstarphen also promised to use the funds to increase individual instruction in math and science, with a special emphasis on the secondary schools. This campaign information was printed in the district's four most-spoken languages—English, Spanish, Hmong, and Somali. Carstarphen also promised that all future district communications would be printed in the four languages, ensuring that the benefits of such programs were made equally available to all members of the community.

Identifying how the money would be spent met part of the chamber's requests, but Carstarphen had also committed to complete transparency. For those still skeptical about how the additional millions would be used, Carstarphen's team drafted a document outlining in detail exactly how much each school would receive from the referendum, and published it in the paper for the entire community to examine (see Exhibit 3.4 on the CD). The school-by-school analysis made clear what programs would be cut if funding were not approved.

With only four months between taking the helm as superintendent and the referendum vote, Carstarphen didn't have time to craft a detailed plan of action for reporting the results or accounting for spending. Nevertheless, she continued to adamantly express to her constituents that she would tackle these issues in her work. At every community forum she repeatedly explained that she would offer a clear and accurate picture of how well the district was serving all student groups, even if the results were not what she expected.

For Carstarphen, this high level of accountability and transparency was required not only of her but also of her staff. She expected everyone to be accountable, from herself down to the classroom teachers, school staff, and even parents. During the school district's 150-year anniversary celebration, one month before the November vote, Carstarphen committed to these new practices. She assured,

> There is no doubt that I will take it to the next level. We will talk more about accountability; we will set targets and benchmarks. We will map out our goals and strategies for every year down to the percentage gain points that need to happen for all students to be successful.

Going Door-to-Door

Carstarphen was weary but invigorated by her conversations with the people of St. Paul. Together she and her director of community relations Dan Rodriguez discussed the game plan to visit homes and how she would work phone banks and fundraisers. As Carstarphen explains, "I wanted my voice to be heard. I was asking a lot of the people of St. Paul. I was asking for their trust and for the dollars. I wanted to do whatever it took to earn their vote." Carstarphen opted to lead by example and explain—in person—to as many citizens as possible how the approved bond measure would help improve SPPS. She contributed $500 of her own money and was directly responsible for raising more than $120,000 in campaign support. Rodriguez explains Carstarphen's dedication to the referendum:

> To say she was enthusiastic doesn't quite capture it. She made it her mission to get the referendum passed, and she went above and beyond what any superintendent has done ever since I began here. She was very explicit about what that meant. She said, "I want to door-knock. I want to be on the phones during the phone banks. I want to go door-to-door with leaflets. I want to raise money. I want to put in yard signs." She did all of that, and people noticed. People took note of it. There was never a request we made of her that she didn't honor, and she raised the bar herself and raised her own expectations of what her role was going to be.

Carstarphen's belief in the referendum wasn't just about money, it was about what the schools could achieve with the community's support. Included in the written and spoken campaign was a commitment that SPPS leadership would periodically report back to the public about how the additional tax dollars would be tracked and spent. It was part of Carstarphen's vision to partner with the community in this work, and this level of transparency was critical to the partnership.

Passing the Referendum and "Coloring the Money"

On November 7, 2006, just four months into Carstarphen's brief but busy tenure, voters passed the $180 million referendum by a resounding 62 percent. For SPPS, the positive vote reflected the community's belief in the new vision, their appreciation for accountability and transparency, and the growing relationship between the city and their hardworking new superintendent. Rodriguez explained, "In the end, the referendum passed by margins exceeding previous referenda, and in no small measure because of Carstarphen's personal commitment."

Carstarphen thanked the community publicly for showing their support of SPPS by approving the referendum. She reiterated her commitment to transparency and results, sharing her plans to include the community in, and keep them informed of, decisions to spend money. Specifically, she described a public accountability process of "coloring the money." In public record-keeping graphs, referendum monies were "dyed" to easily track spending. "We made a commitment to the community when we asked them to support the referendum," Carstarphen said. "I'm a taxpayer too; I want to know, if you're getting $30 million, how you spent it on the things that you promised that you would spend it on."

PARLAYING THE VISION INTO PRACTICE

With the district's newly created vision in hand, Carstarphen undertook to reconnect the district with its stakeholders. A focus on community relations was a new concept for the divided city that had felt ignored by the school system prior to Carstarphen's arrival. During the vetting process, Carstarphen had attended several board meetings and district-wide forums in which people vehemently expressed their frustrations with the school district, with public comment lasting for hours:

> During the interview process, it became clear that the community felt unheard and frustrated. I started forging new relationships by having large leadership group meetings with what I call affinity groups. Whether it was about special education, African American student performance, gifted and talented students, or our Hmong population, I was ready to listen and work with them on their concerns.

Affinity Groups

One of SPPS's most fragile relationships was with the African American community. Reacting to their third consecutive African American superintendent, this historically disenfranchised community wondered if Carstarphen would finally respond to their pleas. A group of African American parents and supporters had compiled a list of multiple offenses and drafted a complaint of twenty-five pages outlining their frustrations over district disservices to their children. The injustices included their children being overidentified as special education students, having lower graduation rates than their white peers, and remaining the object of low expectations by teachers and administrators. Reminded of the civil rights fight in her home in Selma, Alabama, Carstarphen was distraught at their plight. She was committed to repairing and rebuilding this relationship, and she hired a professional facilitator to distill the report and bring people together for genuine two-way conversations. These were not simply listening sessions, however. The meetings resulted in a frank discussion around personal responsibility that had not previously existed in St. Paul. Just as important for real improvement, a shared accountability system establishing loci of responsibility grew out of these conversations. Responsibilities were delineated not only for administrators but also for students, parents and guardians, teaching staff and nonteaching staff, the school board, and the community. The framework laid out specific expectations for each group. For example, teachers were expected to have high academic and behavioral expectations for all students and treat all students fairly and consistently when enforcing rules.

Carstarphen encouraged parents to think about their role in providing a high quality education for all students, and she explained that eradicating achievement gaps in SPPS would take the efforts of all. She said,

> Part of the reason why we have a big gap is because we never talked to the families and people that we serve directly. If we are to close the achievement gap in SPPS, we need the families to support us by teaching early childhood development skills, by encouraging our students to enroll in after-school and summer programs, and by demanding a high-quality, rigorous curriculum in our classrooms.

As parents' responsibilities increased, they were expected to "establish a positive relationship with someone at the school—this may be a teacher, social worker, counselor, or adviser—and ensure that [their children got] 8 to 10 hours of sleep and other basic needs." (St. Paul Public Schools, 2008, p. 8). This radical change in practice was met with mixed reviews. Teachers union president Mary Cathryn Ricker said she heard positive reviews from some of her members, namely how much they appreciated Carstarphen's direct and honest message to parents and community groups. According to Ricker, "Basically, Carstarphen said, 'Get the kids to us on time and ready to learn so we can do our jobs.' Teachers are just amazed there is someone out there explicitly delivering that message on their behalf" (Belden, 2007c, paragraph 11).

For others, Carstarphen's straightforward approach was somewhat alarming. Rodriguez explained,

> We had some very startling, disturbing, brutal facts. She had to find the right way to affirm this district that is doing some things well while also challenging them. "Don't be too complacent about the job you're doing, because you have some real challenges. And here, let me point them out to you." Quite frankly I think some people initially didn't know what to make of that.

Reorganization of the Central Office

The quick and significant focus on community engagement and shared responsibility immediately became the linchpin of SPPS's communications, and Carstarphen wanted to refocus the priorities of the central office to engage families rather than simply informing them of district happenings.

MOVING FROM COMMUNICATIONS TO COMMUNITY RELATIONS. Carstarphen commissioned an audit to understand the strengths and weaknesses of the communications department's internal systems. In a nutshell, according to chief communications officer Christine Wroblewski, the National School Public Relations Association conducted an audit and found "we did a pretty good job of communicating to, but not communicating with, the community." Realizing this external work was vastly different from internal communication, Carstarphen and Wroblewski became determined to restructure communications.

To shift the central office's communications focus and engage the community in conversation, Carstarphen deployed family liaisons and greeters at each school who actually reflected the school's demographic makeup and spoke the majority of the student body's home language. Staff members, regardless of race, were expected to serve all families in St. Paul—a departure from previous practice in which Latino staff interacted only with Latino families, Hmong staff only met with Hmong families, and the same held true for all ethnic groups.

Again Carstarphen experienced some push-back from her staff and the community for this radical change, but she asked her board to support her vision of an inclusive school district. Her board was there for her, fully supporting and adopting the shared accountability framework, which established their own responsibilities. Carstarphen did not apologize for speaking frankly about the district's struggles. Instead, she encouraged teachers, administrators, and staff to act: "It is urgent that we do what is necessary to ensure all children's success."

IMPROVING INTERNAL COMMUNICATION. After requesting new responsibilities from all stakeholders, Carstarphen needed to ensure that the communications office was service-oriented. She renamed the Department of Communications as the Department of Community Relations, and she made chief communications officer Wroblewski a member of her cabinet. By having her communications officer involved in her executive meetings, Carstarphen expected her internal communication with SPPS staff to be clearer and faster than if she alone were the messenger. Communicating the vision of SPPS to the larger community would also be clearer and more accurate:

> I need [Wroblewski] to understand and communicate my vision internally first so our employees are clear on our expectations. We have thousands of ambassadors inside the system, and I committed to keeping them informed and engaged in a two-way communication. If they can share our vision and work with coherence, our work will be tremendously improved. They are the main voice and communication tool of SPPS, much more than any newspaper or Web site.

Carstarphen believed that if she wanted different outcomes from the revamped department she must first engage staff in a three-part process. The first step was to talk openly and honestly about the work of improving outcomes for students in St. Paul in order to help the department staff reorient itself to the new responsibilities. She both talked with staff members about SPPS's vision and inspected district data with them. As one teacher noted, "It is powerful to examine data together and explore what it is telling us about our students and our methods." Soon teachers and administrators started talking about the district's work with a close focus on improving student outcomes. Carstarphen knew the doorway was open for them to think about their own work differently. Even if they disagreed with her methods, they were now thinking and talking about the real work of the district. When these conversations began, Carstarphen started to see changes in her staff's beliefs and expectations—the changes she would look for across the district.

STATE OF THE DISTRICT

As she promised the community in her campaign for the tax referendum, Carstarphen prepared an annual report of the 2006–2007 school year detailing progress, achievements, and the ongoing struggles in the district of St. Paul. The twenty-six-page report was the first of its kind for SPPS, outlining the district's strategic plan framework and presenting up-to-date data on students, staff, schools and programs, resources, and the community. Most important, the annual report presented the district's progress in meeting specific targets on measurable outcomes.

When she presented the report, Carstarphen knew the data would be unsettling. The number of schools not making annual yearly progress (AYP) more than doubled, and the district as a whole did not make AYP. This sudden drop was expected, due in part to changes in the test design and technical problems for English language learners, who made up 40 percent of the district's student population. In her first-ever State of the District address to community leaders, Carstarphen publicly announced that 70 percent of the district's benchmarks had not been met. Holding herself and the district's employees responsible for the outcomes, she again referred to the new accountability system and argued that their jobs were on the line. They were responsible for student outcomes. Explaining the district's progress and lack thereof, Carstarphen asserted, "If we don't tell our story, if we don't help people connect the dots, if we don't stand out there and take the kudos and the lumps, then people don't feel like there is real accountability."

Carstarphen had set the tone of transparency and accountability from the very beginning of her tenure. She fulfilled her promise to establish accountability systems for referendum spending and began her regular reporting schedule with her first annual report and the annual State of the District speech. At times the message was both difficult to deliver and difficult to swallow, but Carstarphen did not shy from it. She believed unwaveringly that the district could achieve its new vision. While giving her first State of the District address, she stood before the citizens of St. Paul and encouraged the entire community to rally behind their children: "We have the talent, the team, and the partners to accomplish our goals. With the support of our families and community, we can also create the collective will and the courage to do so" (Belden, 2007a, paragraph 6).

REFERENCES

Belden, D. (2007a, November 9). "Pockets of success" notes St. Paul superintendent in State of the School District speech. *St. Paul Pioneer Press*. Retrieved October 10, 2009, from http://twincities.com/archives.

Belden, D. (2007b, September 1). Taking on the gap. *St. Paul Pioneer Press*. Retrieved October 10, 2009, from http://twincities.com/archives.

Belden, D. (2007c, June 2). Vigilance and vision. *St. Paul Pioneer Press*. Retrieved October 10, 2009, from http://twincities.com/archives.

Gewertz, C. (2006). Race, gender, and the superintendency. *Education Week*, *25*(24), 1–24.

St. Paul Public Schools. (2008). *SPPS Shared Accountability Framework*. Retrieved February 18, 2010, from http://accountability.spps.org/sites/f42ee0d1-1629-4940-887c-d0d839c0eedf/uploads/REVISED_FINAL_SHARED_ACCOUNTABILITY_FRAMEWORK_-_6.16.08.pdf.

St. Paul Public Schools. (2008). *SPPS vision statement*. Retrieved February 18, 2010, from http://boe.spps.org/Mission_and_Ends.html.

Communicating to Change the Culture

Brian G. Osborne

When talking about effective teaching, to emphasize the import of and accountability for classroom instruction, we often say, "If the kids didn't learn it, then the teacher didn't teach it." When visiting classrooms, we gather much more insight into instructional effectiveness by talking with students about their learning than by watching the teacher teach.

For the leader focusing on communicating the vision, there are clear parallels: just as the teacher's instruction is only effective if students learn, the leader's communication of vision is only effective if the culture of the organization changes. If the culture doesn't change in ways that move reality toward the vision, then the leader didn't communicate it. Public school districts, especially diverse ones that have perpetuated disparate outcomes for students along race and class lines for decades, need leaders whose ability to communicate the vision effectively creates a new norm and a new reality.

Visionary leadership that truly pushes a school district toward equity requires an ability to communicate in ways that inspire and empower others. At the Harvard Graduate School of Education, the Urban Superintendents Program (USP) requires its students, who are aspiring superintendents, to deliver a vision speech to members of the program's advisory board, who then immediately offer a frank critique. Advisory board members, who are sitting superintendents of major urban districts, take this role seriously because they know that those emerging leaders who have the desire to bring social justice to public education from a district leadership position must also have the ability to communicate the vision in powerful ways.

Reflecting on Meria Joel Carstarphen's effective communication in St. Paul and my own work as a new superintendent in South Orange-Maplewood, New Jersey, surfaces a few key dilemmas that develop as the arc of the superintendency unfolds. The *entry* challenge for the new leader is to establish oneself with credibility to gain the ability to lead. The *vision* challenge for the new leader is to infuse a shared vision into the organization deeply enough that other key communicators convey the vision at every level. The *transformation* challenge comes when initiatives and reforms begin to make tangible differences for students, and the leader needs to ensure that the progress becomes part of the new culture so that the organization does not revert. Each of the three challenges applies to every change-oriented superintendent.

THE ENTRY CHALLENGE

At the point of entry, what does the system need most from its leader? How does the leader stay true to personal conviction while also using language and stories that bring others along? How does a leader new to the system create a sense of urgency without repelling others?

Carstarphen entered St. Paul with a powerful sense of personal mission and purpose built around equity. With personal experience of the empowering role education plays in her life; a deep connection to those students she had seen overcome daunting adversity through education; and professional leadership experience in large, stubborn urban systems, Carstarphen entered her first superintendency with a huge amount of drive and seriousness of purpose. She had, in Holly Weeks's language, unshakeable "core truths" that led her to assert, "I was meant to work in public education."

In St. Paul, the challenge presented by the local context was clear. The business community, angered by what it perceived as mismanagement and a lack of transparency in regard to disparate and stagnant outcomes, had mobilized to defeat the referendum. With a referendum defeat, there would be not only a lack of fiscal resources for Carstarphen to use in accelerating the changes needed to bring equity for all children in the school system but also the symbolic repudiation of the system by the larger community. Carstarphen's vision and communication reflected this urgency, and in her frank style she broke through the prevailing Minnesota nice, promised a different future with no excuses for academic failure, and immediately acted on her promises by publishing detailed financial data and leading by example.

Clearly, Carstarphen's personal passion and intellect brought the necessary support that led to a smooth referendum passage. With blunt talk about the system's challenges and an openness to transparently sharing the good, the bad, and the ugly about the district's performance data, Carstarphen led the referendum campaign forcefully and unapologetically. She communicated a vision of an equitable public education system that breaks the links between race, class, and academic performance, and she did so not only by staying on message but also by leading by example, taking that message to every conceivable audience; knocking on doors; and demonstrating through personal action what it means to say that we will do whatever it takes for every student to meet high academic standards with no alibis, no excuses, and no exceptions. Her story epitomizes the power of a visionary and tireless superintendent to compel an entire community—and one in which powerful figures had already become cynical—to invest in the future of its children.

The School District of South Orange-Maplewood, New Jersey, where I became superintendent in May 2007, is a diverse suburban district bordering Newark, New Jersey, that serves 6,400 students in nine schools. The student population is 44 percent African American, 47 percent white, 5 percent Latino, and 4 percent Asian; 20 percent receive free or reduced-price lunch; and 14 percent are special needs students. Frustrated by a stagnant status quo and growing achievement gap across student groups, the board of education hired me in 2007 as a change agent, knowing of my experience in and dedication to urban education. My own core truths mirror Carstarphen's in an unwavering commitment to equity made urgent by my experiences working with young people in Washington Heights, New York, and the South Bronx. The immediate context I entered was of a fractured and wounded school district. Labor, racial, and governance strife had coincided to create a sense of frustration at every level. The board of education mistrusted the prior superintendent to the point where they refused to approve any administrative hires, leaving several schools in limbo with interim principals. Students had staged walkouts at the high school, outraged at the racial insensitivity of the principal, whom the superintendent strongly supported despite board opposition. The board and the teachers union were openly at odds, and teachers, working without a contract for two years, had staged multiple job actions and were working to contract. Parents, many of whom are homeowners in one of the most tax-stressed communities in a state with the highest property taxes in the nation, were frustrated with everyone. In a place where many chose to live out of a desire for diversity, tempers had reached a point of intolerance. The entry challenge for me was to heal the divides while making clear that the status quo, marked by the same substantial differences between the achievement of African American and white students as in St. Paul, must change.

Arriving in May 2007 without the immediate pressure of a referendum campaign allowed me time to closely observe the system in action and listen intently. After all the strife and conflict, people needed to be heard. I fashioned an entry plan with the help of several people who have become key thought partners over the years thanks to the USP program: Larry Leverett, Robert Peterkin, Linda Wing, Andrés Alonso, and Joshua Starr. The May start date and the relatively small size of the district allowed me to meet with every stakeholder group at the district and school levels, including parents, clergy, teachers in grade-level meetings, and students. Spending a full day at every school observing classes and talking with groups of students and teachers was a key opportunity for me to learn the district and listen.

When the school year opened in September 2007, I delivered a speech entitled "New Beginnings" to the entire staff, parent leadership, and elected officials of both towns. After hearing from everyone in the system, I was keenly aware that the local context demanded healing, and that this moment in time called for the superintendent to honor the district's numerous accomplishments, begin to challenge others around equity, and declare that the adults needed to work together in positive ways.

The entry challenge is to find the point of synergy between self and context, and communicate in a way that gains the trust necessary to lead. For Carstarphen, that meant affirming the anger of the chamber and aggressively campaigning for the referendum. For her to meet the entry challenge, she needed to verbalize the impatience so many were feeling and to demonstrate with her tireless actions that she would do whatever it took to secure the resources needed to make real change. For me, meeting the entry challenge meant acknowledging the healing that needed to take place; demonstrating through action an ability to listen; and realizing that firmly rooted change in this district would take time. The greatest tension in the entry phase, for me, was in taming my personal tendency to rail impatiently against the inequity embedded in the district and, instead, seeing my leadership work through a long-term strategic lens. Although I often wonder if my initial communications were too soft on equity and too tolerant of the status quo, my entry plan and the "New Beginnings" speech helped me meet the entry challenge and establish the credibility needed to deepen the vision and work toward genuine transformation.

THE VISION CHALLENGE

Once the superintendent has established an effective entry, the very next challenge is to inculcate vision and mission in others. How does the superintendent secure buy-in for the vision? To what degree does the superintendent define the vision and facilitate the process? How does a district create a shared vision that serves to build aspiration while modeling accountability?

In St. Paul, Carstarphen worked with her board to create a poetic vision with a compelling tagline: "Where imagination meets destination." She accomplished this while campaigning for the referendum, a strong way to show not only that she could manage the district to the type of business standards that won her the confidence of the chamber but also that she understood the magic of education and the poetry needed to awaken creativity. She modeled the role of lead teacher by facilitating a process for the board to generate a vision that aligned with her personal mission and would resonate with others.

Prior to my arrival in South Orange-Maplewood, the district had engaged community stakeholders in a prolonged, eighteen-month strategic planning process resulting in a vision and goals document called *Vision 2010: Rigor, Relevance, and Relationships*. The document was a source of tension, with some board members having actively participated in its creation and others having been recently elected in hotly contested races in which part of their platform was to criticize the document for lacking any measurable milestones. Within the schools, the document had no relevance to the day-to-day work, and as a result there was no systemic approach to accountability for improvement. Yet within it I saw the high aspirations that the community held for its schools, and the fact that there had been such an in-depth community planning process suggested that it would be advantageous to build on the work product, honoring the involvement of hundreds of people and conveniently avoiding the need for further collection of stakeholder input in regard to the district's direction.

Like Carstarphen, I began building the vision with the board of education. This was a continuation of the work started in my first interview for the job, when I told the board that if they were not prepared to address the achievement gap head on and make changes that would anger those who felt well served by the status quo, then they needed to find someone else to serve as superintendent. Once I was on board, we crafted a document that built on *Vision 2010: Rigor, Relevance, and Relationships,* capturing its aspirations for our schools while adding to it measurable milestones that would serve as the basis for evaluating the superintendent. The resulting *District Goals* document provided tangible and measurable targets for our work, including narrowed gaps across student groups on test scores, higher-level course taking, and participation in electives and extracurricular activities. We also followed Carstarphen's move to publish detailed information on performance, measured against all the goals, objectives, and milestones, in a thorough State of the District report, providing data to all stakeholders with complete transparency.

In meeting the vision challenge, the superintendent must communicate clarity about direction, establish mechanisms for accountability, and inspire others to carry the vision forward at all levels of the organization. Unlike the entry challenge, the vision challenge is ongoing: it takes constant repetition and renewal to infuse the vision throughout the organization. A shared vision enables the district to implement changes and reforms, but does not by itself lead to cultural transformation.

THE TRANSFORMATION CHALLENGE

The superintendent, having met the entry challenge and understanding the vision challenge as ongoing, confronts the more difficult work of cultural transformation. With sufficient leadership credibility and a vision shared with key stakeholders, the superintendent can initiate various reforms for change. However, even when they are well implemented, reforms do not necessarily lead to cultural transformation. How does the superintendent use communication to ensure that the very DNA of the organization changes?

In St. Paul, Carstarphen laid some radical groundwork by initiating new approaches to community conversations and the use of transparent financial, program, and outcome data. Her approach to accountability and clarity of vision set the stage for sustained transformation in beliefs, culture, and results.

In South Orange-Maplewood, after three years, we are steeped in the transformation challenge, and it is still unclear how much the culture is changing. Many of the pieces of reform are now in place and held together by a clear theory of action. For example, the building and district instructional leadership team now has a clear focus on teaching and learning, and administrative meetings consist of instructional rounds rather than "administrivia"; schools are implementing a core curriculum; teachers use common and frequent formative assessments to monitor the progress of each individual student; and we have overhauled the way we support, hire, and evaluate teachers to ensure a commitment to equity in every classroom. These reforms have led to dramatic gains in such key indicators as student participation in advanced placement courses and reductions in the achievement gap.

Yet we are far from having transformed the culture of our system into one that prepares every single student for success in higher learning in the twenty-first century. After three years, the brutal truth is that too many in our school system and our community still carry outdated beliefs that student learning outcomes are inevitably tied to race and class. The transformation challenge greets us every day, as we work to use even our most modest successes to deepen our belief that public education can and must break the links among student learning, race, and class, and that it is our work and moral responsibility to make meaningful learning come to life for every child, in every classroom, every day.

CHAPTER 4

Strategic Planning

Planning to Succeed: Strategic Approaches for Every Superintendent

Janice Jackson

Public education continues to be an institution everyone loves to hate. Individuals who choose to lead public school districts often find themselves twisting in a series of tensions as they chart a course to success. These days the honeymoon for new superintendents is short-lived, if it exists at all. The key tensions that seem to swirl around the work are explained below.

1. *Public school superintendents arrive new to a district ready to live in the shadow of past leaders while charting a new pathway for the future.* The development of a plan occurs under the watchful eyes of many different stakeholder groups. There are usually differing public perceptions about the effectiveness of the past superintendents. Upon arrival, one is often met with stories of what was or was not done in the past and who did or did not benefit. Some superintendents are much loved and leave before the community is ready for their departures. Others exit in clouds of distrust. In some cases the new superintendent enters with the expectation that she will never be able to live up to the accomplishments of their much-admired former leader. In other cases she enters with many assuming that she is simply more bad news, just like the superintendents who came before her.

A new superintendent cannot allow either notion to shape who she is as a leader. She must be aware of, but not held hostage by, the emotional state of the community.

To avoid falling into this trap, a superintendent is wise to enter with a well-thought-out plan for coming to know the district and helping the district come to know her. As she listens to the stories about past leaders she must be aware of former leaders' roles in shaping the current state of affairs. She should have a clear sense of the kind of leader she will be in this context. She must convey to everyone that the core work of the district is to ensure that each child who crosses the threshold of a school door is engaged in a rigorous and well-balanced curriculum. Achieving this work calls for a systematic and strategic planning process that looks at how well the district is meeting its primary purpose and at how efficiently the district is operating. In planning, the superintendent must use data that is uncovered in a systematic way to balance what she will bring forward, what she will change, what she will eliminate, and what she will add that is new. That requires being aware of hot-button issues and sacred cows.

2. *The need to balance the urgency for improvement and deliberate, data-driven decision making often places the superintendent at odds with those who are expecting immediate change and quick fixes.* There is no question that something dramatic and positive needs to happen in U.S. public schools. In many school districts across the country the evidence is overwhelming that a significant number of children are not learning at levels that will prepare them to graduate on time, enter the economy and make a living wage, participate in the civic life of the community, and live with a sense of fulfillment.

The superintendent, as the chief advocate for children, must be guided by an unwavering sense of purpose and commitment to a set of core values that will serve as the foundational building blocks for a vision of the future. A primary task for the superintendent in bringing the vision to fruition is developing a plan to guide the operation of the organization as individuals work to meet the goals. The development of the plan must recognize key elements of the organization's history, pay attention to data about the organization's current state, and put people in the picture. Far too often strategic planning is treated as an intellectual exercise. Planners who fail to give thought to how people will actually use the strategy and plan are likely to have set themselves on a path of tremendous resistance. The superintendent is responsible for guarding the vision and ensuring its successful implementation. That requires being disciplined and standing strong in the face of the resistance that is a natural consequence of any call for deep change or transformation. In the case of public education, the superintendent is charged with interrupting the sense of mediocrity that allows for underachievement by large numbers of children in the district's care.

Many people do not understand the importance of taking the time to plan. History is on their side. Too often plans are made that promise improvement, but little noticeable change actually happens. A superintendent who is new to a district or one who is making a major shift in focus must be able to demonstrate a commitment to making things better. The manner in which the superintendent conducts the planning process sends a message about whether this is a new day or business as usual. A process that involves stakeholders in ways that make them feel heard will help ease some of the resistance. However, it will not cause this resistance to dissipate entirely.

3. *The planning process rarely occurs in the time frame allotted.* It is in vogue for a superintendent to enter a district with a thirty-, sixty-, or ninety-day entry plan. If a superintendent is going to come to learn about a district deeply and formulate a long-term plan for success, however, these targets are too short. A superintendent must allocate a sufficient period of time, whether planning occurs at entry or later in a superintendent's tenure. Quite often it takes nine months to a year to complete data gathering and analysis, develop a path forward, and gain the support of the local school board. Further, it takes time to have internal and external experts gather information that provides a robust picture of the district. Once gathered, data should be carefully analyzed to ensure the validity of the picture they paint of a very complex organization. The superintendent should seek input from a wide variety of sources, being certain to include those who are usually tapped and those who are often overlooked. It is important to gather data that put the district in a positive light and data that expose the warts. The pathway forward should be grounded in research-based approaches to improvement and benchmarks that are matched with what is possible given the current state of the district. It is sometimes difficult to convince people that success for all children is possible. The superintendent must be relentless in pushing for success for each child.

Once the improvement plan is designed, the superintendent must pay close attention to implementation. The goals of the plan should be clear, and the superintendent must carefully delineate criteria for measuring success.

4. *The superintendent undertakes the planning process while the system is still fully engaged in its ongoing, day-to-day operations.* School districts are complex organizations. Although their primary goal is student learning and the main tool of delivery is teaching, school superintendents often operate physical and mental health services as well as transportation and meal services for children. Planners cannot shut down schools while they decide on a new course of action, and the district continues to deliver on its commitments while it engages in a planning process.

Like work continues inside the district during planning processes, life outside the school system goes on. Laws change required practices, funding formulas adjust to the economy, and priorities shift as new information about improvement is discovered. The superintendent does not control many factors that affect the attainment of the district's goals. Further, outside factors, such as sudden political shifts, at times cause major disruptions in the organization's regular business. There is no time to pause and begin anew.

GIVEN THESE TENSIONS, WHAT IS A LEADER TO DO?

It behooves a superintendent to embark on this journey guided by a strategic approach that is based on a proven framework for organizational improvement. To be effective, such a framework should focus on the core business of the organization. In the case of school districts, the core business is teaching and learning. The framework should guide the organization in a systematic path to align all that the organization does in meeting its primary purpose, while helping the superintendent align the major functions of the district in supporting the core work. Future decisions should be in concert with the goals and guiding principles in the plan to ensure coherence among the many parts of the district, which requires focus and regular attention. The framework should also help the superintendent pay attention to factors in the external environment that affect the organization. The case of Maria Goodloe-Johnson provides insights into a superintendent's thinking and planning as she leads an improvement effort in her new district. The analysis below explores how Goodloe-Johnson navigates the tensions of collecting data and crafting a five-year strategic plan in Seattle.

SUPERINTENDENT MARIA GOODLOE-JOHNSON

The ghosts of superintendents past were very much alive when Goodloe-Johnson's tenure began in 2007. Goodloe-Johnson was the first "traditional educator" to take the helm of Seattle Public Schools (SPS) since 1995, following three males who had not come through the teaching ranks. The successes and missteps of each of her predecessors were mentioned frequently, and Goodloe-Johnson was aware of these stories. This was superintendent Goodloe-Johnson's second superintendency of a major urban district, after serving as superintendent of the Charleston County Public Schools, the largest urban district in South Carolina. She was known to be deliberate in her approach to leadership, and she was undaunted by the stories of her predecessors that surrounded her, realizing that after several difficult years it would be crucial to win the trust of her many stakeholders.

Balancing urgency for improved student achievement and her training of making data-driven decisions, Goodloe-Johnson held fast to a set of core values of accountability and achievement. She embarked on a six-month plan to learn about the hopes and dreams of the internal and external SPS community. She wanted to get a sense of what people thought about the district, and she developed a host of opportunities to hear from the community, employees, and other stakeholders. She listened closely for ideas about improvement from all of these individuals. Her commitment to listening and learning did not end with entry, however. She continued to provide opportunities for hearing from others as a regular part of her work.

She used the framework developed by the Public Education Leadership Project (PELP) at Harvard University (Childress, Elmore, Grossman, & King, 2004) to organize the work of the district. This framework places student learning at the heart of a district's focus. It provides a systematic approach to looking at key elements of the district's improvement strategy to ensure organizational coherence in the support of teaching and learning. Goodloe-Johnson had a vision of excellence for all children served by the district. She knew from looking at initial achievement data and from her informal conversations that there was a substantial disparity in achievement between and among groups of children. Her commitment to substantial improvements in student learning compelled her to develop a plan to eradicate the problem. In order to make the radical change that appeared to be in order, Goodloe-Johnson put in motion a series of activities that would result in a comprehensive picture of the state of the district. In line with her vision of a district that was equitable in its service to children and in which people held themselves and each other accountable for meeting their responsibility to support children's learning, Goodloe-Johnson developed a multipronged strategy to engage as many people as possible in shaping the district's new direction.

She knew that she would need the help of the philanthropic and business communities to raise the money for the formal process of data gathering. She worked with a local nonprofit whose mission was to support Seattle Public Schools to raise the money necessary for the audits, and the collaboration with these two stakeholder groups enabled her to take the message of improvement to a very important constituency outside of the district. In doing so, Goodloe-Johnson was adamant that those who contributed were doing so in support of the development of the plan, with the sole purpose of educating all students to the highest of levels. But working with these communities was not without a price. Goodloe-Johnson had to work hard to assuage the fears some of the other stakeholders held about potential ulterior motives of outside stakeholders or the benefits of committing time to the strategic planning process instead of rushing to put ideas to paper.

Goodloe-Johnson took great care to present the data she was gathering in a variety of ways that were understandable to all segments of the community. Goodloe-Johnson was cognizant of the importance of making the data usable and widely available, and it was important to her to see that the central office staff and personnel in the schools engaged the data in ways that helped them apply these to their own work. Goodloe-Johnson tapped her staff to take the data to the streets. They began a major outreach initiative to contact families where they lived. This meant recognizing that families were at different levels of sophistication in making the data meaningful. It was critical that the district conduct the outreach in ways that were respectful and helpful, representing a major shift in how it engaged families. Transparency about the state of the district was an important element in rebuilding trust, and essential to the future success of the plan.

The efforts of many people in the planning process over an extended period of time led to the plan "Excellence for All" being put forward to the board and adopted unanimously. The plan centered on a set of focus areas that grew out of the inclusive data-gathering process, each of which incorporated a set of strategies that would help navigate the way to success. Although there was wide support for the plan, the length of time it took to bring the plan forward left some doubting that Goodloe-Johnson would make good on her promise to improve achievement for all children. Parents who felt their children had been poorly served were growing impatient. Others who assumed that there would be swift action once the state of the district was clear to the superintendent grew frustrated with the absence of a quick shake-up. Goodloe-Johnson frequently found herself making the case for the importance of taking the time to gather complete data.

From the very beginning, she was aware that the planning process sets the stage for implementation. The PELP Coherence Framework provided a roadmap to accomplish this task and helped her think strategically. She knew that the staff and board would need a way to manage and monitor the implementation of the plan, and as the strategic plan was being developed, Goodloe-Johnson trained her leadership team and board in performance management. When "Excellence for All" was approved for use, central office staff and the school board were able to track the progress of various parts of the plan using performance management tools. Individuals were assigned areas of responsibility and were held accountable for success. The plan that took a year to fully develop was now used to guide the day-to-day work of the district and influence short- and long-term decision making in Seattle. The case study here describes the complexity, leadership, and commitment required to see the process through.

REFERENCE

Childress, S., Elmore, R. F., Grossman, A. S., & King, C. (2004, November 4). *Note on the PELP Coherence Framework*. Harvard Business School Publishing. Available from http://hbr.org/product/note-on-the-pelp-coherence-framework/an/PEL010-PDF-ENG.

Maria Goodloe-Johnson, Seattle Public Schools: The Strategy Behind the Plan

Leslie Boozer and Laura Kelley

Maria Goodloe-Johnson looked out into the unsettling scene in the crowded boardroom, where many members of the standing-room-only crowd were angrily protesting, yelling, and even crying. Schoolchildren and parents held up signs that demanded and begged for the schools to remain open despite their struggles academically and financially. She could hear more protesters chanting outside the sets of double doors to the meeting room. As the police removed unruly audience members from the meeting, the school board chairman tried to calm the crowd, banging his gavel on the wooden desk and requesting their attention. This public showing was the culmination of weeks of district preparation and community discussions, yet the meeting was not going as smoothly as she had hoped.

Goodloe-Johnson knew this was the first test of her strategic plan. This meeting's outcome could determine whether or not the Seattle community would remain on board with the agreed-upon goals for Seattle Public Schools (SPS) students. She thought about the year of work that went into developing the district's plan—all of the data collection, the input from parents and community organizations, the collaborative goal setting with stakeholders, and the unanimous vote of approval from her school board. She listened to the fractured board support for the school closure proposals she was presenting and wondered if district leadership would be willing to make the hard, unpopular choices it would take to achieve the high expectations required in the strategic plan. She believed in the process and the resulting plan, and was ready to make decisions that were guided by its goals. If the plan was successful, Goodloe-Johnson believed that the systemic changes would offer all children, including her own daughter (a rising kindergartner), better school options and a more relevant, challenging curriculum.

Implementing the strategic plan would no doubt be difficult, but the unrest in the boardroom was too palpable to be quickly forgotten. Would Seattle remain focused on the goal of excellence for all, even when it required difficult decisions like tonight's school closures? Could the district transform from a decentralized collection of schools to an aligned system focused on raising student achievement for every child? Was it wise for her to spend her entire first year developing a deliberate, data-driven five-year plan?

THE DISTRICT: ITS STRENGTHS AND CHALLENGES

Seattle Public Schools is the largest district in Washington state. When Goodloe-Johnson was appointed superintendent in April 2007, SPS had 45,276 students. The student population was diverse, with 42.4 percent white, 22.2 percent Asian, 21.6 percent African American, 11.7 percent Latino, and 2.1 percent American Indian; 38 percent of students were eligible for free or reduced-price meals; and 23.3 percent of students were classified as English language learners (ELLs). Overall, 14 percent of students were enrolled in special education, and a disproportionately large number of African American students were represented in this number (see Exhibit 4.1 on the CD).

SPS was one of the very first urban school districts to recruit a noneducator to lead the district. In July 1995 the Seattle school board hired John Stanford, a retired major general from the U.S. Army. Calling himself the "children's crusader," Stanford became Seattle's spokesman for children and their education, and under his leadership the district experienced three years of rising test scores.

Following his untimely death, the district tried to recapture the magic of Stanford's leadership by appointing two more noneducators, the first being Stanford's chief financial officer, to serve as superintendent of schools. In the five years that followed, the district suffered from significant financial issues when the budget was overestimated by $34 million, resulting in a vote of no confidence by unions and the superintendent's resignation. Following the same pattern, the next appointed interim superintendent was also an SPS chief financial officer.

The board offered the position to the interim after a nationwide search in which all four finalists withdrew. The interim led the district until 2006, during which time he worked to correct the district's financial situation with controversial school closures.

SPS received national attention during the tenures of these nontraditional educators. A momentous lawsuit, entitled *Parents Involved in Community Schools* v. *Seattle School District No. 1,* was filed in response to the district's student assignment plan in 2001. Specifically, white parents sued SPS, claiming its use of race in assigning and sometimes transferring students violated the Equal Protection Clause of the U.S. Constitution. SPS had struggled since the 1960s to voluntarily desegregate its schools and to correct its perpetual problem of racially imbalanced schools caused by the city's segregated housing patterns. To increase diversity, the SPS school board adopted an open choice plan in the 1998–1999 school year, also referred to as "controlled choice." Under the terms of the plan, each student entering ninth grade was allowed to select any high school in the district. Race was used as the third tiebreaker if a school was oversubscribed. According to the court pleadings, only 10 percent of high school students were denied a choice because of race.

Although both the local district court and the Court of Appeals for the Ninth Circuit determined the plan was constitutional, the parents continued to fight all the way to the United States Supreme Court. In the court's 5-to-4 decision on June 28, 2007, SPS's plan was determined to be unconstitutional. As Goodloe-Johnson prepared to take on the superintendency, she was faced with the challenge of designing a new student assignment plan that would prevent racial isolation, raise student achievement for all students, bring the community back together, and meet the constitutional requirements as interpreted by the sitting Supreme Court.

A NEW SUPERINTENDENT FOR SEATTLE

Goodloe-Johnson was quite different from the three nontraditional leaders who preceded her as superintendent. A lifelong educator who has always been deliberate in her decisions, her decisive style and reflective leadership began at the classroom level. Although her mother was a teacher in Nebraska, Goodloe-Johnson did not choose the same career path until she visited a psychiatric ward while a high school student. Furious that any child or adult could be forgotten and ignored, she decided to help those most vulnerable by turning this passion into a career as a special education teacher.

Goodloe-Johnson has been a trailblazer in education. After leaving the classroom, she served as an assistant principal for two years, and then was selected to serve as the youngest African American female high school principal in the state of Colorado. She then served as a director of secondary instruction and as an assistant superintendent while earning a doctorate in education from the University of Colorado at Denver and becoming a member of the 2003 Broad Superintendents Academy. In 2003 Goodloe-Johnson was the first African American and first female superintendent selected to lead Charleston County Public Schools, the largest urban school system in the state of South Carolina.

After fighting racial politics and a divided board in Charleston, Goodloe-Johnson was recruited to lead Seattle Public Schools in 2007. The second female superintendent and the first African American woman to lead the district, Goodloe-Johnson had the experience Seattle's leadership was seeking in a candidate to initiate change. As school board member Michael DeBell noted about what made Goodloe-Johnson stand out from the other candidates,

> Everybody talks about the achievement gap and strategies, and every urban district has that near or at the top of their agenda, and so that was kind of a constant among many of the leading candidates. I was looking for what was evidenced—that they could actually make some progress.... [Goodloe-Johnson] had the courage to reconstitute failing schools.

This courage would be necessary as Goodloe-Johnson embarked on a mission to improve Seattle Public Schools.

A WINDOW'S VIEW

The multitude of complex challenges in SPS at the time of Goodloe-Johnson's arrival in Seattle caused many in the community to push for a quick fix. However, from the moment Goodloe-Johnson began her tenure she wanted to be deliberate in her planning. Her first area of business was to get to know the Seattle community. She decided the best way to become acquainted with the city, its leaders, and the needs of its citizens was to embark on a "listening and learning" campaign, which included a series of bus tours of the district.

Goodloe-Johnson went on a bus tour of each of the district's seven geographical regions with its corresponding board member. Also on the bus were ten to fourteen community members who shared the community's history, their insights on district challenges for families, and points of pride. Following each tour, Goodloe-Johnson invited the community to an informal lunch at a local school to engage in conversation and allow them to directly ask questions of the superintendent, their local board member, and community leaders. According to Goodloe-Johnson, this experience greatly informed her work:

> On the bus tours, I heard the good, the bad, and the ugly. This was probably the best thing I've ever done in my career. It was fabulous because I learned the neighborhoods, I saw the schools, and heard stories directly from the people, which informed me of their perception and their beliefs. Now whether or not it played out to be accurate or not was really irrelevant. It was that it helped to build the capacity for me about why the communities were that way and what the political or community conflicts were in each geographic area.

Goodloe-Johnson was particularly moved by the community's explanation of the injustice, prejudice, and discrimination that they and their children had faced. Parents were frustrated that teachers and administrators were not holding many of the students in the district to high standards. They longed for diverse neighborhoods in which everyone got along while encouraging and supporting the children.

A STRATEGY TAKES SHAPE

From her cursory review of the district's data and her bus tours, Goodloe-Johnson was keenly aware that the district needed a clear direction—an enlightened and transparent path to guide the work. Goodloe-Johnson explained the importance of balancing the desire for quick, necessary change with a need for lasting systemic change:

> The process that deliberately takes you through the big picture of all the challenges, where you need to start, what you need to accomplish, means we had to build a foundation first. It's not sexy, it's not exciting, but we had to do that first or we couldn't build a strong foundation resulting in the improved educational outcomes of all children.

To begin the process, Goodloe-Johnson developed a detailed entry plan around her motto, "Every student achieving, everyone accountable." Covering July 2007 until January 2008, this document revolved around Goodloe-Johnson's deeply held belief in listening and learning.

After years of questionable leadership in SPS, Goodloe-Johnson focused on increasing confidence in Seattle Public Schools. She believed this process was necessary to win the trust of the people of Seattle: "My entry plan was a fit for Seattle because they like to process and talk things through." However, her slow, steady pace of gathering information and developing a relationship with her constituents had some worried. As Goodloe-Johnson recalled, "There were some people that started getting nervous about my pace—they wondered, 'When am I going to do something?'" To ease this tension, Goodloe-Johnson regularly talked about the importance of gathering data before making decisions.

Some district leadership felt that despite Goodloe-Johnson's deliberateness, they weren't being heard as much as they would have liked. Seattle Education Association (SEA) union vice president Olga Addae said the following about Goodloe-Johnson's arrival:

> Union leadership Steve Pulkkinen, Wendy Kimball, and I arranged a meeting with her. It wasn't her coming to meet us. It was us saying, "Hello, we're the leadership of SEA," and we brought her the bargaining contract. She had some basic questions about interest-based bargaining versus traditional bargaining. I did not feel that it was an outreach to come get to know us as important players.

GATHERING THE DATA

Goodloe-Johnson was not content with merely gathering data through bus tours, community forums, and one-on-one meetings with her executive leadership team. She recognized that systemic change required systemic knowledge. To gain this insight, she commissioned ten audits conducted by national experts, such as the Council of the Great City Schools, to provide objective, detailed analyses of the district's strengths, challenges, and best practices. Specifically, experts conducted audits on the Academic Safety Net (alternative education programs), bilingual education, communications, curriculum, special education, operations, capital projects, gifted education, and stakeholder engagement. In addition, McKinsey & Company carried out a district-wide diagnostic audit to analyze all aspects of the district's operations.

Audits cost money, and SPS had only recently recovered from its financial crisis thanks to the work of the previous superintendent. Goodloe-Johnson felt it was critical to have the support of philanthropic groups in order to fund the many audits she deemed necessary for the district to create a data-driven strategic plan. To secure this funding, Goodloe-Johnson worked with the independent Alliance for Education, a nonprofit organization that sought to build community support for SPS. Together they acquired over $9 million in grants from the Bill & Melinda Gates Foundation ($7.2 million); the Eli and Edythe Broad Foundation ($1.2 million); the Boeing Company ($308,000); and the Stuart Foundation ($254,000). This support was an integral piece of Goodloe-Johnson's plan for SPS.

Although most leaders would welcome outside money to support district initiatives, the money came at a cost to Goodloe-Johnson's budding relationship with the teachers union. Goodloe-Johnson believed push-back from SEA "stemmed from an anti-philanthropy, anti-big-business mentality because of what's happened in the past when groups, including the Alliance, said, 'We're going to give you this money, but we want you to use it this way.'" Goodloe-Johnson worked to convince the union that the district was not being bought off. To the contrary, she made it clear to anyone offering money that the district's vision was to create a strategic plan. If groups were interested in supporting this work, informed by the district research and audits, then SPS would accept benefactors' help.

THE PROCESS

The operations report by McKinsey & Company pointed to fragmentation among SPS departments and included hundreds of recommendations for improvement. Goodloe-Johnson hired Carol Rava Treat, who had previously worked at the Gates Foundation, to work across departments to prioritize goals and lead the strategic planning effort. Goodloe-Johnson had a specific goal in mind for her work: "I wanted to impact student achievement, and you can't impact student achievement if you don't have an aligned system." Treat was hired for just an eighteen-month period to pull the strategic planning efforts together in a coherent plan and support initial implementation.

For Goodloe-Johnson, this alignment work required specific, clear benchmark goals for the district. The strategic plan had to be detailed enough to guide the daily work of the district if she was going to raise the achievement of all students. As she explained,

> You have to be strategic, and you have to execute, and you have to be set up and organized to execute. People have to understand that expectation of alignment, everything from your evaluation to data dashboards to your meetings to the daily conversations [has] to be aligned to your strategic plan. I learned from my previous experience that you have to be deliberate about execution and benchmarking that execution. Otherwise nothing will be accomplished.

Goodloe-Johnson felt that the complexity of system-level leadership should be guided by a framework everyone in the district could understand and use. The SPS Board of Education adopted the Public Education Leadership Project Coherence Framework, which business and education leaders collaboratively designed (see Exhibit 4.2 on the CD). The framework assists with attaining and maintaining coherence by placing the instructional core as the focus of a district-wide strategy for improvement; emphasizing district elements that can support or hinder effective strategy implementation and their interrelationships; and recognizing and considering environmental factors that can have an impact on the implementation of a strategy.

Using the PELP framework, Treat began to work on establishing specific benchmarks and district-wide goals. As she explained, "You have goals, then you have strategies, then you have tactics. We first needed the board to support the goals and the strategies, and then the district needed to really figure out those individual tactics to raise achievement."

Developing tactics meant that the district had to carefully examine specific areas of the curriculum or operations and devise a plan for change. Treat began leading this inquisitive process by asking such questions as What's the timeline? What are the deliverables, and how will we know that what we're doing is going to affect student achievement? What are those connections? As Treat described, "That's been my job—to try to tie all things together and make sure we're always coming back to How do our actions interact with each other, and how do they lead us to impact on student achievement?"

Having one person focused on developing the tactics of the strategic plan was a pivotal initial step in establishing the aligned system Goodloe-Johnson desired. The overwhelming amount of data from the formal and informal audits, which Treat was culling together and coordinating, facilitated decision making across departments. Although Goodloe-Johnson had someone internal to work through understanding and making use of the collected data, she needed to involve the participatory Seattle community in setting direction for the strategic plan as well. The district also had to ensure that the tactical plans were managed properly once they were devised.

"SHAPED BY THOUSANDS OF STAKEHOLDERS"

While Treat was organizing the audit information across departments at the central office, the director of public affairs, Bridgett Chandler, worked to collate the audit findings and communicate them to principals, teachers, and the Seattle community at large. Goodloe-Johnson believed that "good ideas can come from anywhere in the organization, they can come from anywhere in our community." She felt the district could forge better pathways to success by including different perspectives throughout the planning process, and she charged Chandler with bringing this message to the community as inclusively as possible. According to Chandler, "We had a very deliberate plan to involve stakeholders from the beginning of the process, and to be transparent as we went through the process of making sense of the audit data and crafting a strategic plan."

The technical language, length, and multiple recommendations of the various audit reports were overwhelming to many in the central office, so one of Chandler's first priorities was crafting high-level summary reports for schools, families, and community organizations to enable more stakeholders to access the audit data. She posted each audit report on the district Web site along with an easy-to-read four-page summary report. All reports were translated into multiple languages to offer access to Seattle's many non-native English speakers. The overall plan was to be as transparent as possible about where SPS was performing well and where there was need for improvement.

"We put it all out there—the good, the bad, and the ugly," said Chandler. "We made it easy for people to be satisfied with whatever level of detail they were interested in learning." Part of the overall communication strategy was also to keep building-level staff regularly informed, to include them in the work, and to tap into their expertise. Goodloe-Johnson continued her listening and learning well beyond her initial entry via direct e-mail with various SPS employee groups; online interactive chats with teachers, principals, and community groups; the district Web site; and even the district television studio. Through these channels, as well as in face-to-face meetings, the superintendent sought input from those closest to the work of classrooms as she strove to put together a plan that would build a more effective and efficient system for all students.

According to Chandler, Goodloe-Johnson's stance was an active yet cautious one:

> She really didn't believe in coming in, guns blazing, with "This is my idea and I'm here to rescue you all." It was more, "Let me really understand what's happening here in Seattle, what works, and where the challenge is. Then, let me help figure out, together, [from] what I believe from my past experience and from my knowledge of where K–12 is going, what Seattle really needs to do." It was a big shift in culture for the city.

After a decade of overspending, a very public disruption in the student assignment plan that attempted to integrate the school system, and given a looming economic recession, many in Seattle wanted more decisive and speedy action from Goodloe-Johnson. The very deliberateness she touted as a virtue of a well-crafted strategic direction was not appreciated by some in the community who felt that for too long their children had been underserved. They pointed to the audit data themselves as evidence that swift action was needed, particularly for special education students and English language learners in SPS.

In large part Goodloe-Johnson empathized with the dissenters, for she, too, had been "appalled" by some of the audit findings. "The audits confirmed what I suspected, but I cried when I read that ELL audit because it was horrible. I mean, I knew that we needed to do work, but I didn't know it was that bad," she said. The former special education teacher was even more surprised by the audit of district practices for special education students:

> I could not fathom how some of [the special education] practices were still in place. It was just incredible to me how disconnected the practices were to what the research says about how we should serve students with special needs.

Increasing Family Involvement

Goodloe-Johnson was not solely interested in tapping into the educators of the system. She believed it important to include families in the data analysis and decision-making process that would build the strategic plan. Having the Seattle community on board was another way to ensure the plan was not about her as the leader, and would encourage system-wide implementation.

Coordinator of family and community engagement Bernardo Ruiz's suspicions were confirmed by a major audit finding that SPS was not doing a good job of informing families of what was going on in the district. In his process of reporting to and involving families that were representative of the district's population, Ruiz intended to make good on the recommendations of the engagement audit.

Breaking into groups over several community meetings, Ruiz and his department led families and community members in exercises for understanding the multiple audit reports, after they had viewed high-level PowerPoint presentations by Goodloe-Johnson. "First we said to the groups, 'This is the finding. What do you think about it? How can the district go about addressing this? What is your feedback?'" said Ruiz. "Families sat down with the data, and they were analyzing the schools and everything."

According to Ruiz,

> The empowerment that we give the families by sitting down with them and showing the complexity of making those decisions and all the things that we were looking at—that helped us a great deal. The other beautiful part about it is families had the opportunity to share with us what their recommendations were or if they had new ideas. We were able to make amendments to the first plans due to the feedback we received from families. That was a powerful thing that we did.

Crafting "Excellence for All" as a Community

What Goodloe-Johnson had predicted to be a six- to eight-month process of creating the strategic plan stretched out to a year before the board unanimously approved "Excellence for All" in June 2008, one year after her tenure in SPS began. Although the plan offered the promise of specific increased student achievement targets and benchmarks for tracking progress toward those goals (see Exhibit 4.3 on the CD), complaints rumbled about how urgent the district was about creating better outcomes for students. Protested one principal,

> It took her a year to put this together? We have a graduation rate of 63.2 percent, down from the last couple of years. Instead of talking and planning, why aren't they doing something tangible like providing more support to our classrooms?

The vast majority of the community, however, was on board with Goodloe-Johnson's plan. Patrick D'Amelio, CEO of the Alliance for Education, explained the public's appreciation of Goodloe-Johnson's frank discussion:

> She was quite willing to speak the truth and speak it plainly, and to be able to say to folks, "Look, this is where we are today, but here's where we're going," and so [there was] that marriage between an honest, candid assessment that wasn't always positive and a real vision for where the system needed to go in order to deliver on the promise of excellence for every student. I give her high marks for that.

"Excellence for All" outlined a vision for a coherent and consistent system, and Goodloe-Johnson promised to focus on a few key priorities at a time, to work within the district's means, and to assess their progress and report out to the public regularly and frequently. She also repeatedly reminded the community how valuable their input—combined with the experience of educators and practice-based research—was in shaping the plan.

At the core of "Excellence for All" was a solid framework to guide the district's work that promised an improved educational system for SPS students and that comprised five major areas of focus:

- Ensure Excellence in Every Classroom
- Strengthen Leaders System-Wide
- Build an Infrastructure That Works Well
- Improve Our Systems
- Engage Stakeholders

Each area of focus included two to five specific strategies for achieving the exponential academic growth the plan promised by 2013. Like the audit reports that contributed to the overall plan, "Excellence for All" was presented in a user-friendly format as well as more detailed versions.

Goodloe-Johnson's commitment to transparency was at the forefront of the presentation. Anyone in Seattle could easily find the strategic plan on the Web site, in schools, or in the district office, and she made countless presentations on the radio, in television news, and in school and district meetings. Schools hung and distributed posters throughout the district, and brochures with a high-level description of the plan were shared with the entire community. Chandler's staff trained principals to explain the strategic plan to teachers and parents, and gave them talking points for discussing the plan with various audiences. Chandler was also committed to a consistent "visual message" in the form of an "Excellence for All" "brand" that she and Goodloe-Johnson created and made easily identifiable in each SPS building.

For Goodloe-Johnson, the approval of "Excellence for All" was a critical step in the system-level improvement she hoped to make in Seattle:

> This strategic plan is specific to Seattle, and it is really shaped by the audits and the input of over three thousand people in the community, because there are some very unique things in the context of Seattle and work that we have to do here. I absolutely think there is a need for this kind of plan, because otherwise how do you determine how you help schools? And my premise is [that] the district office job is to help schools be successful. In order to help schools be successful we have to understand what the best practice is, what the best research is, and then what the expectations are for all students. This work will now be aligned to a guide that helps us make good decisions along the way.

MONITORING THE PLAN: PERFORMANCE MANAGEMENT

Keeping on top of the process of coordinating the audit data and crafting a district strategic plan, all while maintaining the day-to-day operations and shorter-term decision making, required an organized method of monitoring that was unfamiliar to SPS. Although Treat was charged with assessing and managing the overall strategic planning process, her temporary position was never intended to establish continuity throughout the entire system. To begin tackling some of the fragmentation, Goodloe-Johnson began reorganizing her executive team and senior leadership teams, starting with determining who needed to be at the table to create a coherent, high-functioning system.

Weekly meetings with her executive team revealed some holes in processes and procedures, gaps Goodloe-Johnson intended to close by changing the face of the team. Treat assumed her place on the team, which facilitated her understanding of other departments, their roles and responsibilities, and how she could arrange a coherent plan for her work. Goodloe-Johnson made other key adjustments, stating,

> I changed the structure of how we work together. I expanded the folks that sit on my executive team that I meet with every Monday because I felt like HR was key and was missing. I felt like communications was key and missing. Holly [Ferguson] became my policy and governance person, and she sits on the team. My strategic outreach and partnership person sits on the team. Research and evaluation sits on the team. The CFO and general counsel were there, and I expanded the team to include these other folks, as well as technology. I've got everybody at the table that's connected in the systemic work that we do, and we talk every Monday to keep everybody on the same page about the work.

As the composition of the executive team was changing, so was that of the senior leadership team of central office middle managers, composed primarily of instructional directors. Goodloe-Johnson felt that the previous setup was "ineffective," and she included this senior management team in the new process for implementation and monitoring of district-level work.

The central office staff was trained in performance management activities that were tailored to help streamline their work and improve efficiency as they moved toward the goal of improving student achievement in SPS. Aligned with Goodloe-Johnson's push for accountability, the overall process not only outlined the steps and tasks required to implement initiatives and work goals but also designated the managerial and intellectual capital necessary to get work done. Every project required an SPS executive project sponsor who brought a specialized knowledge and expertise, and a project manager who oversaw the overall progression of work, managed needed resources, and monitored the timeline of completion. The sponsor was ultimately accountable for the successful outcomes of a project, and the project manager was the work "catalyst," responsible for the planning, coordination, and communication required to execute. Together they created a defined work plan with clear goals, responsibilities, and monitoring points that allowed the SPS team to make adjustments as needed to ensure the project's successful completion.

Although this strategy greatly assisted the leadership team, Goodloe-Johnson wanted a tool that could provide anyone in the district with a quick understanding of district priorities. They therefore created the district strategic plan project dashboard, which at any given time displayed between twenty and forty projects on which SPS was working, all directly connected to the goals of "Excellence for All" and prioritized according to immediacy. The dashboard served as a tool for assessing the overall work of the district at a glance and used stoplight color coding: red to indicate "late or over budget," yellow for "schedule or budget concerns," and green for "on schedule and within budget." The phase of work for each project was also color coded to display how far along that project was in terms of definition, planning, execution, or closing out. To ensure alignment, every single project also listed which of the strategic plan's five major areas of focus it was addressing.

Weekly executive team meetings resulted in executive project sponsors' sharing reports and status updates based on the stoplight dashboard. Coherence became clearer as all of the projects were dictated by the strategic plan and prioritized on the district dashboard of implementation. With a formal process for monitoring implementation on an ongoing basis, Goodloe-Johnson believed the district could answer critics and step up the pace, resulting in higher-quality instructional programs for students.

REPORTING TO THE PUBLIC AND THE BOARD

The performance management training didn't stop with the executive and senior leadership teams. Goodloe-Johnson used the same process to keep her board informed of progress in SPS. In quarterly strategic plan updates, she briefed the board on the stage of implementation for each of the various projects prioritized in the strategic plan. Projects in various phases of implementation were discussed with the board using the same stoplight color coding (red, yellow, green) that the district staff used to indicate progress and areas in need of further resources, support, and attention.

The district also established an annual scorecard that tracked growth over time, again aligned with the strategic plan goals and initiatives (see Exhibits 4.4 and 4.5 on the CD to view the district scorecard and student achievement results). Used as a public reporting measure and also as a way to share progress and struggles with the board, the district scorecard offered a system-level overview of movement toward the 2013 goals.

Everyone having a clear understanding of progress increased the pressure to achieve. When SPS was not on track to meet 2013 goals, Goodloe-Johnson and her team members were responsible for sharing strategies for accelerating progress, and SPS prepared additional or revised strategies for action when original plans were not meeting benchmark targets. Not only the central office but also individual schools felt this pressure. Each school's annual improvement plan was aligned with the district scorecard, and schools that were not making gains and that displayed low performance on state measures were scheduled to receive more structured guidance and support from the central office than were schools that were meeting benchmarks.

TESTING "EXCELLENCE FOR ALL"

The hallmark of performance management is adapting successfully to unexpected change. Despite SPS's ranking of all the projects outlined to implement the strategic planning goals, the state funding crisis projected in late summer 2008 meant reorganizing priorities. Even though the courts required a new student assignment plan, school closures moved ahead on the dashboard as the budget shortfall required a reduction in schools.

The community struggled with closing its schools, even those that were underenrolled and underperforming. D'Amelio described the public sentiment: "These are tough, tough decisions, and any time you make decisions like these, there are perceived winners and losers and people that feel like they've lost in the process." However, Goodloe-Johnson believed that these decisions were necessary; the district simply could not financially support all of its schools. As she noted, "Why would I cut teachers and programs to spread our resources so thin as opposed to, let's use our facilities better, let's improve our programs, increase that market share, and increase the academic expectations?"

However, parents, students, and community members did not share this opinion. They believed that closing schools was tantamount to giving up on their community, even if SPS promised to relocate successful programs to other buildings. Some believed that Goodloe-Johnson's business-like approach to the painful process of school closures they had experienced under previous superintendents demonstrated a lack of compassion and understanding of their needs.

District staff experienced the decisions—termed "capacity management"—very differently. The careful planning in "Excellence for All" framed all of the decisions pertaining to school closures, and central office leadership asked,

> How do we achieve greater excellence in programs across the district? How do we not just count seats and compare that with demographics, but how do we really look at this as an opportunity to improve instruction and access for all of our kids to the excellent programs that we have going?

As the personal attacks on her began, Goodloe-Johnson looked to her strategic plan for the strength to stand up for her convictions:

> The thing about school closures, at least that helps me, is I feel like we're making really good decisions for our kids, and the system is going to be stronger as long as we execute and do the work around the transition and the change and building stronger programs. Because no matter what your criteria [are] for school closure, or your rationale or what data you have, people aren't going to like it. They are going to be angry, they're going to be mad, they're going to come talk to you about it, they're going to call you names, so you just have to be ready for that. And having the data and the strategic plan just really helps because in my head I'm clear about what we need to do, I'm clear about where the inequities are, where we need to increase our programs, what we need to do to [achieve more] success, provide access, all of that.

As Goodloe-Johnson prepared to speak at the heated board meeting, she carefully weighed her convictions with those of the families before her. To be successful, a district must not only carefully plan for success but also earn the respect, understanding, and support of its constituents as it makes the difficult choices required to improve the system. But Goodloe-Johnson also realized a strength in strategic planning is to not be swayed by emotion—to stay true to the plan, its goals, and the pursuit of desired outcomes. Balancing these two requirements would take all of her abilities as a system leader.

"We are working to deliver on the promise of an excellent education for every student," Goodloe-Johnson began. As she explained her thinking to protesting families, the question for the SPS public remained—Would they embrace the change required by the plan or demand a return to the status quo?

The Best Laid Plans . . .

Maree Sneed

As legal counsel for multiple urban school districts and as a former principal and central office administrator, I learned that at any given time superintendents are faced with competing commitments—to students and families, communities and businesses, and district partners and financial sponsors. Managing these commitments, while providing students the opportunity for a high-quality and diverse education, is challenging. Success is only achieved through creativity, thoughtful planning, and collaboration and flexibility by superintendents committed and determined to carry out their instructional, legal, and financial obligations and responsibilities.

On any given day, headlines throughout the country fill papers with news of superintendents losing their jobs over controversial decisions, such as school closures, student assignment plans, and budget changes. Unable to please everyone, effective superintendents make difficult choices that they believe will result in the best potential educational outcomes for all students. These unpopular decisions, however, often result in superintendents being ousted from their positions. In addition, a superintendent's race and gender often become hot-button issues further complicating the decision-making process in such controversial matters.

Like most superintendents, SPS superintendent Maria Goodloe-Johnson began her tenure in the Rainy City with a myriad of competing commitments and challenges. Goodloe-Johnson had to balance her commitment to equity and "excellence for all," providing high-quality instruction for all students, with an obligation to maintain fiscal responsibility in the midst of a distressing financial climate. She also wanted to continue implementing a student assignment plan that included school choice for students and their families.

Goodloe-Johnson began her superintendency in the aftermath of a decision by the Supreme Court in June 2007 in *Parents Involved in Community Schools (PICS)* v. *Seattle Schools District No. 1,* which is the Supreme Court's most recent ruling on voluntary integration. In *PICS* several parents of SPS high school students challenged the district's choice plan because their children were not assigned to the high schools of their choosing. This was because more high school students wanted to attend some of the SPS high schools than these schools could accommodate. In assigning students to these oversubscribed schools, the SPS plan took into account a number of factors, in addition to choice and available seats, including keeping siblings in the same schools and allowing students to attend schools closer to their homes. In very limited circumstances, the plan also used race as a factor.

THE IMPORTANCE OF CONTEXT

Like in many other urban school districts, the enrollment of SPS has decreased steadily since the 1970s from approximately eighty-five thousand students to approximately forty-five thousand students, while the number and percentage of African American, Hispanic, and Asian students has increased. Unlike in many other urban districts, however, SPS began implementing voluntary integration plans in the 1960s to address issues of racial isolation. By implementing these plans, SPS avoided a court-ordered desegregation plan.

Over the years, the SPS board members, in consultation with their legal counsel, adopted voluntary integration plans that included a variety of strategies, such as voluntary transfers, mandatory student assignment, magnet schools, controlled choice, and the open choice plan that was challenged in *PICS*. The board recognized that implementation of voluntary integration plans was necessary because of Seattle's segregated housing patterns.

SPS began implementing the open choice plan in the 1999–2000 school year and continued to implement the plan until 2010, with modifications throughout the years to address a number of issues, including those raised by parents and changes in the law. As part of the open choice plan, the SPS board adopted a "Statement Reaffirming Diversity Rationale" that outlined the board's reasons for their efforts toward voluntary integration. This statement affirmed the board's belief in equity and their dedication to providing a high-quality education for every child. The board took this opportunity to explain to the entire community the educational benefits of providing diverse enrollments in schools. According to the board, diverse student enrollment "fosters racial and cultural understanding" by "increase[ing] the likelihood that students will discuss racial or ethnic issues and be more likely to socialize with people of different races." In addition, the board stated that diversity "enhances the educational process" by "bring[ing] different viewpoints and experiences to [the classroom]" and has "inherent education value from the standpoint of education's role in a democratic society." Diversity is therefore "a valuable resource for teaching students to become citizens in a multi-racial/multi-ethnic world" (*Parents Involved in Community Schools* v. *Seattle School District No. 1*, 2007).

Despite the long-standing commitment of the SPS board in providing diverse school enrollments, a number of the schools have remained or have became racially and ethnically isolated. Like many other school districts, SPS found that its racially and ethnically isolated schools had higher teacher turnover and fewer experienced teachers. SPS struggled to counter these trends, because research has shown that high teacher turnover and concentrations of inexperienced teachers in such schools have a negative impact on the achievement of their students.

A STANDARD OF EXCELLENCE

Goodloe-Johnson assumed the superintendency of SPS about the same time that the United States Supreme Court announced its ruling in *PICS*. Although the *PICS* decision did not invalidate all voluntary integration efforts or plans, it did rule that the SPS open choice plan was unconstitutional. The Supreme Court's decision, however, did not require any changes to the current SPS plan because, at the time of the decision, SPS was using only race-neutral factors in assigning students to schools and had not been using race as a factor for several years.

Nevertheless, Goodloe-Johnson began her superintendency in a city that continued to be divided racially and ethnically, with the north part of Seattle far whiter and wealthier than the central and south parts, and with many of the schools in the north part of Seattle perceived as being "better" than those in the central and south parts. She also faced a looming budget crisis, the need to redesign the student assignment plan to ensure equitable opportunities for students no matter where they lived, and the necessity of developing a comprehensive strategic plan to address her priorities of equity and excellence.

As the above case study described, Goodloe-Johnson spent many months listening to stakeholders and reviewing previous strategic plans and studies of issues and problems in SPS before she and her staff developed a five-year strategic plan—"Excellence for All"—that focused on providing the best education to every child in the system. According to "Excellence for All," SPS "will achieve excellence" by ensuring that there is excellence in all classrooms; strengthening leaders throughout the system; building an infrastructure that works effectively; improving district systems; and engaging stakeholders.

With "Excellence for All" in place, Goodloe-Johnson faced some difficult choices. These included determining which schools should be closed and how to increase equitable access for students in order to address the "Excellence for All" goal of high-quality instruction in every classroom. Based on Goodloe-Johnson's recommendation, the board approved the closing of five schools for 2009–2010. The school closures allowed the superintendent to focus resources on fewer buildings, place programs strategically so that all students had equitable access to programs no matter where they lived, redraw attendance boundaries to address demographic changes that had taken place over the last decade, and revise the student assignment process to make it more transparent and understandable and to reduce transportation costs.

Some of the schools slated to be closed included programs that benefited their students, despite being underenrolled or failing to meet the academic needs of all. For example, a program supporting special education students, one of SPS's most vulnerable student groups, was housed in one of the schools recommended for closure. Another school due to close had been created in reaction to the resegregation of Seattle: the African American Academy supported students and families academically, culturally, and socially. Many parents and teachers worried that students might not receive the same kind of support in other schools.

Not surprisingly, closing schools was not popular. Angry protestors regularly appeared at board meetings. Parents and students pleaded with Goodloe-Johnson and the board to save their schools. District leadership, however, did not succumb to political pressure, choosing instead what they felt was in the best interest of all students, committing to re-create successful programs and supportive school environments in the remaining schools in SPS.

With more tough choices ahead, Goodloe-Johnson decided to work with her legal team to use the law to the district's advantage instead of seeing it as a hindrance. The result was a student assignment plan that addressed SPS's commitment to diversity by using socioeconomic factors in drawing school boundaries "because of the potentially beneficial impact on the diversity of a school's population." In addition, the plan

> uses [a] socioeconomic tiebreaker for assigning students to open choice seats at high schools [to] create some opportunities for greater diversity. After the second year of high school assignments under [the] plan, the [s]uperintendent will report to the school board and the public on high school demographics. Based on that analysis, a determination will be made as to whether an economic diversity tiebreaker should be instituted in a subsequent year.

The example for superintendents Goodloe-Johnson provides in the development and implementation of "Excellence for All" is important. She has not only modeled for SPS how to use data to drive a plan for improvement but also set a course beyond what the law requires: her vision of excellence for all extends further than the minimum the district is legally required to provide for students. For example, Goodloe-Johnson took into account Justice Anthony Kennedy's suggestions in *PICS* for pursuing diversity, such as the purposeful placement of programs to give students the educational benefits of diversity. This included the strategic positioning, for instance, of Montessori and gifted programs in southern and central Seattle and other underserved sections of the city so that all students could have equitable access to these programs. Goodloe-Johnson was also willing to recommend the use of socioeconomic factors in order to promote diversity and avoid racial isolation.

In all ways, Goodloe-Johnson strove to meet a higher standard, believing in the students of Seattle and the adults' ability to deliver on the promise of a high-quality and diverse education for all. Articulating the educational benefits of diversity is politically challenging for any superintendent, but it is particularly difficult for African American superintendents. Those who already benefit may see themselves losing slices of the "privilege pie" as a result of the efforts of African American superintendents to fight for diversity and equity.

Some superintendents contend that pursuing such strategies as those Goodloe-Johnson implemented leads to too much political instability. Superintendents, however, should follow the example set by Goodloe-Johnson and others in promoting the educational benefits of diversity and avoiding the harms of racial isolation. The law is not stagnant, and leaders who believe in equity and diversity consistently work with their legal teams to design opportunities for the advancement of all children. To reduce the political volatility and improve student achievement, superintendents should consider implementing these strategies as part of a multiyear strategic plan that has been developed with input from stakeholders throughout the district and is based on research and best practices.

WHEN PLANS CHANGE

After she became superintendent, Goodloe-Johnson had to rethink her well-organized, carefully designed strategic plan when the budget crisis grew significantly worse. In other districts, constituent desires, budget cuts, and unexpected legislation changes can hinder even the most proactive of plans. Maintaining the integrity of the district strategic plan despite shifts in resources and support is the primary focus of a district leader. If a plan has been devised to increase and improve educational opportunities and outcomes for students, the superintendent must find ways to see that goal through, often by doing more with less. Keeping the focus on students and student achievement must always be the top priority, even if it means disrupting the status quo.

Throughout the last thirty years, SPS has had the benefit of in-house counsel to guide it through the complicated legal landscape when it needed to make difficult decisions related to voluntary integration, diversity, equity, and school closures. Unlike in many other districts, these decisions were more difficult because SPS was not under a court mandate to desegregate. Without a court order to leverage action, Goodloe-Johnson's work was harder. Many sophisticated superintendents and boards, such as in Lee County, Florida, and San Francisco, California, have used such orders to bring about systemic change in their districts and to ensure equity and diversity for every student.

By incorporating lawyers and their expertise into planning processes, districts and leaders are better poised to be proactive about their strategic plans and advancing reform agendas. Although superintendents should not feel limited by the law when research and expertise inform what is best for students, lawyers and policymakers also can influence and help districts design new policies. The law is often tested and changed due to the innovative thinking of educational leaders who frequently are called upon to testify about their practice before policymakers.

The relationship between law, policy, and practice remains a balancing act for superintendents. The most effective practitioners are those who maintain a healthy respect for the law's potential to assist them in their goals while understanding that policies are malleable and can be adjusted as circumstances change. As in the case of Goodloe-Johnson, these superintendents are in the best position to craft and successfully implement strategic plans that pursue equity and excellence for all.

REFERENCE

Parents Involved in Community Schools v. *Seattle School District No. 1*, 551 U.S. 701 (2007).

CHAPTER 5

Instructional Improvement

Leading Learning in Urban Schools

Richard F. Elmore

Not so very long ago, in an era that might be called "B.A.," or Before Accountability, I recall sitting in a large meeting of school administrators listening to a speech by a distinguished and nationally recognized school superintendent in which he described his job, with pride, as operating one of the largest construction authorities, transportation systems, and food service organizations in the country, and doing it with laser-like precision. I remember thinking at the time, without really knowing why, that I was witnessing the end of an era. I was.

It is still possible to become a school superintendent without knowing (or caring) much about instructional practice, but this is not something most superintendents would admit in public. In fact, most superintendents would say publicly that they are, in the tired lingo of the time, "in it for the kids," by which they mean possibly something about the conditions for teaching and learning for children in schools. School superintendents are now required, as a condition of their work and as an artifact of the accountability system, to take some responsibility, however indirect, for student learning. This is in itself a major transformation in the job description, if not the practice, of the superintendency.

EXAMINING INSTRUCTION

I am something of an anthropologist of superintendents' meetings. I am often called to address large groups of superintendents by their association leaders, to speak to them about the centrality and urgency of large-scale instructional improvement and its importance to the role and practice of the superintendency. In every such group there is a faction of true believers who sit near the front, attend to my remarks with a certain ferocious dedication, and come equipped with difficult-to-answer questions. The proportion of these superintendents has, indeed, increased significantly since the advent of performance-based accountability. But I would say from my experience that they are FAR from the majority of practicing superintendents. When I sit at tables in the rear of the room for lunch, as I intentionally do after I have given my speech, the topics of conversation have a certain regularity, regardless of the setting. The themes, in rough order of frequency, are: (1) who is moving from one job to another; (2) retirement and benefits packages recently secured by those who have moved; (3) school board politics; (4) budget; (5) the latest absurdity emanating from the state department of education; and (6) warm-weather golf destinations. Depending on the season and the region, number 6 can get as high as number 1. Even when I am the featured speaker, and even when I am present at the table, the topic of instructional improvement rarely, if ever, lands in the top ten.

I also have the luxury now of spending a great deal of time with superintendents who are committed to the practice of instructional improvement in their districts. They are a self-selected bunch, a statistically small part of their professional cohort. They are committed and good at what they do. They practice their work, and they teach other people how to do it. They are considered to be outliers in their profession. And they are aware of how difficult it is, even in a policy environment that focuses on accountability for student performance, to hold the attention of their boards and school systems on the work of continuous improvement of instructional practice and student learning. It is exhausting work. They are routinely criticized by their boards for the work they do on instruction because, by definition, it upsets the routine expectations of what a senior leader in a school system should be. In the hallways outside our meetings, before we get together for the "real" work, their topics of conversation are not so very different from those of the superintendents who sit at the back tables in the professional meetings, but when we begin the work of instructional improvement they are highly focused and competent.

Let me be blunt. Although it is obvious to anyone who is paying attention that accountability for student performance requires people in leadership positions who actually know something about instructional practice and are qualified to lead its improvement, it is far from clear that most of the people who are being hired for leadership positions in local school districts, mostly by local boards, are in fact qualified to do the work. They undoubtedly have many talents, or they wouldn't be hired. They may be required to espouse views about high-quality instruction as a condition of employment. It is painfully obvious to me, however, that the majority of people in the superintendency are neither qualified for nor particularly interested in the hard work of instructional improvement. It is equally clear to me that, with a few notable exceptions, the programs that purport to train people for the superintendency are equally uninterested in the work. I am enough of an institutionalist to understand the harsh reality behind this phenomenon: leaders are not qualified to do the work because the people who hire them are not interested in these qualifications. If the system were as rational as accountability advocates think it should be, the qualifications for the superintendency, and for the incumbents of these positions, would have changed markedly by now. They haven't.

For the past twenty years, the Harvard Urban Superintendents Program (USP) has been the most persistent voice in preparing senior leaders for urban school systems for whom the improvement of instructional practice is the centerpiece of their leadership. Over this period we have learned a great deal about the knowledge and skill requirements of the work of leading instructional improvement and about how to prepare people to do it. We still have a great deal to learn, but in order to learn it we have to have people who are willing to practice it so we can participate in building the knowledge base that goes with the practice. The point of view about the superintendency that USP represents is a decidedly minority view, but it is a strong and increasingly coherent one.

The work of the superintendents represented in this book makes clear that transformational leadership in the public education sector is possible. These exemplars also demonstrate that the knowledge and skill required to do the work of transformational leadership are very different from anything required in the past. They are the generation that has taught us it is possible to do this work. The commitments of these leaders are large—nothing less than equal access and educational success for all students, regardless of their social circumstances. It is also evident, from the record of their achievements, that most of what they have done has been accomplished *in spite of,* rather than *because of,* the institutional systems in which they work. It is the rare transformational leader who is able to sustain a mandate within the existing institutional structure long enough to make a deep impression on that structure. These are defects of the system more than of the people who choose to do the work.

SUPERINTENDENTS AND THE INSTRUCTIONAL CORE

The central premise of the leadership of large-scale instructional improvement is a focus on the instructional core—the student and the teacher in the presence of content. The work of improvement consists of providing the resources, pressure, and support to raise the level of content, to expand the knowledge and skill of teachers, and to increase the active engagement of students in their own learning. That's it. Any action at the classroom, school, or system level can be evaluated by whether it increases the level of cognitive demand for students through changes in content, whether it increases the knowledge and skill of teachers in their work with students, and whether it provides opportunities for students to exercise control over their own learning. If an action doesn't meet these criteria it should be the subject of intense scrutiny, because it is probably serving some purpose other than the core one of student learning.

USP has consistently taught people to see the work of leadership in terms of its impact on the instructional core and to measure their success in terms of their capacity to orchestrate the resources of the system around the core, with a strong commitment to improving the prospects of underserved students. School systems, especially large urban systems, are not built to do this work, and they do not easily accommodate the work. American school systems (most decidedly *not* the educational systems of other countries) have, since the late nineteenth century, been viewed as institutional receptacles for whatever the prevailing political idea is, rather than as places where adults and children engage in learning over time. So the typical urban school system is a collection of pieces that accurately represents a geological profile of the sedimentary layers of shifting political agendas over time. Elected officials at the federal, state, and local levels add functions to the system, often without paying for them, and never take any away. The structure of urban school systems, in its default mode, is built to process political demands, not to manage instructional practice.

It should surprise no one, then, that superintendents who aspire to lead instructional improvement in their systems almost immediately get into conflicts over the purpose and organization of the enterprise.

They are upsetting a carefully crafted set of political bargains that are Byzantine in their complexity and often invisible to those who are their beneficiaries—until that critical moment when organizations realize that their institutional interests are threatened and move quickly into self-preservation mode.

TRANSFORMATIONAL LEADERSHIP

The seemingly obvious idea that the purpose of urban education systems is to manage conditions that promote quality and improvement in the instructional core is, it turns out, a very subversive one. It requires a coherent strategy, the purpose of which is not to "change" the system in ways that are acceptable to everyone in it but to fundamentally transform the set of institutional agreements, commitments, procedures, and routines that represent the congealed residue of accumulated bargains over the past century. The work is fundamentally cultural, but it is also heavily managerial. The cultural work entails changing the furniture inside people's heads. The managerial work is designing the organization that supports this transformation. Everything about the existing institutional structure is geared toward resisting this transformation—always in the interest of perfectly reasonable claims of the accumulated baggage of the old system.

A short list of the kind of transformations required to do this work should make my point. The work of improvement makes heavy demands on people's time, it requires them to work together in unfamiliar ways, and it asks them to reexamine their established practices. This work necessitates a different structure for the workday—one that accommodates people working in groups as opposed to as individuals. It demands knowledge and skill about how to work in groups, which typically don't come with the work experience of people in schools. And it requires a different kind of practice on the part of individuals in teaching and leadership roles. When schools and systems start the process of transformation, it is fair to say, almost no one in the organization knows how to do this work or how to manage it. Furthermore, the work requires a significant intrusion on some of the organization's most sacred cultural norms—the inviolable norm of privacy for teachers' practice, for example. Most people in schools experience the initial stages of serious school improvement not as some sort of *kumbaya* spiritual epiphany, but, quite the contrary, as a direct assault on the core values of the institution and their roles in it. They experience it that way because it *is* that way. The reflex action of the default culture, no matter the good intentions and values of its incumbents, is to protect itself. The practice of improvement, at least in the early stages, involves a kind of zen-like persistence and a body of knowledge and skill that is about transforming not just people's work lives but the contents of their heads, hands, and hearts. Most people in the field of education have coped with generations of "change" initiatives by a skillful combination of resistance, subversion, and relabeling. Cultural transformation, like that of Richmond Public Schools in Virginia and of New York City's Chancellor's District presented herein, requires them quite literally to change their understanding of themselves and their practice in the face of altered circumstances. Not surprisingly, the reflex response is quite powerful.

Large-scale improvements in instructional practice and student learning require mastery of a well-defined body of knowledge and skill: using structures and processes to redefine the work and provide a safe environment for adult and student learning, managing the resources of the organization to support the learning and performance of adults and students, creating and sustaining accountability for high standards of practice based on defensible evidence, fostering an environment of reciprocal accountability in which every demand for increased performance is accompanied by support for the development of the knowledge and skill necessary to meet the performance target, developing and using information about the organization to make deliberate decisions about its work, and managing relationships with the external environment to create a stable mandate for the work. This knowledge and these skills are teachable. We see evidence of this work in Rudy Crew's Chancellor's District in New York City and his School Improvement Zone strategy in Miami-Dade. The issue is not so much the knowledge base that attaches to strong instructional leadership, although we can always use help in developing it, but the *demand* for the skills and knowledge that powerful transformational leaders have. Let's just say the American education system has its enthusiasm well under control for the kind of leadership required to do the work of transformation.

The best models we currently have to learn from of highly effective urban superintendents within traditional models of education are those who have managed, as Deborah Jewell-Sherman did in Richmond, to sustain a relentless focus on improving conditions of teaching and learning in schools over a long enough period of time to convince the adults who work in schools that students can learn at much higher levels than they previously expected. However, it must be said that, as the Jewell-Sherman case demonstrates, this unwavering focus on teaching and learning rests largely with the superintendent, and occurs largely *in spite of,* rather than *because of,* the surrounding governance and bureaucratic system.

MOVING LEARNING TO THE CENTER

The successful urban superintendent is required to treat learning—of adults about their work, of students in their daily lives in schools—as a "new" concern of the system, as an "initiative" rather than as the central responsibility and work of the whole enterprise. Instructional improvement is viewed by people in the system—including elected and appointed board members—as a series of "initiatives" associated with the leadership agenda of a particular superintendent, and as imposing a "new" set of demands on people (principals, teachers, support staff) "in addition" to their already-onerous responsibilities (which would *be* . . . ?). So the superintendent's learning agenda has to be vetted through the existing collective bargaining agreement to make sure it doesn't impose noncontractual responsibilities on affected parties. The superintendent's learning agenda has to be funded by the board through special, marginal, discretionary funding decisions that can be reversed at any time by a majority vote for any number of reasons. This agenda has to be reviewed and evaluated through many bureaucratic processes by other jurisdictions, especially in districts that have large numbers of underperforming schools by the metric of state accountability systems. And the superintendent's learning agenda has to pick its way through the multitude of procedural and structural requirements that urban districts impose on themselves by virtue of being complex bureaucratic organizations, usually without regard for whether these processes actually improve the final product, which they typically do not. The superintendent who doesn't consult with all the interests in and around the organization about any important facet of her learning agenda will quickly become an ex-superintendent. Pause for a moment and consider a world in which a school superintendent's focus on teaching and learning is considered to be a "novel" or controversially innovative idea. Hmmm.

The challenges to urban educational leaders are the same as the challenges to all educational leaders in the future, only larger and with higher stakes. Moving from a system in which a focus on teaching and learning is considered to be a novel and controversial initiative to a system in which it is considered to be the central work of leaders will not be either easy or quick. But the future of organized learning depends on it. I think the issue of who will be the kinds of transformational, instruction-focused leaders like Jewell-Sherman and Crew of the education sector is up for grabs. The work of USP has been a beacon in an otherwise fairly bleak landscape for the development of transformational leaders—one of three or four exemplars, and probably the oldest. The ground is shifting under the sector in ways that are not necessarily conducive to the long-term improvement of traditional public school systems, or the traditional institutions that have trained their leaders. I greet this prospect with concern and, I confess, a degree of anticipation.

Deborah Jewell-Sherman, Richmond Public Schools: Getting to the Heart of the Work

Kristy Cooper, Laura Kelley, Leslie Boozer, and Aaliyah El-Amin

Deborah Jewell-Sherman, superintendent of Richmond Public Schools (RPS) in Virginia, was preparing to speak at a news conference. It was her birthday, April 7, 2008, and it would be a day she would never forget. In the audience was a select group of school board members, supporters, and colleagues. As she considered the gravity of the news she was about to share, she couldn't help but reflect on her tenure in Richmond: the progress over the last six years she and her leadership team made, the improvements to schools, the gains in student achievement, and the numerous partnerships RPS had forged with the community. In fact, earlier that morning she had participated in the unveiling of a partnership with Virginia Union University that would result in many Richmond high school students receiving college scholarships. As the press anxiously greeted her, wondering why they had been assembled, she stepped forward and announced that she would not accept an extension on her contract because she planned to retire from the superintendency. Explaining her decision to leave Richmond, she said, "I can say with both humility and with pride that I have accomplished, and in many instances exceeded, what I set out to achieve."

Jewell-Sherman and her team had good cause to be proud. In 2001, just a year before she became superintendent, Richmond had been the second-lowest-performing school district in Virginia. In 2002, only ten of the district's fifty-one schools had the required number of students performing at or above proficient on the Virginia Standards of Learning (SOL) test to earn full accreditation by the state. Under her leadership, this number jumped to twenty-one schools, then to thirty-nine, and finally to forty-three schools by 2005. In 2008, 87 percent of district schools were accredited, including all eight of the district's high schools, for the second year in a row.

Yet Jewell-Sherman's tenure was fraught with high-profile political battles. A divided school board, a public battle with the mayor, and multiple audits by the city auditor plagued her superintendency and prompted some to question her leadership. The crowd at the press conference wondered, Were these the reasons that Jewell-Sherman was deciding to leave, despite the tremendous growth in student achievement? As Jewell-Sherman prepared to address the media, she paused. She knew that leaving was the right thing to do. But what would happen to the progress she led? Would her commitment to "protecting the instructional core" be maintained? Had the vicious public political battles made it difficult for the community to trust the school system? Would her successor be able to sustain and exceed the growth she and her leadership team had made?

THE STARTING PLACE: RICHMOND IN 2002

A report produced by the Council of the Great City Schools (2003, p. 11) noted that Richmond faced challenges common to urban districts in the United States: "low student achievement, high poverty rates, disparate funding, high dropout rates, and fragile public support." Instability also plagued the district as Richmond prepared to lose its sixth superintendent in fourteen years. RPS served just under twenty-five thousand students, which included 88 percent students of color and 61 percent qualifying for free or reduced-price lunch.

When the nine-member school board debated options for a new superintendent in summer 2002, the associate superintendent for instruction and accountability, Deborah Jewell-Sherman, was among the candidates. Despite her seven years of service in Richmond's superintendent's office, her doctorate from Harvard University, and her previous success as an elementary school principal and classroom teacher, Jewell-Sherman's suitability for the open superintendent job was hotly debated. Amid grumbling about the rushed and incomplete nature of the hiring process (only two of thirteen candidates were interviewed), and some of the board members' publicly expressing a lack of faith in her abilities, Jewell-Sherman was elected to the superintendency by a 5-to-3 vote.

However, her appointment came with stipulations. Jewell-Sherman had to increase the number of accredited schools in Richmond from ten to twenty within one year, or her contract would be terminated for cause. Among the requirements for school accreditation was meeting the 70-percent-or-higher passing rate on the Virginia SOL exams. Jewell-Sherman's contract was one of the first in Virginia and one of only a few in the nation to tie a superintendent's job security to student test scores on standardized tests. Because the "all or nothing" stipulation was a highly unusual contract requirement to make of a superintendent, some thought Jewell-Sherman was foolish to accept these terms. Many people publicly questioned not only Jewell-Sherman's leadership abilities but also the children of Richmond's potential to achieve at high levels.

Jewell-Sherman recalled, "It was clear in many people's minds that this was not doable."

But Jewell-Sherman was confident that she and the children of Richmond could meet this challenge, and her first step was to rally her staff. She called a meeting of all RPS employees and shared her faith that they could do this:

> There are people who don't believe that we have the collective will, the resolve, or the knowledge to get this done. But I signed that contract for three reasons. First, the work has to be done, and I dedicated my life to making a difference for children. Second, contrary to what some might think, I am the woman for the job. And third, I believe in all of you. Collectively, we can get this job done. And I will put in motion the supports to do it.

Despite her adamant resolve to boost student achievement, Jewell-Sherman's responsibilities as superintendent also included managing a dysfunctional district office. She inherited a bureaucracy renowned for accounting errors and budgetary coding mistakes. An efficiency report of district operations conducted at Jewell-Sherman's request by the Virginia Office of the Secretary of Finance (2004) concluded that the district could potentially save over $2 million annually through more efficient fiscal management. The report noted, for example, that the district had needlessly spent over $30,000 on late fees and missed on-time payment discounts for electricity, gas, and other bills in 2003. The report also revealed that, in comparison with nine other Virginia school divisions serving populations similar in both size and demographics, RPS's per-pupil spending for the 2001–2002 school year was the highest overall and the highest in seven out of ten expenditure categories.

Although she acknowledged the need for district-level housecleaning, Jewell-Sherman prioritized increasing student achievement as her first order of business as superintendent. What Jewell-Sherman did not realize, however, was that despite her sharp focus on instruction, financial troubles would consistently compete for her attention.

FROM THE BRONX TO THE SOUTH

Born in the Bronx and having spent her elementary years in a public housing community there, Jewell-Sherman was no stranger to hard times. Her divorced mother, who worked two jobs to send her and her siblings to parochial schools, stressed the importance of education throughout Jewell-Sherman's life, and it was no surprise she decided to become a teacher upon graduation from NYU. It was in the classroom that she learned one of the many lessons that would carry her through her tenure in Richmond: students would always come first. Jewell-Sherman quickly moved through the education ranks, becoming known for both her charisma and relentless pursuit of equitable outcomes for all children.

As an elementary school teacher and then a principal in Fairfax County, Virginia, and Hampton, Virginia, Jewell-Sherman honed the instructional leadership skills on which she would rely as superintendent. She believed in continuously improving her skill set as an educator and enrolled in Harvard's Urban Superintendents Program to further develop her ability to lead a district to academic success. She also believed in children's ability to learn and perform at high levels, and she was determined to lead children of all demographic backgrounds to increased levels of achievement. She was quite familiar with "boutique" schools that served some students well. For Jewell-Sherman, success meant providing high-quality educational opportunities for all children. Radical reform was not new to the seasoned educator.

STEPS TO FOCUSING ON INSTRUCTION

Jewell-Sherman's first action was to promote to her previous position, associate superintendent for instruction and accountability, Yvonne Brandon, whom Jewell-Sherman described as "a brilliant, courageous RPS career educator, whose commitment to reform and ingenuity mirrored my passion for exponential improvement." Jewell-Sherman's next step was to commission an audit by the Council of the Great City Schools, a coalition of districts committed to improving urban public schools through research and advocacy. The purpose of the audit was to identify shortcomings and prioritize district needs. Jewell-Sherman recalled,

> Having an outside entity conduct the audit was risky. Facing the "brutal facts" is challenging for a school district, especially one like ours where change had been very incremental and where there was a belief that we were doing all things right. But I wanted us to have an objective overview of our strengths, our weaknesses, and where we could do a better job.

The council's audit identified numerous challenges for the district, including poor student performance, low graduation rates, and problematic student discipline. They reported,

> The school district has a highly fractured program to boost student performance, the legacy of too many initiatives piled on top of one another over too many years. Its efforts had become incoherent and unintelligible; its moorings had loosened, and its unity of purpose had splintered. [Council of the Great City Schools, 2003, p. 11]

The council's 110-page report recommended a battery of strategies aimed at instructional coherence, accountability, professional development, funding allocation, and data monitoring. These recommendations provided Jewell-Sherman and her team with needed leverage to enact a blueprint for improvement.

The First Priority: Instructional Coherence

Even before the council's report, Jewell-Sherman and other district leaders recognized that instructional effectiveness and efficiency varied tremendously across the district. Thus, developing instructional coherence was crucial. Jewell-Sherman knew, however, that she also needed a chief financial officer (CFO) to get the district's spending under control, and a national search for a CFO would not be easy, requiring her to throw much of her energy into the search process. She noted that "it was really hard to get someone of quality to come to a district as dysfunctional as RPS."

Looking at the sea of papers before her, Jewell-Sherman's eyes fell to the number of Richmond schools that were not meeting basic-level student achievement benchmarks. She thought of the children she'd met that morning during an elementary school visit and the stipulations of her contract to improve the number of accredited schools immediately. "I have to focus on instruction first," Jewell-Sherman thought. She took one last look at the news articles before setting them to the side to draw up a plan for Richmond's instructional improvement.

For help with instructional improvement, she looked to an effort she began as associate superintendent for instruction and accountability. Working in concert with Brandon before her promotion, the curriculum and accountability department had started to establish curriculum guides that were created by district teachers and focused on Virginia's SOL exams. Now, with the power to implement this reform across the district, Jewell-Sherman pushed it to the forefront:

> We have what we call a "Curriculum Compass," which has a lesson plan for every objective in math, science, social science, and language arts, pre-K through 12. And working with stellar teachers, we developed lesson plans that outlined the essential knowledge, anticipated outcomes, vocabulary, technology integration, texts to be used with specific pages, resources to be used, field trips to augment the learning, remediation and enrichment activities, and assessment tools. Each teacher gets a CD-ROM with the information pre-K through 12.

Resources and technology innovations also accompanied the curriculum guides. Jewell-Sherman ensured that schools were able to access the instructional advantages of video streaming, providing short Internet video clips to demonstrate learning concepts that were aligned directly to the curriculum maps and guides. Instructional technology resource teachers worked within schools to provide professional development and logistical support for infusing technology into lesson plans.

Soon some acknowledged the coherence and accountability that the "Teaching by Design" curriculum guides, nicknamed Richmond's "treasure chest," brought to RPS. Fairfield Court Elementary School principal Irene Williams noted,

> We were provided a roadmap, a specific report from central administration with curriculum guides, pacing charts, workshops to follow up, lots of professional development, lots of resources that were updated every year. There was actually something in writing, a document that supported the district expectations. Those supports were critical and assisted principals in their buildings with having everyone be on the same page.

Despite the clarity of the curriculum guides, instructional practice did not immediately change throughout the district. Jewell-Sherman's expectation was that everyone would use the lesson plans included in the guides, yet some teachers objected to the mandate. They worried that the curriculum from the district wasn't necessarily better than what they had already been doing, and that the new curriculum was simply teaching kids to take a test rather than to love content. Jewell-Sherman expected that this transformation would require some coaxing: "There was some chasing because we were pulling teachers and principals into the science of teaching."

To ease this radical change, Jewell-Sherman deployed central office personnel into the schools. They were in classrooms, modeling expected behavior and coaching teachers and principals on what it meant to be an effective teacher. Attitudes began to change as classroom teachers witnessed their peers improving their practice during "walk-throughs" and professional development by teacher leaders and central office staff.

Jewell-Sherman also developed a new vision for district curriculum specialists, turning their focus from compliance with district mandates to instructional development and excellence. Her hope was that a focus on additional capacity looking at instruction on a daily basis and providing one-on-one support would help teachers and principals improve. She adjusted time allocations of curriculum specialists and demanded they spend more time in classrooms than in the district office. Curriculum specialists met monthly with department heads and helped schools figure out how to gather curriculum resources. Jewell-Sherman insisted all curriculum specialists come together to share teaching best practices, stating that collaboration was the only option if the district was going to achieve cohesion and widespread instructional success.

Measuring District Progress

After revamping the district's instructional materials and reallocating instructional staff, Jewell-Sherman turned to assessments. How would her leadership team and teachers know what was best for students if they didn't use data to inform their instruction? The board expected her to increase achievement in all of Richmond's schools, and Jewell-Sherman knew the district needed benchmark measures to rate their progress. To this end, another dominant focus of Jewell-Sherman's district reform was the collection and analysis of data through teacher-created bi-weekly classroom assessments using EduSoft software and district-created, nine-week assessments. Jewell-Sherman spoke highly of this process:

> Assessments are a part of life for us. We purchased a software package that allows teachers to create their own tests. We're not asking for them to be onerous. We're not asking that every Friday become doom and gloom test day. But if you've taught certain objectives, then you ought to be able to give them two questions on each and know whether they've mastered them. The software is loaded with questions that we have aligned to our objectives. So a teacher who's teaching Algebra I can access the software and put in [Standard 4.7] ALG 4.7. And it will ask you, "How many questions do you want?" And then the program randomly selects from the database.

Jewell-Sherman's leadership team constantly refined the tool, ensuring that the questions were of high rigor and demanded critical thinking from students. They asked principals to collect and analyze the data, and expected teachers to share assessment data in team meetings. As Jewell-Sherman explained,

> You can no longer use the excuse that we're dealing with kids that come from an impoverished part of the city, so nobody is expecting them to pass. We now have to have a more explicit conversation about why someone may be having difficulties.

Norrell Elementary School principal Mary Pierce similarly emphasized the change in planning during grade-level meetings:

> I have found that the conversation has gone from a very general discussion about instruction to a very specific conversation about remediation of individual children and what we will do for an intervention or prescriptive

> lesson for a certain child. So the whole tone has changed. We were no longer gathering data just for the sake of collecting it. Instead, within your teaching teams, you were really using that data to drive instruction. That was a huge change for all of us.

Principal Gregory Muzik of Mary Munford Elementary School acknowledged, however, that some teachers questioned the increased focus on testing as a measure of their effectiveness in the classroom:

> Resistance was related to the methods used to gain "accountability." Many of the teachers felt that the use of multiple choice tests, especially in the early grades, was not developmentally appropriate and was not providing accurate data. Some teachers felt the emphasis on testing was taking away from instructional time. Even so, teachers went along with it.

Teacher Wayne Ellis, math department chair at Huguenot High School and a former union president with a thirty-three-year history in RPS, commented on the intellectual limits of district-guided instruction when he noted,

> With the idea that no child can be left behind, one way to do that is make sure you slow up the ones in front. And I think that's what we've done in education. We've slowed up the curriculum. I have an AP calculus class of three students this year. That's ridiculous. But it's not fair to those kids to say there's no AP calculus when you have three students that are capable of doing it. And those kids really weren't as prepared as I'd like them to be because, as I said, they haven't had the rigor all the way through to get them prepared for a course like AP calculus.

Supporting Principals, Building Schools

Because the work of administrators had shifted from compliance to support, individual schools were not left on their own to implement the various new aspects of Jewell-Sherman's plan. District-led trainings taught principals to share "power" with teachers and to get them invested in helping the schools meet expectations through school planning management teams. Jewell-Sherman noted, "Our principal meetings are opportunities for best practices to be shared and, as a result, some really great practices have migrated across the district." And as another principal remarked,

> We evolved. Now we're all really good at taking any type of data and really looking at it. Attendance data, mobility data, incidents in the lunchroom. We can analyze anything. We have greatly improved our analytical skills, which helped to drive instructional improvement because we knew right where our weaknesses were.

In November 2003, just one year after Jewell-Sherman assumed the superintendency, everyone was able to see how her changes had paid off. The results on the SOL tests were the best that they had been in Richmond for six years. Twenty-three of fifty-five schools had received full accreditation, which was more than double the accredited schools from the year before. Jewell-Sherman would keep her job as superintendent, but she was determined to continue making progress: "I just felt with every fiber of my being that if I could get these children educated then nobody could take a brighter future away from them."

Continuing to Reach for Achievement, Students First

Jewell-Sherman continued her efforts to buffer Richmond's instructional core. In 2004 a change in graduation requirements put numerous students at risk of not completing high school. For the first time, the Virginia Department of Education would be requiring seniors to pass specific content courses and six of the Virginia SOL tests to earn a high school diploma. The change was severe, and some members of the board immediately questioned Jewell-Sherman's ability to ensure the district's students would graduate. One central office staffer recalled a board member suggesting Jewell-Sherman "didn't know what she was doing," claiming RPS would be "lucky if 50 percent of the kids graduated."

Undeterred by political mudslinging, Jewell-Sherman focused on overcoming this new hurdle. She worked with her leadership team to establish a process for meeting with every rising sophomore, junior, and senior in RPS. Everyone in the district except those with clerical responsibilities and in the financial and human resources departments was trained on how to look at a student's transcript and determine what he or she needed to meet the new requirements. To fuel the efforts, Jewell-Sherman secured a $25,000 grant from the state department of education to bring in additional personnel.

Retired guidance counselors worked on weekends and at night to meet directly with parents who couldn't meet during district hours. Jewell-Sherman and her leadership team also joined the effort, meeting with parents at Huguenot High School. For two weeks straight Jewell-Sherman and her team met with families to explain what their children needed in order to graduate. Jewell-Sherman expressed,

> That is an example of the kind of focus needed to do what was right for our kids. Everything else stopped, and it wouldn't have worked if I said, "This is what I want all of you to do, but I'm going to stay in my office and do my work, because I've got to run the district." I was leading by example, and when you're asking people to do something new or about which they are skeptical, you've got to put your own skin in the game.

As Jewell-Sherman's staff worked diligently outside the RPS office, several other district priorities arose. Allegations of financial mismanagement continued, and journalists reported concerns with the expense of the resources needed for Jewell-Sherman's instructional priorities. Her current financial staff was working to ensure compliance, but Jewell-Sherman still had not found the time to begin looking for the right CFO. She said of her decision to continue prioritizing instruction despite these concerns:

> It was hard fighting from day one and still trying to keep my hands on everything. But the one area that I protected to the exclusion of everything else was teaching and learning, to make sure that we would see different results there.

The results she hoped for came. In 2004, 94 percent of the senior class graduated from Richmond Public Schools with the new diploma. Performance improvements on the SOL resulted in 76 percent of the district's schools earning accreditation in preparation for the 2004–2005 school year (see Exhibit 5.1 on the CD to view accreditation trends and Exhibit 5.2 for SOL scores at three district schools). Jewell-Sherman had proven that academic achievement for all children in Richmond was not beyond reach. When her contract came up for renewal in 2005, this time the board's vote was unanimous in her favor.

Being Data Driven, Charting the Course

With encouragement from Richmond's academic progress and teacher and staff satisfaction, Jewell-Sherman continued to push forward her efforts to reform instructional practices. The district created Charting the Course—a non-punitive evaluation process in which school administrators were encouraged to maximize the potential of their data. Jewell-Sherman explained,

> It starts with the principal, administrative, and leadership team looking at their school's data. You're looking at data for at least a three-year period, and you're analyzing it from multiple perspectives. First you look at core areas, and then drill down deeper and look at subgroups. Now you drill down even deeper and review the data by classroom. That way, you know where the learning is taking place and where there are gaps in achievement. You can then identify where you need to focus, where there are . . . either needs in direct instruction or professional development. We then set district targets.

Once the school identified its needs and established its action plan, a team of district-based instructional staff and administrators visited each school to meet with school-site administrators to focus their work.

This was new to Richmond, so Jewell-Sherman trained her staff on collaborative teaming and taught them a common language around effective teaching.

Through extensive professional development, the instructional staff at both the district and school levels became better able to analyze quality teaching, discuss pedagogy, and identify gaps in the curriculum and the corresponding strategies necessary to close them. Brandon and the instructional team went to each school monthly or quarterly depending on its needs, and schools presented their analyzed data. The visiting teams pushed and investigated the data presented, striving to ensure that each school considered its context and information thoroughly. The expectation: if there is a gap in the student data, your action plan should be aligned to that gap.

Principals acknowledged that being accountable to the Charting the Course team intensified their work. Principal Muzik recalled, "Before the visiting teams came to each school, people from central administration just weren't really in the buildings. Now I feel personal accountability. I do think it makes a difference when someone is coming in and checking on me."

By contrast, former union president Ellis questioned the value of Charting the Course in light of what some considered the district's already excessive spending: "Such micromanagement has got to go. That's wasting too many resources. If these people have all this time to go around and spend an hour in each building every month, do we really need them?"

Through internal restructuring and the addition of new resources and capacity, Jewell-Sherman's leadership team had laid a solid foundation for Richmond's instructional improvement. However, even with these changes and the growing investment of students and school administrators, Jewell-Sherman had not convinced everyone. The constant tension between balancing the district's need for financial restructuring and developing instructional coherence would finally come to a head with the election of a new mayor.

BARRIERS TO THE SUCCESS OF THE FOCUS

As diligently as the instructional personnel of RPS worked, they could not shelter themselves from the ever-present and turbulent political climate of the City of Richmond. Most notable were the ongoing accusations of excessive per-pupil expenditures. The numerous initiatives put forth by Jewell-Sherman and her cabinet—the curriculum guides, the improvements in technology with on-site technological support, the curriculum specialists, extensive professional development, and the many other resources devoted to supporting Charting the Course—were expensive and required reallocation of human and fiscal resources. For Jewell-Sherman these expenses were a part of running an effective school district and were necessary for pulling the district out of its achievement crisis. For others in the community, however, the district budget seemed unwieldy, overstressed, mismanaged, and a problem requiring immediate intervention.

Budget Crisis

Among the most vocal of the critics was Richmond's mayor and former Virginia governor, L. Douglas Wilder. From the start of his tenure in 2004, Mayor Wilder publicly expressed interest in taking authority over Richmond's public education system, specifically in naming the superintendent. Yet the school board and many in the community disagreed with the mayor's position and rejected his push for an appointed school board. Determined to have a hand in running the public schools, Wilder launched a public campaign that questioned the spending habits of the system. Wilder demanded that the school system "reduce their costs immediately," stating as much in a letter to Jewell-Sherman in 2005.

He accused Jewell-Sherman and her team of inappropriate and excessive spending despite their knowledge of the city's declining resources. The school board was outraged, and one member, speaking about the new mayor's encroaching request, said, "I think they're trying to balance the budget on the backs of schoolchildren." Although there were considerable improvements in SOL scores since Jewell-Sherman became superintendent, Wilder did not believe those improvements were enough to warrant the increased spending. He stated, "The bottom line is, what do you do with what you have to make things better for the kids? Rather than cry and bemoan: 'Oh, we don't have this, we don't have that'" (Ress & Kastner, 2005, p. A-1).

Jewell-Sherman and her team proposed a leaner budget for the 2005–2006 school year, making cuts to programs, increasing class sizes in grades 4 and 5, and cutting ten teaching positions. However, the cuts did not meet the mayor's standards, and he rejected the budget, saying the methods proposed were not the "right" ways to save money. Then, in April 2005, the city reduced its quarterly payment to the schools by $9.2 million, indicating that the money had not been designated for a specific use by the school board. After much negotiating and protest by community and municipal leaders, the city restored the funding in June of that year. The mayor's dissatisfaction with the school district and Jewell-Sherman were just beginning. He continued to criticize the school system's funding well into the 2005–2006 school year.

To ensure that they had a clear picture of the district's financial management, the city council and school board requested an audit of district spending to look for areas in which the district could trim costs. City Auditor Umesh Dalal explained the need for the audit:

> The City of Richmond funds Richmond Public Schools to the tune of about $161 million a year. And since this is a sizable investment in the public schools, my job as city auditor is to verify accountability over that substantial resource. When I came to the City of Richmond in March of 2006, there were significant doubts about how [our schools] operate. People were not satisfied. The business community was accusing schools of wasting money. Per capita, we were spending the highest amount in the area.

Richmond Public Schools was funded about 33 percent, or about $70 million, higher than what other comparative districts received per pupil. So all this added up to quite a bit of concern for the city council.

City auditor Dalal concluded his six-month study of district finances in February 2007 and released a report with recommendations for trimming up to $20 million in excess spending each year. Dalal's recommendations for change included reductions in custodial staff and administrators, replacement of vehicles, and reconfiguration of bus routes. The school board also proposed to cut the number of guidance counselors, and the mayor even recommended the closure of a number of underenrolled schools to save money.

Dissatisfied with the pace of the city auditor's assessment, the mayor sought an independent audit to be performed by an external firm his staff had secured. At a press conference, the mayor and supporters announced that this audit would focus more on central administration operations as opposed to school-based spending. Wilder punctuated his frustration with the district by threatening to withhold future city funds if RPS failed to cooperate with the external auditor. Wilder stated to the press, "Now, they are going to be held accountable to provide the information. If they can't provide it, bye-bye. There ain't no money coming. And I mean that, as seriously as I mean my name is what it is" (O'Rear, 2007, paragraph 2). After considerable complaints about the redundancy of the audits, the mayor eventually dropped his request. The multiple audits and their publicly published results not only diverted Jewell-Sherman's attention from her instructional reform but also caused a downward spiral of the public's perceptions of Jewell-Sherman and RPS. Dalal summed it up,

> The results of the May 2007 audit got a tremendous amount of publicity, and again, people attacking Richmond Public Schools, that they are wasting $20 million. Well, that was not quite the way we said it. Actually, we identified opportunities of savings of up to $20 million. And there were recommendations

that they needed to implement to get those savings. But people wanted the savings now. They were not willing to give Richmond Public Schools an opportunity to implement the recommendations.

Political Mayhem

Wilder also spoke publicly about the location of the district offices for RPS. The school system occupied five floors in Richmond city hall, and Wilder believed the city could save $1 million if RPS retrofitted a recently closed school site, allowing other city offices to use the five floors the school district occupied. In 2004 Wilder served the school system notice that he was going to take the space. He also indicated that the city would provide the funding both to make the move and for the new space. However, the mayor and the school board never reached agreement. Jewell-Sherman and her employees remained in city hall a year after receiving the notification while trying to negotiate a compromise with Wilder. Voicing frustration with the district's failure to move out, in November 2005 Wilder issued a statement alerting district officials that they had until the start of the new year to move their offices. The school board pleaded with Wilder to give them until April to come up with a plan for such a large operations shift. Wilder, who refused to meet with any members of the school board, denied the request, causing Richmond's school board to fervently protest.

Despite the board's interest in relocating to a refurbished school or a rental property downtown, the mayor insisted that these locations were too expensive and a closed school "as it was" would suffice. Unable to reconcile their differences, the school board and Wilder sought mediation from the city council in 2007. The city council ruled that RPS could remain in city hall for an additional year at a modest rent. Even with this ruling by the city council, the school board and Jewell-Sherman feared Wilder might lock them out. Copies of the renewed lease were hung outside every office door and on the elevators of every floor. As suspected, Wilder ignored the ruling and sent another letter to Jewell-Sherman. The letter indicated that the move should be completed by September 30, 2007. The school board and Jewell-Sherman relied on the city council's ruling—they would not vacate. However, no board member, district employee, or even Jewell-Sherman herself could imagine what would happen next.

On September 22, 2007, RPS officials were hard at work. A brand-new school would open its doors to students in just two days. Final preparations for the opening were under way to ensure a smooth first day. Other staff members were helping another school team relocate to a temporary space because their school had been damaged by a recent hurricane. That afternoon as Jewell-Sherman and her staff managed the two priorities among their other daily responsibilities, they received word from the city that Wilder had ordered RPS's central office to be forcefully evicted from city hall. Jewell-Sherman recalled, "We were told to be out by 5:00 P.M. and that we wouldn't be allowed back before 8:00 A.M. Monday morning." When school employees left that Friday evening, they did not realize their work documents and personal items would be lost in a sea of chaos only a few hours later.

As Jewell-Sherman left that evening, she saw trucks, platforms, lights, moving vans, and a police command center vehicle lining the streets in front of city hall. Over 150 movers, armed with the mayor's permission, worked in tandem to remove the district's belongings from the building. Within hours, the workers removed file cabinets, furniture, technology, and personal items belonging to RPS. Student records, employee files, and state records littered the halls and streets in carelessly packed, unlabeled boxes.

Vendors lined the streets selling food and drinks to the workers and the growing crowds who watched as the school district was displaced. To flashing cameras, a spokesperson from the mayor's office, Linwood Norman, defended the scene:

> Having seen no indication that the school system intended to be out of City Hall by September 30th, the action being taken tonight and continuing through the weekend, is aimed at minimizing disruption for the school system personnel, who can resume work at their new offices, with their furniture and equipment on Monday, September 24th. [Martz, Meola, & Ress, 2007, paragraph 8]

A phone call at 4:15 P.M. that afternoon had brought Jewell-Sherman the news of Wilder's decision to forcefully evict. Immediately Jewell-Sherman, Brandon, and the rest of the leadership team walked from floor to floor and to each office alerting any employees who were left to take their personal belongings with them. The floors were relatively desolate because it was so close to 4:30 P.M.—the school district's closing time. Angry and devastated, Jewell-Sherman headed home, hoping that the morning would not bring what had been forewarned. Yet within an hour of leaving the office, Jewell-Sherman received another call confirming that her school system was being forced out.

Returning to city hall for a hastily called emergency board meeting, Brandon and Jewell-Sherman sat together in Jewell-Sherman's car a block away from the building watching the scene unfold. They held hands in a moment of prayer and solidarity, considering what would come next. Brandon squeezed Jewell-Sherman's hand just before they exited the car, saying, "You can do this Deborah," adding, "Put your face on." Reporters and camera crews immediately surrounded the pair. Jewell-Sherman said of this moment,

> I just knew I had to deal with it and that I had to be strong. I literally remember pulling my shoulders back and walking with my head up, and striding—just walking with strength, because I would not allow the students and the teachers and the principals to see anything but strength. But I also remember that it took everything that I had in me to walk from that car to the end of the corner where all of the reporters were.

As the public looked on in shock, Jewell-Sherman addressed the city and her priorities: "I just know I have 24,000 students and I have a job to do, and this is not making it easy" (Martz et al., 2007, paragraph 18). Seeing all of her hard work tossed into boxes, Jewell-Sherman felt momentarily defeated:

> It was like a military coup, and I knew it was one of those leadership moments when I had to make sure I was making sense of what was happening for the people who I cared about and who I led. I wouldn't have shed a public tear then if my life depended on it. I might have been crying on the inside, but not on the outside.

Dalal shared his dismay, "I have never witnessed anything like that in my entire career." Many other city stakeholders weighed in. Councilman Chris Hilbert called the attempted eviction "inexcusable and a disgrace to our city." At the school board's emergency meeting they were able to hire an attorney and awaken a judge who agreed to meet them in court later that night. At one o'clock in the morning the judge issued a cease-and-desist order that required RPS to immediately "be made whole." However, disconnected computers, piles of mislabeled documents and resources, incorrectly boxed materials, and tainted public opinion made it impossible to undo the damage. News reporters, anxious to hear from Wilder, found him at a party celebrating the opening of a new shopping venue, dancing happily to a song in the background. "Two years, it's over.... Enough is enough," he told cameras (Martz et al., 2007, paragraph 3). The total cost to the city for Wilder's eviction—an estimated $1 million.

MOVING FORWARD: A LEADER'S CHALLENGE

Despite the mayor's public resentment, Jewell-Sherman focused RPS staff on the students. Calling her entire staff into a mandatory meeting at an alternate location Monday morning, Jewell-Sherman, in addressing the crowd and exhorting them to stay focused on the critical instructional work ahead, said, "Is it going to be difficult? Unbelievably. Does this take us off task? Very much so. But will we allow this or any other distraction to take us off our primary mission of educating students? Absolutely not."

To the principals directly in charge of Richmond's students, Jewell-Sherman issued the following direction: "All I need from you all is to focus on our paramount mission." She instructed them to ignore the media and sent her communications team to field all questions. As the morning came to a close, Jewell-Sherman looked into the faces of her team and said, "It's not fair, but our work is bigger than any challenge, and we're going to work together to get this done."

Jewell-Sherman's instructional focus brought national attention to Richmond. Yet even with praise from federal policymakers and colleagues in other districts—many of whom looked to Richmond as a model of success—local public perception of the district continued to lag. There was concern about diminishing parental support for city schools, as close to one-third of all school-age children within the city limits continued to attend private schools. Attacking the district from another standpoint, former union president Ellis voiced the concerns of some teachers by questioning the assumption that increased test scores meant students were learning more. He argued,

> Kids are wonders at working backwards from multiple choice answers, especially in math. You give them a graphing calculator, which everybody has, and you give them a list of four answers, they can figure out which three are wrong more times than not. And they get a passing score for it.

Despite these concerns, the news media began to recognize and celebrate Richmond's accomplishments, thereby broadening the local support base for RPS. For example, in June 2007 the *Richmond Times-Dispatch* ran a front-page article extolling the performance of Fairfield Court Elementary School. The paper reported on Fairfield's 98 percent passing rate for its 96 percent free-lunch-eligible population, relaying the hard work of Fairfield students. For Jewell-Sherman, the student success at Fairfield exemplified her dreams for the district. She explained,

> I wanted my legacy to be that a stranger could look at our district and not be able to tell, based on student achievement, whether a school was in a poor area or a more affluent one. Fairfield Court Elementary is in the middle of a housing project in the East End. It's a community where parents have told me that before they go to sleep at night, they put a sofa in front of one door and a chair in front of the other to keep safe. It's a place where kids don't go outside to play—where school really is a safe haven. It's a really impoverished part of the city. Last year, Fairfield Court had the highest achievement levels—98

> percent — of any elementary school in the City of Richmond. I shared with the school board and the district that this is not just an affirmation of Fairfield. This is an affirmation of *all* of our work.

A SUPERINTENDENT'S REWARD

At the press conference she called on her birthday, Jewell-Sherman stood in the crowd waiting to be called to the podium, smoothing her skirt. After years of battling to protect Richmond's instructional core and guarantee learning for all students, she had finally seen the success she had hoped for. The members of the Virginia Association of School Superintendents sat around her as her name was announced. Association President Don Ford introduced Deborah Jewell-Sherman as Virginia's chosen Superintendent of the Year. He continued,

> During the past several years, we have watched with pride in Deborah's accomplishments as she has improved her schools' accreditation rate. [She] has accomplished this through her inspiring leadership as she implemented her vision, raised expectations, involved her community and produced results under pressure of local politics and economic deficiencies. [Reid, 2008, paragraph 4]

After hearing of Jewell-Sherman's honor, Richmond leaders spoke out. "The board is not surprised but very happy and very proud of her and all the work she has done in Richmond," said school board vice chairwoman Lisa Dawson (Reid, 2008, paragraph 2). Other Richmond leaders agreed. "We offer her our congratulations," said William Pantele, city council president. "She took a job a lot of others wouldn't, and she agreed to key her compensation to performance. There is no question that Richmond Public Schools in that time period has improved significantly" (Reid, 2008).

And data agreed. With five years of budgetary battles, a public eviction, and continuous disagreement between Jewell-Sherman and the city's mayor, RPS showed remarkable gains in student outcomes on the Virginia SOL tests each year of Jewell-Sherman's tenure (see Exhibit 5.3 on the CD to view 2006–2009 academic performance trends). In 2008, 87 percent of Richmond schools were accredited. In addition, two schools were selected as national Blue Ribbon Schools, and four schools were bestowed with the state's highest performance honor, the Governor's Award for Educational Excellence. Jewell-Sherman received the Flame Bearers of Education Award from the United Negro College Fund, and both Jewell-Sherman and deputy Brandon had been called to address the House Education Committee and the Senate Committee on Health, Education, Labor, and Pensions to outline the district's reform efforts in the hope that their successes could be replicated elsewhere. In contrast to his previously vocal role during Jewell-Sherman's tenure, when the news of Jewell-Sherman's superintendent's award broke, Mayor Wilder was not available for comment.

WHAT'S NEXT FOR RICHMOND? JEWELL-SHERMAN DEPARTS

After announcing her planned retirement from the superintendency, Jewell-Sherman stated at her news conference,

> I have accomplished what I set out to do for Richmond and its students. We've had challenges, things I'd do differently. But we never shied away from what works. However, the time has come for me to take on a new challenge, and I will continue the fight to ensure that all kids have a quality education.

As Jewell-Sherman finished her speech, the crowd was moved to their feet. Some members of her leadership team shed tears as they realized their city's loss. As she stepped down from the podium, the crowd wondered what was next for Richmond. Would the system be able to sustain its growth while transitioning its leadership? Would RPS plateau as a new leader faced continued allegations of financial mismanagement and irresponsibility? Most important, would the culture of an absolute focus on student success and the instructional core be maintained?

REFERENCES

Council of the Great City Schools. (2003). *Charting a new course for the Richmond Public Schools.* Report for Richmond Public Schools, Richmond, VA.

Martz, M., Meola, O., & Ress, D. (2007, September 22). Chaos erupts at city hall; city evicts school officials; police ban public from attending emergency school board meeting. *Richmond Times-Dispatch.* Retrieved December 15, 2010, from Lexis-Nexis Universe/General News.

Office of the Secretary of Finance, State of Virginia. (2004). School efficiency review: City of Richmond Public School Division. Retrieved November 30, 2007, from www.doe.virginia.gov/school_finance/efficiency_reviews/richmond_city.pdf.

O'Rear, C. (2007, February 14). Attack of the audits. *Richmond.com.* Retrieved December 15, 2010, from http://www2.richmond.com/news/2007/feb/14/attack-of-the-audits-ar-594365/.

Reid, Z. (2008, May 7). Richmond school superintendent is honored. *Richmond Times-Dispatch.* Retrieved December 15, 2010, from Lexis-Nexis Universe/General News.

Ress, D., & Kastner, L. (2005, July 20). Wilder creates watchdog panel for city schools; he vows to "end the complacency and dysfunctionality of the district." *Richmond Times-Dispatch.* Retrieved September 21, 2009, from Lexis-Nexis Universe/General News database.

Building New Structures and Options for Success

Rudy F. Crew

It is a truism to say that a superintendent does not succeed without deep and significant support from the educators and community around him, certainly not Richmond Public Schools or in a district as large as Miami-Dade County Public Schools. Similar to the work of Deborah Jewell-Sherman, the work I led reshaped that dynamic and continues to influence the district.

When I arrived in Miami-Dade in summer 2004 as the first superintendent hired from the outside in fifty years, this vital ingredient for success in improving the lives of students was largely absent, or at least buried in the rubble of the district's difficult recent past. The public distrusted the administration in the wake of well-publicized scandals in the construction and maintenance department that led the state to appoint a special oversight panel. Many employees believed that connections rather than merit drove advancement. The inability to address chronic poor performance in a minority of schools was overshadowing respectable results in most schools. The mayor of Miami was seeking control of the city's schools, and the teachers union was beset with internal problems of its own as its leader was found guilty on federal corruption charges.

In Miami-Dade we had over 350,000 students in nearly four hundred schools. From recent immigrants to youths from some of the wealthiest communities in the nation, our student population was racially and economically diverse. I treated our teachers and unions as partners, working with them first to create a School Improvement Zone, encompassing thirty-nine schools historically marked by poor performance, and I used collective bargaining that focused on our common interests and resulted in a landmark three-year deal that benefited employees, parents, and students.

The Zone students represented groups who had been truly disenfranchised by poverty and discrimination, and, strange as it may seem, by people who came from a country that had disenfranchised them. The children bore the brunt of this bias. Having the district focus on these children not only improved their lives but also changed the public's belief in the school system as whole.

Starting with the lowest-performing schools was the core of my overarching theory of change in regard to instruction. Change is about relationships—between adults and children, specifically teachers and students. When a unit of change happens in a classroom, it spreads through the school and beyond, altering the culture throughout the district. The lowest-performing schools are always the most challenging, but they are also the ones on the edge of change in which radical improvement will happen and can be leveraged throughout the system. This culture moved everybody into a new zone of thinking, behavior, and core assumptions of what it takes to educate all children.

I have demonstrated that performance matters more broadly among employees by promoting those who get results for students. I moved principals directly into regional superintendent posts, which was unprecedented in Miami-Dade, and promoted strong contributors who had been overlooked to move up in the administration. The signal was unmistakable. I communicated regularly with employees to keep them informed and to congratulate them on our progress; I was shocked in my first year in Miami-Dade by the flood of thank-you replies I received to a simple note wishing employees a restful and happy Thanksgiving. Clearly, my outreach to school-based employees did more than just build morale. I was looking at the big picture, and my feedback was based on data that showed what was happening in the classroom. This informed and improved instruction, and, most important, it made change happen.

In the community we forged "education compacts" with municipal governments in our large county, again focusing on our common interest in the development of competent, competitive graduates and the actions each partner would take to ensure that we reached our goal and that graduates became part of the local workforce. I met monthly in "CEO briefings," both to share the district's story with the private sector and to hear back from them about how we were doing in shaping Miami-Dade's future workforce. The central focus of every discussion was the important role the public school system played in sustaining a successful community. Business leaders at every meeting voiced their willingness to help the district in a sustained and meaningful way.

INSTRUCTIONAL IMPROVEMENT: IT DOESN'T JUST HAPPEN IN SCHOOLS

Parents are at the heart of student learning, and with strategic changes at the district level they are at the core of the conversation. I held a series of town hall meetings for parents at the start of each school year, giving them a chance to hear directly from me; that's not unique. What was different in Miami-Dade was that we created the means by which parents and others could enter that conversation as empowered, knowledgeable participants. We opened the Parent Academy, which offered more than one hundred classes in convenient locations across Miami-Dade to help parents be better partners with schools, better parents generally, and better citizens. The response was overwhelming, both in terms of the community's support for the effort, which was funded entirely by donations, and in terms of the more than one hundred thousand parents served. The success of the Parent Academy is legendary—the model is being replicated throughout the nation.

We summed up this idea of pulling together for the benefit of students in a branding campaign, *It Takes . . .* , to make clear that my leadership as superintendent was effective only to the extent that others believed in it and worked hard to follow my direction. This campaign was critical to improving instruction in the classroom. The faces of children everywhere not only told the story but also reminded us daily that students are more than data points—they're the inspiration for why we do this work.

PREPARING OUR STUDENTS FOR THE WORLD, IN AND OUTSIDE OF MIAMI-DADE

In my first address to administrators, I had asked them to embrace change, to make good choices, and to show courage. These were the marks of leadership that were evident in Miami-Dade, along with the results that come when the force of those "3C's" is brought to bear—whether they be fifty thousand new students seats built, more high school students than ever in advanced and college prep classes, or an improved balance sheet and bond rating.

In a school district as large and diverse as Miami-Dade County, communicating with all members of the public presented many challenges. Yet, with the proper planning and meaningful collaboration between district offices, school sites, and the community, the goal of engaging all stakeholders ensured the successful development and approval of the *2005–2008 District Strategic Plan.* A primary goal of the strategic plan was to educate and inform stakeholders. A culture was established: community engagement became an entrenched value, and the community played a significant role in lifting the bar on academic excellence and providing critical resources to schools, students, and their families.

Our work in Miami-Dade embodied the new reality that students today face a world of jobs that require not only higher levels of reading than ever before but also communications, critical-thinking, and math skills. We understood that the world is not static and that time is speeding on, forcing us into a race with destiny fueled by rapid change, global competitiveness, and international relationships.

REINVENTING PRACTICE, WITH SUPPORT

I fostered an understanding in the Miami community of the need to continually improve and, when necessary, reengineer the system. In a district that had long-held, ingrained ideals, this was a challenge. Through professional development and mentoring, district faculty and staff soon believed that unless improvements were made, Miami-Dade students would not be competitive.

My priority was to put in place a system that addressed this issue. We constructed a professional development plan aimed at delivering research-based learning experiences that would advance performance for all teachers, administrators, and noninstructional personnel. I strongly believe that for professional development to have an impact on student learning it must be embedded within jobs and aligned with a district's goals. Our plan directed relevant professional development for educators that supported the instructional needs of students and incorporated essential elements for adult learning, focusing on knowledge, modeling, and practice with feedback. To influence administrators and noninstructional personnel, the plan also charted on-the-job professional learning that enhanced workforce capabilities and promoted advancement.

We know that giving students the necessary skills, insight, and imagination to succeed is essential, and that those who are unprepared will sit on the sidelines, facing poverty, dead-end jobs, and hopelessness. I introduced the Secondary School Reform initiative that encouraged all students to take rigorous courses and align what they learned in the classroom with real-world experiences through an internship program. The effort was not focused on the already high-achieving students but on raising the aspirations of the students who were in danger of slipping through the cracks.

But with much success there is always the unexpected twist. Late in summer 2005, three forces of nature bearing the names Katrina, Rita, and Wilma stole more than 15 percent of the school year. These conditions created a dire situation, but with the view that this was an opportunity for the community and district to funnel the strongest winds into winds of change, we resumed the business of schooling with renewed vigor.

Yet one of my greatest concerns during my tenure in Miami-Dade was the accountability provisions attached to the 2001 reauthorization of the Elementary and Secondary Education Act, better known as No Child Left

Behind. This focus on test scores came at the expense of other content that was significant in its own way. I understood the value of an assessment that measured how our students were achieving against state standards and of accountability for results in promoting improvement, but we could not overlook the value of physical education in a nation beset by childhood obesity or the value of arts education in a global economy driven by creativity and innovation. Test results are descriptive, not predictive. They can tell us only where students have been, not how far they will go.

I wanted Miami-Dade students to take the test and do well, but passing it could not be the driver of expectations—that would simply have set too low a target for the district's students in several ways. Academically, we needed to worry less about how students in Miami-Dade County fared compared to other districts in Florida and more about how they compared to students in other countries. An international city like Miami made it abundantly clear that the district's students would live, work, and need to compete in a global economy. We knew that our students couldn't yet measure up to those international standards, but even passing the Florida Comprehensive Assessment Test would not ensure that they did; the math required to pass the high school exit test generally is taught in middle school in the rest of the world. Just as significant, a standardized test could not assess important things Miami-Dade students should master—the ability to write a term paper or to analyze the writings of others in deep ways, for example.

As we worked to improve schools in Miami-Dade, our goal was a simple one: to ensure that the district's schools delivered an education that would enable students to graduate ready for college and the careers of a global economy. To be sure, that meant far more than passing a state test. It meant academic preparation that rivaled that of the young people from around the world with whom Miami-Dade students would compete economically. It meant an "occupational competency" that connected students to the careers in which they would strive. It meant a "civic competency" that allowed students to place themselves in the community as informed, participating citizens. And it meant a "personal competency" that empowered students with the social graces they need to comport themselves with dignity.

MOVING FORWARD

The real challenge for a superintendent is that the demands students face today are being dictated by a world in which change comes nearly as rapidly as information travels on the Internet. To meet these new demands, we have to think beyond our traditional constraints, to move beyond tried-and-true perspectives that don't hold up to what we understand our students need. One of the great democratic values of public education is that it provides most of us with a shared experience that binds us; but we can't let our fond memories of what school "is" stand in the way of delivering the right education for children now and tomorrow.

Finally, a challenge most superintendents face, and one that cannot be overlooked, is the politics of education—namely, dealing with the school board. Too many boards and other politicians spend more time haggling, whining, regulating, and politicizing classrooms than focusing on the real issues that lead to educational success. Miami-Dade was no exception; politics got in the way of progress.

As in Richmond, Virginia, in Miami-Dade, there was much to celebrate. Many schools throughout the district were tremendous success stories, and we implemented promising strategies that continue to help students achieve higher levels of reading, writing, math, and science, preparing them to be productive contributors to the world market and responsible citizens of the global community.

With this success came national attention. As the spotlight strengthened, the glare from the school board intensified. They lost sight of the fact that they brought me to Miami and shared in those accolades. Instead, the game became "Take Rudy Down." Politics trumped what mattered most—student learning. For a superintendent who truly cares about teaching and learning in the classroom, this broken relationship meant it was time to move on. Like Jewell-Sherman, I have no regrets, and I was not complacent. We both set challenging expectations for our districts to ensure that all students were engaged in learning and were prepared for the demands ahead. The results for students speak for themselves.

CHAPTER 6

School Boards and Unions

Moving Ahead with School Boards and Teachers Unions

Susan Moore Johnson

Many large school districts these days no longer have superintendents. Instead they have CEOs. The title, chief executive officer, is designed to signal to the public and stakeholders that the person holding it is like a titan of industry—fully in charge of a large and complex organization. Whatever respect the title of CEO may elicit, it cannot mask the reality that ultimately the superintendent's authority is ambiguous and the power of her position limited. Being a superintendent today requires at least as much political savvy as it does executive skill. Those who succeed, whatever their titles, manage creatively with the opportunities and constraints that their roles and local contexts provide.

When a superintendent fails to achieve promised change in the schools, two groups typically are blamed for blocking progress—the school board and the teachers union. One of the first things that a new superintendent must do is take stock of each and devise an effective approach for moving ahead together, ideally in a constructive partnership, but at least in a respectful and informed working relationship.

SCHOOL BOARDS

School boards are meant to ensure that the public schools serve the public interest. In keeping with the very local nature of public education in the United States, every district has its own board setting policy for its schools. The board hires and fires the superintendent and, therefore, technically has the "upper hand." However, board members also depend on their superintendent to assess the district's program and chart a plan for improvement. Thus the superintendent must at once guide and be responsive to the board.

A century ago, school boards were composed largely of local business and community leaders—mostly men, mostly white—who believed that school districts should be run like efficient companies, deliberately distributing resources to achieve clear outcomes. The members of a local board typically held similar expectations for what their schools should do and how the superintendent should lead them.

In the past seventy-five years, however, with increased immigration, residential and financial mobility, and social progress, more and more local urban communities have elected school boards that are diverse racially, ethnically, socially, and economically. Members typically bring to their board priorities grounded in their own political and cultural backgrounds. Often members on the same board introduce different (sometimes competing) expectations for their schools and how the children whose families they represent should be educated. Over time, as the composition of a school board changes, so too do the district's goals and strategies for improvement.

Until recently, most school board members were elected by wards—sections of the district in which residents had similar ideas about what the public schools should do and provide. As a result, school board members had to be responsive to residents in their ward, and a superintendent needed to recognize those obligations, because ignoring the concerns of a member's constituents could mean quickly losing that board member's vote. In many districts today, however, at least some school board members are elected district-wide, an approach designed to discourage provincialism and enable the district and superintendent to pursue broader change on behalf of all students. The trend seems to reverse itself every twenty years or so.

District-wide elections, however, have not put an end to divided boards because candidates often still run on narrow issues of self-interest—increasing programs for the gifted, opposing school closings, ending or supporting bilingual education. A superintendent who once might have monitored his standing with board members ward by ward now must assess how he's faring district-wide on a shifting array of issues. The process is no less political, just more challenging.

The most notable change in recent years, however, is the increasing number of districts—for example, Boston, New York City, and Chicago—in which the mayor appoints the board. Citizens still have their say in school governance, but they now express themselves indirectly by electing the mayor who appoints the local school board. Mayoral appointment offers both the possibility of rising above partisan politics and some assurance that members will take the community's broad educational needs into account, rather than focusing on a series of single issues. Such changes may improve a superintendent's chances of making progress on a reform agenda. However, with mayors increasingly asserting that they should be judged by the success of their schools, superintendents become responsible for not only effective education but also the mayor's reelection. In this way, mayoral control of the board also increases the political demands for the superintendent.

In Baltimore, when Andrés Alonso became chief executive officer, the school board's educational and political responsibilities were unusually complex. Because a city-state partnership governs Baltimore City Public Schools, the state board of education vets school board candidates, who are then jointly appointed by the mayor and governor. This approach, which requires agreement, if not consensus, across several jurisdictions, encourages broad support for the schools. Those making the appointments are required by law to attend not only to the demographics of the community but also to the knowledge and expertise of candidates. As a group, those on the board must bring, among other possible attributes, a high level of managerial experience, knowledge of regular and special education, and firsthand experience as parents in the system. Such requirements decrease the role of patronage and the likelihood that narrow interests will control Baltimore City's approach to reform. They make it more likely that the CEO-superintendent will be able to build support for a district-wide agenda to improve instruction.

These assurances all seem warranted in such a low-performing urban district as Baltimore, which for many years has been demographically divided and mired in political rancor. However, even these requirements, which are meant to stabilize school governance, cannot guarantee that the new CEO can act independently, no matter how effective he might be as a manager. Because in this district, as in others, politics remains central to the superintendent's work with the school board. Alonso, like superintendents everywhere, must continue to weigh the possible impact on board members' support as he decides to hire new administrators, introduce a new program, or reallocate resources to the schools. Across the nation, superintendents continue to report that they must routinely "count votes" on their school board before those votes are taken. They must anticipate that support for their initiatives—and thus for them—might shift suddenly with a mayoral or school board election. A superintendent is hired by the school board, yet expected to lead that board. It is a relationship that is both promising and precarious.

TEACHERS UNIONS

"The Union"—like "The Board"—often is blamed when a superintendent's reforms encounter resistance, and the superintendent's relationship with the union is similarly ambiguous. Despite having a position at the top of the organizational chart, the superintendent cannot count on top-down managerial control of teachers, because those teachers are often unionized and have the right to bargain in regard to their wages, hours, and conditions of employment.

Teachers in forty-five states are entitled or permitted by state law to unionize and bargain. Because "conditions of employment" are often broadly defined, negotiations may cover a wide range of issues with important instructional consequences, from class size and performance evaluation to school-site governance and discipline. The scope of issues for bargaining—those that are mandated, permissible, or prohibited—is set by state statute and past practice in the district. Once signed by labor and management, the contract is enforceable by law. New superintendents who plan to fundamentally change the work rules that affect teachers often discover that their predecessors negotiated away important management prerogatives long ago and that they have less discretion than they expected. They can only hope to renegotiate the contract, not rewrite it.

Often the union is treated as if it's an outside troublemaker. However, locally the union retains the authority to negotiate its own contract, even though it is affiliated with state and national unions. In exchange for having the right to represent all teachers in a district, the local union is legally obliged to fairly represent those teachers' interests, not only those of its members. Teachers in many states and districts are required to pay a service or "agency" fee to the union for negotiating their contract. Because that fee often approaches the full cost of union membership, all teachers—even those who choose not to join—have a financial stake in the local union's work and, therefore, pay attention to the relationship between the superintendent and the union president.

Although there have always been teachers who chose not to join their union for professional and personal reasons, new teachers today express less support of union priorities and practices than in the past. Their veteran colleagues tend to view the union more favorably because they were involved in negotiating the first contract, know the details of union-management history, and routinely do the union's work in committees and elected office. Many early-career teachers today are said to doubt the need for a union, to take the terms of their contract for granted, and to expect service from their union rather than standing behind it. More experienced teachers tend to oppose performance-based pay and dismiss professional development as ineffective, whereas early-career teachers would like to see teachers rewarded for their accomplishments and want their union to find ways to support them in the classroom.

Superintendents might be tempted to favor new teachers' priorities over those of veteran teachers, but those who explicitly do so risk being branded anti-union and, therefore, anti-teacher. Nothing can more quickly drive ambivalent teachers to stand behind their union leaders than administrators who seem disrespectful or unfair. Thus superintendents, like union presidents, must find ways to bridge the divide between the cohorts of veteran teachers who endorse traditional union values and priorities and new teachers who are attracted by more progressive change.

There is no more important union-management relationship than that between the superintendent and the union president. Although the school board actually holds the legal obligation for negotiations, it is the superintendent and union president who maintain an ongoing relationship. These two individuals typically have very different histories in the district. The union president often has many years of local experience, having begun as a classroom teacher and worked her way up in the organization. By contrast, the superintendent is often new, having been recruited from another district across the state or across the country. Being new means not knowing the history and traditions of local labor relations or understanding what meanings others may attribute to established practices. It's important for a new superintendent to spend time understanding local labor relations—the union, its leadership, and its contract—before pursuing changes that will require support from the teachers and their union. It is best, superintendents say, to have a strong and principled president who understands the responsibilities of the union to its teachers and the opportunities for progress through partnership.

In the end, union presidents and superintendents have a shared stake in school improvement, and together they can make change. If one's gain becomes the other's loss and power is treated as a zero-sum commodity, both will suffer when the standing of public schools diminishes. Alternately, if each recognizes the need to substitute joint ventures for adversarial jousting, they can advance the interests of the schools and children.

The local teachers union in Baltimore lacked the sophistication and standing of some of its counterparts in neighboring Montgomery County or Prince George's County. Repeated turnover in the superintendent's office coupled with seasons of political and labor combat meant that there was no viable union-management partnership. The contract, although detailed, was not particularly pro-teacher and actually imposed few constraints on management. But the union president was not accustomed to collaboration or to an action-oriented superintendent, and she resisted Alonso's early initiatives by calling for a vote of no confidence and urging a work-to-rule. That teachers did not respond to her political move reassured the superintendent that he could build a strong relationship with the teachers, whose support he would need to change practice in schools and classrooms. Yet he also could not count on a partner in the union president, someone who might encourage her members to take risks on behalf of new initiatives and to accept compromises in the interest of moving forward with the district's stated mission and goals.

MOVING AHEAD

Faced with enormous demands in urban public schools, superintendents today understandably seek to acquire more authority in directing school reform and exercise more autonomy in using teachers' time and talents. However, because making progress on each of these goals is tied to another organization—the school board or the teachers union—superintendents cannot move unilaterally as powerful CEOs might. Rather, they must find ways to assess differences, identify common interests, build alliances, and bridge boundaries—all activities that call for ongoing diagnosis and effective action. Often it is the superintendent's skillful politics, rather than executive skill, that makes the difference between a short, troubled tenure and a long, productive run.

Andrés Alonso, Baltimore City Public Schools: The Superintendent and Board Partnership

Laura Kelley and Leslie Boozer

Wanted: *Chief executive officers and board members for growing, complex enterprise in highly regulated industry. Must stay focused on core business despite disparate stakeholder demands, uncertain funding, critical labor shortages, and politically charged environment. Must be highly skilled at dealing with sensitive and divisive issues that may jeopardize family relationships, health, and/or career. Must be able to withstand intense media scrutiny of professional and personal life. Typical workday: 7 A.M. to 10 P.M., plus weekends and board meetings. College education required; doctorate preferred. Pay significantly below market rate. Future of nation at stake.*

Nora Carr, "Leadership: The Toughest Job in America," 2003, p. 14.

It was a warm spring night in 2007, and the excitement in the room was contagious. The nine members of the Baltimore City Public Schools Board of Education, called commissioners, had just finished dinner with Andrés Alonso, the deputy chancellor of the New York City Board of Education, and he seemed to be the right fit for the city school system. He understood urban children and cities, he was intelligent and articulate, and he was someone the board believed could "sell the system" as a strong public relations agent for the school district. After his experience in New York, he had the skills to manage the scale of Baltimore, and his substantial background in special education and his law degree would most certainly help with the stipulations emanating from the settlement of the *Vaughn G.* legal case, filed in 1984 on behalf of seven Baltimore special education students, which the school district had been unable to meet for the past two decades. As the board members prepared to call their search consultant, they wondered: Had they found their next leader?

"We weren't sure if we wanted an idea person or an executive to implement ideas, but with Alonso, we would be getting both," said board president Brian Morris. "He has the pedigree, he's done the superintendents program, he's been in New York, so he has dealt with the type of scale where you can't say, 'Can he do it here?'" Morris continued, "We want someone to come in and be a change in culture and to expand people's ideas of what's possible in Baltimore, and I think he can do it."

Nods of agreement spread around the room. Another commissioner agreed with Morris,

> The question will be, Why would somebody leave the largest district in the country to come to Baltimore? I think he is the CEO who can help us actualize our priorities. But he's not from here, and he's Hispanic. How will the city react to him?

As the board continued to balance the long list of pros against the weighty cons of selecting Alonso as the next CEO, a similar process was taking place on a train ride back to New York. The commissioners had given Alonso a lot to think about. The profile of Baltimore certainly wasn't the profile of the city school system he thought he would lead one day. He had always imagined he would be a superintendent in a city with a large Latino population because of his Cuban identity and knowledge of the culture. Baltimore also had more than its fair share of troubles, with inconsistent school leadership and low, if increasing, standardized test scores. He would have to consider his family and the fit before talking to the board again.

THE CONTEXT—BALTIMORE CITY PUBLIC SCHOOLS

In the ten years prior to Alonso's meeting with the board, Baltimore City Public Schools (City Schools) saw tremendous turnover in the district's leadership. Already on their fifth CEO in a decade, the current interim CEO, Charlene Cooper Boston, was quite popular with many of the city's educators, who saw her as a colleague because she had risen up through the ranks in City Schools. Many expected the board to name Boston the permanent CEO at the end of her interim appointment. However, the board questioned her managerial skills. The district had experienced a string of CEOs who the board felt had not exhibited the strong executive or management skills City Schools needed, as indicated by the swaying deficit of $16 million to $58 million over the past five years.

In several ways, the board had become actively involved in the day-to-day operations of the school system. CEOs whom the board perceived as having weaker skill sets or whom the board did not completely trust spurred members to step beyond their policymaking duties. Board chair Brian Morris explained,

> We had a commissioner who was the de facto facilities person. At times, I was the face of the system. That is not a good scenario, because when everybody's in charge, nobody's in charge, and then nobody can be held accountable.

The desire for a CEO who could both establish a vision for the system and execute and deliver results grew over the six years of Morris's tenure, as his voice became "the voice of the board." The self-described "face of the search," Morris was looking for someone who would be very flexible with the board and understand their various agendas and characteristics, but someone who was a strong leader and could take the reins of the district.

Student achievement had gradually improved each year from 2004 to 2007, while enrollment continued to decline (see Exhibit 6.1 on the CD). In fact, enrollment had been in decline in City Schools for over forty years. As the decline worsened, the school district cited more and more underused school buildings, and announced a proposal to consolidate several high schools in 2006. High school students across the district held a three-day strike against the consolidation, claiming extra building space was due to large class sizes rather than low enrollment. The Maryland State Department of Education intervened later that month, threatening to take over eleven seriously underperforming Baltimore City middle and high schools. The entire district, which had been in "corrective action" since 2003, was simply not showing enough progress, according to state superintendent Nancy Grasmick.

Prior to 1997 City Schools operated under mayoral control as a function of the city government. According to Grasmick, several events precipitated a change of governance that resulted in the city-state partnership. In 1994 the American Civil Liberties Union of Maryland filed suit against the Maryland State Board of Education in *Bradford v. Maryland,* charging that the state was not providing an adequate education to Baltimore City schoolchildren as guaranteed in the Maryland State Constitution. Children in City Schools had the lowest test scores in the state from elementary school to high school, the lowest graduation rate in Maryland, and the highest number of children classified as at risk.

A second significant lawsuit against City Schools was the *Vaughn G.* case, filed in 1984 by the Maryland Disability Law Center on behalf of seven City Schools students. The petitioner argued that City Schools had failed to meet the needs of, and deliver adequate services to, special education students—approximately 15 percent of its student population. The long-standing litigation warranted special attention from the state, and assistance to meet federal compliance requirements has been ongoing.

Another important factor leading up to the city-state partnership was the lobbying and advocacy for accountability in City Schools that were led by a powerful legislator in Annapolis who became the head of the Appropriations Committee in the House of Delegates. Grasmick described "this perfect storm coming together, this very powerful legislator giving a lot of visibility to the inadequacies of the school system, and you had two court suits pending. Something needed to be done." A former special education teacher in City Schools, Grasmick convinced the state to join City Schools as a co-defendant.

The resulting city-state partnership gave City Schools an additional $253 million, but with the funds came additional oversight and accountability from the state. The City Schools Board of Education became one appointed by both the Baltimore mayor and the governor of Maryland. Under this unique format, the state board of education vetted potential candidates, and then the mayor and governor chose from those candidates and appointed the commissioners to the City Schools board each year. Once commissioners were appointed, the board acted independently, setting policy and hiring and removing City Schools CEOs as needed.

To ensure diversity of perspectives and expertise in City Schools, several criteria were set for selecting the commissioners. The nine-member board consists of residents of Baltimore City who, to the extent practicable, reflect the demographics of the city. The voting members serve three-year terms, staggered so that each year three members are up for renewal or replacement. Each commissioner may serve no more than two consecutive full terms, and all commissioners serve without compensation. Every two years the board elects its own chairperson.

According to the law established in the city-state partnership, at least four of the voting members are required "to possess a high level of knowledge and expertise concerning the successful administration of a large business, nonprofit, or governmental entity and shall have served in a high level management position within such an entity" (State Law 3–108.1). To complement the business acumen, at least three members should "possess a high level of knowledge and expertise concerning education" (State Law 3–108.1). A minimum of one member must be a parent of a student enrolled in the Baltimore City Public Schools system as of the date of his or her appointment. At least one commissioner is required to have "knowledge or experience in the education of children with disabilities, which may be derived from being the parent of a child with a disability" (State law 3–108.1).

In addition, a student enrolled in City Schools is nominated each year by the Associated Student Congress of Baltimore City to serve for a maximum of two one-year terms. The student member may not vote on matters of personnel, school closings or reopenings, or school boundaries; collective bargaining decisions; student disciplinary matters; or capital and operating budgets.

With such a complex operating structure, it is understandable that the board would seek a strong, capable leader with strengths in instruction, policy, and management. Alonso's diverse and unconventional background made him a logical choice for CEO.

FROM IMMIGRANT TO SCHOOL CHIEF

Born in Jovellanos, Cuba, Alonso began his American education when he was twelve and had to repeat the seventh grade for being too young. He quickly learned English and flourished in high school, and with the support of a high school French teacher in Union City, New Jersey, he applied and was accepted to Columbia University. He later graduated from Harvard Law School and worked as a corporate attorney before deciding to become a teacher at age twenty-nine.

Alonso began his twelve-year teaching career in Newark, New Jersey, at the Samuel L. Berliner School, teaching adolescents with emotional disturbances. It was at Berliner that Alonso acquired his mantra of "kids come as is," a message he took with him not only to the classroom but also to his preparation to be a superintendent, and to his deputy chancellorship in New York City. At Berliner he met a student he would later adopt as his son, who now lives in Maryland.

From his early years as a teacher, Alonso learned the importance of earned autonomy. The principal at Berliner gave Alonso what he asked for—a place to meet with his students and the authority to make his own rules. His boldness and strong work ethic impressed the principal, as did the growth his students were experiencing. Having faced similar challenges as an immigrant and English language learner, he saw the potential of every child and believed children could overcome economic, social, and language challenges and barriers. He also saw the possibilities for students facing difficult home lives who may require nontraditional teaching and social supports to find success.

Alonso continued to scale up his practice—taking on greater challenges as the opportunities arose. He first returned to Harvard to complete his doctorate in education. Then he worked with the superintendent in Springfield, Massachusetts, to learn how schools at the district level operate. Next he broadened his reach and flexed his leadership in the largest school system in the country, New York City. As deputy chancellor Alonso was given wide authority to implement reform, much like the leeway his former principal at Berliner had given him. His confidence in his leadership ability helped him make decisions for equity without fear or hesitation. According to Alonso,

> The reason why I have no fear is because I literally think I give it my best. As soon as I give it my best, as soon as every decision is stemming from a very strong core, then mistakes are part of the game. Moments of weakness are part of the game. Times when things can be better, messiness, all those things are part of the game. Fear cannot be part of the game, because that impinges on the ability to inhabit the moment with the good of the kids in mind.

When the search firm for City Schools called him to have a confidential meeting with the board, Alonso agreed, but also clearly defined his own working terms, including the authority he needed to make change.

THE MATCH

As Alonso explained,

> The board, because it had conducted a confidential search, was, I felt, deeply concerned about how the community would respond to me. The board was concerned with my outsider status, and that was clear from the first conversation. This topic took a lot more energy in the conversations than specific

> talk about "political players," which gave me tremendous insight about the system, as well as in terms of what the board hoped for from a CEO. Clearly the board hoped for somebody who had great managerial ability, but also somebody who could communicate and who could rally public support for the cause of children in the city, in a way that had not been done before.

The board was also looking for someone who was equally strong in all key areas of the superintendency—instruction, politics, and management. Alonso felt he could deliver in all three areas. "They wanted to ramp up significantly the quality of execution and performance. They wanted somebody who could cut through barriers," he said. "They wanted somebody who could focus the work around performance, who could accelerate what progress there had been, and bring a sense of hope and belief into the district." Alonso continued, "All those things at some level had to do with an ability to communicate and an ability to convey a clear message."

Like in many urban school systems, the board looked for a leader as a change agent. Alonso was not surprised. He looked at Baltimore and saw in the city many of the challenges he had faced in his classroom in Newark, and he felt that the years of preparation and practice he'd experienced had rendered him prepared to be the "transformative agent" the board desired him to be.

NEGOTIATING A CONTRACT

What Alonso wanted, and felt he needed, in order to bring about a change of business in City Schools was an unprecedented amount of autonomy as CEO. As he negotiated his contract in early summer 2007, he contemplated how to balance his need for authority with the needs of the City Schools system. For Alonso the authority was more important than salary provisions. He not only wrote exceptional authority into his contract but also included increased accountability for improvement. As Alonso recalled,

> I already knew that I wasn't going to be very demanding, because I felt that superintendents put themselves in a position of weakness around contractual terms quite often. I asked to see the contract that the previous superintendent had had, and I looked at the contract, and I thought, "Well you know, this is a generous contract." It was more important for me that I felt right about the district, and that the board, especially the board chair, felt right about me. I've consciously tried to create almost unmeetable expectations as a way of pushing the work forward, and what's so remarkable is that we're getting the kinds of outcomes that no one would put in their contract as a performance goal because sometimes it's looked unrealistic.

He made his desire for authority very public, and although some of the community was ready to put their faith in Alonso, others were critical of what they perceived as "excessive" decision-making power. President of the Baltimore Administrators and Supervisors Association Jimmy Gittings, a particularly strong critic of district administration, had concerns about the one-sidedness of Alonso's authority:

> Dr. Alonso has indicated if the board doesn't allow him to do what he wants to do, he'll leave. I don't want to see him leave, but I want to see the board of school commissioners act like a board of school commissioners, and they need to start speaking up.

The board introduced Alonso as the new CEO in June 2007, and he quickly started in July 2007. With all of the deliberateness that went into hiring just the right CEO, the board was signaling a change of pace and practice. However, it was unclear if everyone—even the board members—would be able to sustain the speed with which Alonso wanted to act.

News of Alonso's hire and contractual demand was fodder for public critique. The *Baltimore Sun* ran stories introducing the new CEO to the city while explaining his executive leadership style:

> The policy change is representative of the hands-on leadership style that Alonso has exhibited since becoming chief executive officer of the city schools in July. He has insisted on being personally involved in virtually every aspect of the system's operation, from reviewing the contracts submitted to the school board to interviewing principals before he agrees to appoint them.
>
> Critics have said he is slowing up routine processes, but Alonso — known for working virtually around the clock — says that to reform the system, he needs to understand all its components and be assured that the right people are in place. At the same time, Alonso has said he wants to give more authority to principals, and hold them accountable for the results. [Jones & Neufeld, 2007, paragraph 7–8]

TAKING THE LEAD

Alonso flexed his authority quickly, impressing some and ruffling the feathers of others. Deputy chief of staff Laura Wheeldryer had worked under a handful of superintendents prior to Alonso and wasn't particularly interested in working with another, but when board chair Morris introduced Alonso during a cabinet meeting in early July 2007, Wheeldryer knew things would be different. "I listened to him speak for a little while, and I thought, 'I'm going to stick around a little longer. This isn't going to be the same old, same old,' she remembered. "He was incredibly respectful of Charlene [Cooper Boston], who was also sitting in the room, and so it was a little bit awkward. But he just talked a lot about kids." Morris continued, "He's quite a powerful speaker. And so I was sitting there feeling goose bumps, thinking, 'This is an A-list superintendent.'"

Within his first three months, Alonso started changing long-standing district policy. After seeing the data on student discipline that showed twenty-six thousand instances of suspension in 2004 and 2005, he decided to address the issue head-on to reduce the over sixteen thousand instances of out-of-school suspensions across the district (see Exhibit 6.2 on the CD). Alonso said every suspension over five days had to be personally approved by him, and he literally sat with every single expelled student to figure out what was going on. Some saw this change as micromanaging the schools, but Alonso saw it as his responsibility to truly understand the students and their struggles. The move was also symbolic, signaling a deep interest in students and a shift in values for City Schools. As Alonso described,

> It was so much about the cultural tenets of the district. Taking them on, not necessarily flowing with them, because culturally in the past the city has been about exclusion of kids. It was about taking an oppositional stance to a previous practice and being willing to take the hit for a while because of the conviction that kids aren't going to learn if they're not in school. And the purpose is to teach them, it's not to exclude them.

Another major change of practice Alonso wanted to initiate had an impact on teachers. A dispute over planning time erupted into Alonso's first political battle in October 2007. Alonso wanted to forgo a negotiated contract to require teachers to meet in teams for collaborative planning once a week. However, the Baltimore Teachers Union (BTU) strongly opposed this change and began threatening demonstrations and calling for a vote of no confidence in the CEO just two months into the 2007–2008 school year. BTU president Marietta English talked of taking job actions, asking teachers to "work to rule" just as the school year got under way. The heated conflict with the BTU marked the beginning of Alonso's tenure, and many wondered if he would last any longer than previous CEOs.

Alonso considered the troubles with the union to be a test of his authority, and many advisers suggested he stand down. He explained,

> Every person is saying, "You have a lot of momentum, the community seems to like you, why are you in a fight with teachers over one period of planning a week?" At that point in time, I thought one period of planning a week might

> make the difference between a school succeeding and a school failing, so it's something that I had to assert as a value.

Alonso refused to budge from his position, touting the benefits of collaboration, and the board supported him. Chairman Morris said this embodied the CEO-board relationship in City Schools:

> Our first responsibility is to make certain that there is a system in place that will improve the academic achievement levels of all students, to work with the superintendent to establish the policies under which he would operate, but then let him operate. Our primary role is to look at those policies that need to be in place for the system. Then the superintendent has the responsibility for letting us know what should change, because he's dealing with situations out there. We give him some guidance and support. The superintendent should never be out there by himself. He should always know that his board is supportive of him, . . . that's the collaboration that has to exist between the superintendent and the board.

Determined to put children first in the system, Alonso moved forward with several other symbolic changes that represented cultural shifts in operations in City Schools. His "Kids Come Back" campaign was aligned with his beliefs about student suspensions: "Kids can't learn if they aren't in school." Alonso asked high school principals to make home visits and go door-to-door asking students who had dropped out of City Schools to return. For deputy chief of staff Wheeldryer, this request was indicative of the system's new priorities—the students. "He framed so much of it in terms of 'We have to hold on to the kids, and we have to bring in kids who aren't coming,'" she said. "For two hundred kids, all it took was asking, and they showed back up again. That was one of the rare moments I've had in nine years here where I felt really proud of the system."

Not everyone was happy about the return of high school dropouts, however. Administrators union president Gittings applauded Alonso's efforts to recover dropouts, but had misgivings about the safety of returning the older students to general high school classes.

WORKING BEHIND THE SCENES

Although the public face of CEO-board relations seemed smooth, both Alonso and City Schools commissioners admit to a great deal of work and collaboration in private. Alonso saw great advantages in having a board with diverse perspectives. He believed the composition requirements helped him scrutinize ideas and plans, and their varied expertise allowed him to perfect plans as much as possible before implementation.

In fact, he saw the board less as a single unit than as "different members with different belief systems, different hopes, and different experiences." Alonso was the face of the system and was held publicly accountable for results, but he described the board as a group of partners who pushed him to think about different angles and details, whereas he was the expert educator who taught them about systemic change:

> I would say that I have had tremendous autonomy in the work, but it's been earned autonomy. The work is still hard in terms of every innovation has to be leveraged and platformed, and not being part of the status quo means having to be very careful about ways in which one disrupts the status quo. There's a narrative arc that says, "I've come into Baltimore, and I have been unafraid, and I've made changes," but that's not what the work is.
>
> The work is about coming in and having to be extraordinarily strategic about how to make the changes and what changes to make. I understand that there are some times when I have to work with the status quo, and other times when the status quo has to be shaken to the rafters. The actual doing of the job is always about calibration, and it's always charged with risk. Every board wants things to be great, but every board is also afraid of things not working out as they should. The work is always hard in that sense, and I still consider myself lucky because on the whole the board has been extraordinarily willing to take chances. It's very hard work in terms of keeping that balance between motion and aggressiveness.

Part of Alonso's strategy involved making procedural changes in how the board and district personnel interacted. Alonso felt the need to create a "buffer" or "nonpolitical space" in which district staff could work so he discontinued the practice of bringing numerous staff members to board meetings. Alonso felt the interactions had not always been healthy in the past. By designating himself as the point person for corresponding with the board, he not only streamlined communication but also assumed personal accountability for results.

According to Wheeldryer, many staff members that no longer were allowed to attend executive sessions were upset about the change and felt left out of the loop. Although staff was required to prepare for board meetings, for the first five months of Alonso's tenure no staff members were allowed to speak in front of the board. As Wheeldryer explained,

> The board loved to beat staff up in public, so everybody who's still left in this building and has ever presented to the board has some story where they can tell you about how they got their annual performance evaluation from the board in front of two hundred people and on TV. The board would pick apart staff and totally beat them up in board meetings. Alonso . . . stopped that dynamic, and he won a lot of admiration from staff for doing that. It was literally just the superintendent talking to the board in public for two hours.

Alonso recognized that the care of the CEO-board relationship took constant time and energy. Alonso and the board met for hours each week and had executive committee meetings every two weeks. There were also six standing board committees organized to address (1) teaching and learning; (2) special education; (3) board policy; (4) parent and community engagement; (5) personnel and employment; and (6) payroll finance, including budget and facilities. These committees met monthly or bimonthly, offering numerous opportunities to convene and discuss district progress, concerns, and upcoming initiatives. Noted Alonso, "Their job is to flag for me all the things that could go wrong, which sometimes makes discussion difficult. But I would rather hear that from the board before than hear it from someone else after it's happened."

COLLABORATIVE LEADERSHIP

The room in which City Schools cabinet meetings took place was spacious, with a table large enough to accommodate all of the people Alonso invited to think through the work of the district. Mayor's liaison Sabrina Sutton, district leaders, and staff from the Maryland State Department of Education all sat around the table each meeting, ready to work alongside Alonso in improving the school system. "I want as many people around the table engaging in a process of thinking and questioning. I want the work to be tremendously cross-functional," Alonso recalled. For those concerned about Alonso's unprecedented authority, his commitment to working jointly with other decision makers offered some balance. Alonso described the tension,

> It is dangerous to function as though we live in isolation or disconnected from everything else in the city. Not just dangerous and unrealistic, but also ineffective, especially in a city like Baltimore, which has so many social issues. There's no one agency that can span the extent of the need. When it comes to children, we are the agency that everybody else turns to for the answer. This is because we happen to be the agency that is functioning, at some level, exclusively for the children.

In fact, when the state announced drastic budget cuts to education in late 2008, Alonso appealed to multiple agencies for both organizational alliances and political support. Despite the fact the governor would select a portion of his board, Alonso advocated publicly for reconsideration of the state's proposed funding formulas, teaching the community via radio, on television, and in public meetings how the loss of funding would harm the children of City Schools. Many city residents were reminded of the

Bradford case and the underfunding of City Schools students, and they were not interested in repeating the inequities.

In his challenge to the budget cuts Maryland governor Martin O'Malley proposed, Alonso found tremendous support from various sources. According to Morris,

> Taking away the money was an if-then statement, and because we've built a little bit of credibility and people feel positive about the progress and the direction, we were able to engender the type of support that it probably wouldn't have engendered. Because six years ago or eight years ago, people would have said, "Oh, they're just crying for more money. They're not even managing the money that they already have." Now we have some credibility, and it gave us the ability to say, "Look, our students are getting better. We think we have a handle on this. We're moving in the right direction. But if not, if this funding doesn't happen, then you're saying to us we have to pull back, and you should expect there's some impact to our children, which is unacceptable, which is why we're pushing so hard."

Federal tax stimulus dollars helped defray the loss of funding, and the effort to avert financial crisis was considered a success, even though it might have damaged Alonso's relationship with the governor. Alonso was more focused on the united public front that had developed, noting that this public support and collaboration were not surprising to him. He felt the support of the board, the mayor, and the community who believed in the children and the district. Touting measurable results, Alonso was confident when asking for political support. This partnership developed from Alonso's efforts to keep his partners informed and on the same page. "There is an amazing amount of hard work that goes into taking bold public stances, which appear to be flowing smoothly with relatively little tension," he said. "This hard work allows for me to ask for things when I need it, when the system can't survive without help."

WHAT CAN HAPPEN WHEN WE WORK TOGETHER

The city took notice of the change in daily practices. With the help of a relationship fostered with the *Baltimore Sun,* news of Alonso's reform efforts and the results of change have been heavily publicized—a rarity in public education. From a three-day, consecutive front-page spread about Alonso's leadership and City Schools in early 2009, the community was able to glean insights into the passion and drive of the man behind some of the district's most impressive achievements. The increase in kindergarten enrollment and ninth- and tenth-grade class sizes marked a positive difference in the choices parents and students were making in sending their children to City Schools. The number of City Schools students who exceeded the standard on the Maryland School Assessment in reading increased by 92 percent from 2007 to 2009. Similarly, the number of students who exceeded the standard on the mathematics component of the test increased by 107 percent over this two-year period (see Exhibit 6.3 on the CD). Moreover, the number of advanced students doubled, meaning that the shift had not simply been about moving students from basic to proficient. According to Alonso, "It has been about pushing kids to the high end of the continuum along standards, not just moving to a basic standard of proficiency."

The district also made significant progress in the *Vaughn G.* consent decree. Over one hundred schools were identified for release from the consent decree based on the demonstrable improvement of the system in attending to the needs of its special education students. Wheeldryer summed up the city's reaction:

> I think what they see in him, in this particular instance, is a man with a special education background who's incredibly committed to serving kids with disabilities. I think that across the board people are so relieved at how competent he is that they all are sitting back a little bit.

Although thrilled with some of the progress, board chairman Morris worried about the media attention Alonso was receiving. "I thought the front-page coverage was good, and I also told him I thought that was enough," said Morris of his advice to Alonso. "No more big covers like that, because as much as people like to place you on a pedestal, they then subsequently like to pull you down."

THE REVOLVING BOARD—LOOKING AHEAD

Alonso is painfully aware of how tenuous both the success City Schools has achieved and the support he has enjoyed can be. Even after a successful two years, he plans to continue to push the schools and the city as far as he can to produce results. Even though he is the face of change in the district, he acknowledges that the tide could turn at any time:

> The essence of what I am in the district right now — and it could turn in a day — is the establishment of a kind of partnership with community that allows me to take great risks for the right reasons with a kind of certainty that people

do believe that I am making decisions for the right reasons. There are people out there who think that I'm going to crash at some point. Eventually I will, as all superintendents do, but I do believe that there is a deep-rooted sense of conviction in the city that I'm making decisions in a different way than [others have] in the past, and that gives me great power to do what is right. If it's not for the right reasons then I lose it completely.

Alonso knows that one of the keys to maintaining that partnership will be keeping the support of the board. With its staggered appointment schedule, yearly turnover is inevitable. Morris has been Alonso's biggest supporter thus far, and when he steps down from his position on the board after two years in June 2009, Alonso will have to rebuild relationships with new members and a new chair.

When the new board configuration occurs, moving forward in the culture of change Morris sought and achieved in Alonso is likely to require a very different level of commitment. To maintain the improvement trends City Schools has seen in two years, the behind-the-scenes work that has enabled success for Alonso and the board must become manifest in the kind of public partnership Morris and Alonso established. Explained Morris,

I think we've done some good things since I've been on the board. But for me, bringing him here was the biggest achievement. I think it starts to build the sustainability and starts to build the culture of the system.

Alonso's work will lie in sustaining relationships and adjusting to the new nine-member dynamic. How will processes change when a new board chair is announced and new members are appointed? What will influence the new dynamic of collaboration? Will he be able to convince this new board to continue "running with him," as he marvels in reflection on the board's willingness to work with him during his first two years? Can he continue to convince the new board to take strong risks for the betterment of students? According to Alonso, the pace and process of change in upcoming years will be just as challenging as they were in the beginning, even if different:

In my first two years, if you judge success by outcomes for kids, the risks have been worth the gamble. That doesn't mean that it should be done in the same way in the next two years, because we will be in different places, but when I think of what the first two years have been, I have no regret whatsoever in terms of how I have approached the work. The question is, Am I going to be smarter moving forward? Because the work is going to become more difficult as the district itself accustoms itself to doing better. Doing better doesn't necessarily mean that things are going to get easier.

REFERENCES

Baltimore City Public Schools School Board. (n.d.). Article 1: Board of school commissioners. Retrieved February 21, 2010.,from www.bcps.k12.md.us/School_Board/PDF/Article_1 .pdf.

Carr, N. (2003). Leadership: The toughest job in America. *American School Board Journal Special Report: Education Vital Signs*, *122*, 14–20.

Jones, B., & Neufeld, S. (2007, September 26). Alonso given wider power: Schools CEO must OK suspensions of more than a week. *Baltimore Sun*. Retrieved February 21, 2010, from www.thebaltimoresun.com.

Pragmatic Radicalism: The Superintendent as Catalyst, Capacity Builder, and Concertmaster

Joshua P. Starr

The story of Andrés Alonso's experience as CEO of Baltimore City Public Schools reminds us that in order to be successful, superintendents of schools must strike the balance between that which they want to do because it's the right thing for children and that which they must do in order to achieve their vision within the context of the community. Alonso epitomizes what I call the pragmatic radical: someone who moves seemingly radical ideas through an organization by taking a realistic approach that rests on collaboration, communication, and breaking complex ideas into bite-sized chunks in order to make them digestible for multiple audiences with diverse interests. Pragmatic radicalism rests on the notion that leaders must work to change people's actions while also influencing their beliefs, and it requires that those leaders be three steps ahead of everyone else.

I use the term *radical* to describe a fundamental shift in urban education from a system that serves the interests of adults to a system that supports and makes college-ready each and every student. This shift may not be a radical idea, but when it comes to fruition it will dramatically alter the landscape of American society because we will have drastically improved opportunities for the very students who have been denied opportunities in the American urban public education system. Visionaries like Alonso, who strive daily to implement practices and alter systems to support the new soil of a changed landscape, are true radicals. It's a lot easier to maintain the status quo. I use the term *pragmatic* to refer to a practical-minded approach to change that recognizes and is able to work through the different components—or frames, as Bolman and Deal (2003) would suggest—of our educational systems.

CONTEXT

Although Stamford, Connecticut, is quite different from Baltimore, there as elsewhere the superintendent must have political skills that adapt to the context. Stamford is a city of 120,000 in southwestern Connecticut that serves as a suburb to New York City and a location for many corporations in its own right—particularly in the financial sector. There are 15,000 students in twenty public schools. The student population is 40 percent white, 30 percent Hispanic, 22 percent African American, and 8 percent Asian; 40 percent of students qualify for free or reduced-price lunch; and 15 percent are English language learners, 9 percent are special education students, and 35 percent come from families in which English is not the native language. Since the early 1970s Stamford has intentionally integrated its schools so that school enrollment reflects the overall demographics of the student population within 10 percentage points.

The political structure of Stamford is similar to the New England–style hyper-democracy that pervades much of Connecticut. There is a nine-member board of education (BOE); elections are held every year for three seats, and each seat has a three-year term. The minority party (typically Republican) must hold at least three seats on the BOE, so it is possible for a Democrat to get more votes than a Republican but not get seated if there are only two Republicans on the BOE. The BOE functions in a typical fashion with a committee structure and tries to keep its focus on policy, budget, and superintendent evaluation. In addition to the BOE, there is a board of finance and a board of representatives. The six-member board of finance (BOF) controls the finances of the city and sets the mill (tax) rate. It votes on the BOE's budget after the BOE votes, and cannot add to the budget or vote on individual line items. The board of representatives (BOR) is a legislative body of forty members who vote on the BOE budget after the BOF and sets policy for the city. Both the BOR and the BOF have education committees. All three boards comprise primarily members of the traditional power structure of Stamford—white individuals of Irish, Italian, or Jewish heritage. There is one African American on the BOE, none on the BOF, and a few on the BOR. There is one Hispanic member of the BOR and none on any other boards. This political structure creates two dynamics that I have had to manage as superintendent; one is micromanagement and the other is the "or else" syndrome.

Micromanagement results from having so many elected officials, each of whom has constituents as neighbors. When someone doesn't like her child's bus stop, or when her child doesn't get into a magnet school, she calls her BOR member, who calls a BOE member or the superintendent to take care of it. It becomes difficult for BOE members to avoid micromanagement when the other boards force them to wallow in the details. It also leads to the "or else" syndrome because the BOF and BOR have the final say on the BOE's budget. Hence, the BOE is constantly in a weak position because it must respond to the interests of those other boards "or else" its budget might be cut. And, too often, those interests are not aligned with the needs of the children; they reflect the needs of adults.

When I arrived in Stamford, the district was just beginning to acknowledge that it must take action to address the stark disparity in student achievement among students of different demographics. The difference in student achievement across subgroups as measured by standardized test scores is 40 percentage points in some grades on some state tests. For decades, schools in Stamford had been largely autonomous in regard to curriculum, professional development, and ensuring high expectations for all children. Many students excel in the Stamford Public Schools; we have always offered numerous advanced placement (AP) and extracurricular classes at the high schools, students excelled in the top classes at the middle schools, and our elementary schools served students at the high end of the spectrum very well. However, students who are poor, African American, Hispanic, or learners of the English language fare much worse at every level. And there has been no consistency of curriculum, pedagogy, or expectations between and among schools. Moreover, many people had concerns about moving forward; some wanted to proceed more slowly, whereas others had great interest in maintaining the status quo and refused to confront their own beliefs and practices. Most, however, including the BOE that hired me as superintendent, were clear about wanting to change these dynamics and improve the teaching and learning environment for all students. Thus, as a superintendent who aspired to be a pragmatic radical—and had learned from Alonso while working in New York City—I set about the work of creating a catalyst for transformation, building the capacity of others and aligning all of the different elements within a highly political environment.

CATALYST

The board of education that hired me wanted a change agent. I was thirty-five years old, had never been a principal, and had a background in central office leadership, specifically in designing and implementing comprehensive accountability systems. I was working in New York City when I was offered the position in Stamford. The BOE clearly wanted someone who would shake up the status quo, and I was eager to lead a district that was seeking to deal with the issues of urban public education in a deep and aggressive way. By hiring me, the BOE was sending a clear signal to the community—both internal and external—that it was time for change.

Although many people in Stamford were ready for change, there was great wariness about who should direct change and what it should look like. Like in many other districts, teachers and principals were skeptical of a new superintendent with new ideas, and many took the wait-and-see attitude. During my entry work I heard time and again that the district had tried a program or purchased materials that ended up going nowhere. In addition, because many students had been successful in Stamford for so long and those who were unsuccessful represented particular demographics, many people attributed the failure to parents, culture, or the students themselves rather than their own practice as educators. The work before me was quite clear, but mobilizing others was going to take some effort. The changes we needed to put in place could not be seen as stemming from me alone; others had to own it. BOE members and I went on a retreat, facilitated by outside experts, soon after I started. The major outcome of the retreat was the adoption of five long-term visionary goals for the system, which I used for strategic planning and budget purposes. The game in Stamford had changed; the BOE was putting itself on the line for bringing the school system into the twenty-first century through improved teaching and learning for everyone, focusing its attention on addressing the achievement gap. The catalyst for change was not, therefore, solely my beliefs and desires as superintendent but also a board that had publicly committed to addressing the long-standing issues that had plagued our system.

CAPACITY BUILDING

The autonomy that had existed in Stamford for so long and the dearth of expertise and authority at the central office had resulted in a vast disarray of approaches to teaching and learning. I have often said that Stamford had twenty schools with eighty ways of doing business. In order to change that dynamic, I reorganized the central office within my first few months. Whereas Alonso slashed his central office in order to make a point about resources, autonomy, and accountability needing to be at the school level, I was taking a more centralized approach consistent with what the BOE wanted. Moreover, autonomy had not worked in Stamford. There has always been a highly centralized approach to distributing students throughout the district to comply with the BOE's longtime integration policy. However, what happened in each school and classroom was left largely to the schools, and there was no accountability for student results. For example, an audit of our elementary literacy program by Phi Delta Kappa determined that there were 153 different literacy approaches among twelve schools. I knew that in order to improve teaching and learning for every child in every classroom, the system needed a great curriculum, extensive professional development, and better data to track progress. The central office had to first build the capacity of adults throughout the system, and then gradually release responsibility.

I put my ideas for a new structure on a whiteboard in my office and invited many people to comment freely on it. I then eliminated most jobs in curriculum and instruction and created new ones, forcing people to apply for new positions if they wanted to stay. I also appointed two experienced principals with long and deep ties to the system as assistant superintendents for elementary and secondary education, who directly supervised the principals. Some of the moves I made worked and some did not, and I miscalculated how much time it would take for the changes to bear fruit. In my third year, moreover, due to significant budget cuts, I had to lay off ten people in the central office. However, the message was clear: the BOE had set goals and given me a clear charge, and I was fully prepared to do whatever it took to carry it out.

I was extremely fortunate that the GE Foundation was prepared to invest up to $17 million over five years in Stamford because of its deep business roots in the community. The GE Foundation Developing Futures in Education program (formerly College Bound) was established to improve math and science instruction and increase college readiness in locations where GE had a big presence. For a new superintendent, it was an incredible confluence of events: the board of education hired me to build a system for the transformation of teaching and learning, and a major corporation was about to give me the funding to do just that. In addition, the monies from the GE Foundation were protected from some of the political dynamics in town because they weren't local taxpayer dollars. The purpose of the grant was clear—to create consistency within and among schools, raise the standards for all children, and address the achievement gap. What more could a superintendent ask for?

I was not aware, however, of the depth of the challenge in regard to teaching and learning in Stamford. Many administrators and teachers had bemoaned the lack of a curriculum and adherence to consistent standards, yet no one believed that the central office had the capacity to drive change. We therefore involved teachers and administrators, as well as the unions, in defining and designing what the change would be.

The work before me was abundantly clear, and the pragmatic radical in me had to determine how to take on these issues in a way that would build on the culture and strengths of the system and not throw it into disarray. I was not going to negotiate on what we were going to do—not only had the BOE set goals but also I became a superintendent in order to improve educational outcomes for urban youths—and I was not committed to any one approach to getting there. The outcomes and goals were clear: college readiness for each and every child through consistently high expectations of adults at every school. How we were going to get there and how we would continually improve through good feedback were going to make the change last. Similar to Alonso's aims, the "radical" goal was nonnegotiable, yet the approach to bringing it to fruition had to be both practical and cognizant of the extant structures of the Stamford Public Schools. Thus we have involved multiple stakeholders in the development process through work and oversight committees and collaborative monitoring entities that include union and board members. Engaging multiple teachers and administrators in the process also gave me leverage when I was asked to explain something to any of the three local boards. Because I could show that folks throughout the system had participated in designing the change, it was harder for attackers to argue that the young guy from New York City was imposing the change on Stamford.

CONCERTMASTER

Five years after beginning my tenure in Stamford, my role has shifted from being the relentless communicator of urgency to the designer of a system and teacher of people to learn the skills needed to make that system viable—to a concertmaster who sets the pace and rhythm, knowing that the pieces before me are working within an intricate interplay that has the potential to produce beauty when in harmony. By working with the BOE, the unions, and stakeholders throughout the system, we have completely overhauled our math and science curriculum and professional development for grades K through 12, instituted Professional Learning Communities in all schools, begun to implement a new K–12 literacy curriculum, established multiple opportunities for collaboration with our teachers and administrators unions, renegotiated labor contracts to increase efficiency and innovation, developed new metrics for measuring performance qualitatively and quantitatively, extended our partnership with the GE Foundation and developed a partnership with the Panasonic Foundation and Connecticut Center for School Change, and established an Office of Family and Community Engagement to increase our efforts to engage families in their children's education. All of this has been accomplished with declining local resources. Student achievement has risen as well; more students from all No Child Left Behind subgroups are achieving at the higher end of the state test; the achievement gap is starting to narrow; and more students are taking AP courses, four years of math, and four years of science. Our work is in no way finished, but we are on a good course toward the future.

The challenge going forward will be to align the political will behind the instructional reform that has begun to take hold. The criticisms that were levied against me when I first arrived—too young, never been a principal, doesn't know Stamford, is looking for his next career move—can no longer be sustained because we have results. However, a new political climate is emerging on my board of education and the other city boards. After five years, no board members who originally hired me remain, and some of the new members have distinct agendas or deep, long-standing ties to the district that may compromise the original reform agenda.

As superintendent of schools I must always remember that I work within the cultural and political context of the community I serve. For better or worse, the local voters elect the boards, who set policy and the budget. My responsibility is to find ways to move the reform agenda forward without completely upsetting the apple cart. I have found that new board members who are elected with specific agendas or ideas about what they are going to do often shift their perspectives when faced with the realities of governing within a tight system. Five years ago I began to strategically establish relationships and take steps to dismantle those things that have kept Stamford from performing at its potential while building the supports that are helping teachers and administrators do their jobs better. The state department of education and the GE Foundation have explicitly declared that they will be holding us accountable for the work we are doing, especially around eradicating the long-adhered-to system of tracking students. Therefore, our moves in that area are not the whims of the radical superintendent; they are a response to major organizations that fund and monitor us. Such a large number of our teachers and administrators have become intimately involved in the curriculum design and implementation work, and so many are happy with our professional development and Professional Learning Communities, that it would be difficult to return to the way it was five years ago. Many parents have been mobilized to become more vocal about the need to change the system, so the politicians will ideally have to listen to them. We have taken many small, bite-size steps over five years. They are all part of an agenda that may not seem radical to those who know and understand the changes that must be made to improve urban public education. However, in a community that has just begun to confront change, it has been necessary to make the agenda accessible to many different groups in ways they can understand, and to carry out this agenda by engaging multiple stakeholders in figuring out how to improve the system together.

REFERENCE

Bolman, L., & Deal, T. (2003). *Reframing organizations: Artistry, choice, and leadership* (3rd ed.). San Francisco: Jossey-Bass.

CHAPTER 7

Realigning Resources

Strategic Resource Allocation: The Superintendent's Perspective

James P. Honan

Among the many key challenges facing all public school superintendents and their leadership teams is the strategic allocation and use of the district's financial resources. The current economic climate has made this aspect of a superintendent's work particularly difficult and, in a sense, even more crucial. One way to think about a superintendent's "to do" list in regard to strategic, district-level financial leadership is to frame it using some high-level guiding questions. Such questions may help us to organize and better understand the important work of strategic resource allocation in school districts and schools. For me, three broad questions are particularly significant:

1. *How do the school district's financial resources "work," and can leaders allocate or re-allocate them strategically?*

An obvious but important starting point for any superintendent and his or her leadership team is having a full and accurate understanding of a district's overall financial resources. Based on my own experience teaching nonprofit financial management for a number of years and working with a variety of school leaders in many different settings, I know this is sometimes easier said than done. I am struck by the all-too-common lament that public school financial statements and reports are often unduly complex and hard to decipher and interpret. The sheer length and volume of most public school financial statements and reports certainly affirm this concern. Nonetheless, I think superintendents and their leadership teams have a fundamental responsibility to fully understand how the district's financial resources "work" and to be able to effectively communicate these insights to internal and external constituents. Such work needs to take place in senior leadership team meetings, budget presentations and hearings, and any other venues in which financial matters are discussed and deliberated. A district's chief financial officer obviously plays an important role here, but I would argue that it is essential for the superintendent and other senior leadership team members also to engage in this effort to think more deeply about how a district's resources can be used in more strategic ways.

2. *How can the school district's superintendent and leadership team allocate or re-allocate the district's financial resources to improve student performance and achievement?*

Answering this question has certainly proved vexing for many superintendents and leadership teams, but attempting to do so in a more systematic way is probably one of the most important aspects of strategic resource allocation in public school districts. There are a number of frameworks and models that can aid our understanding of the relationship between financial resources and results and outcomes. For example, a theory of action, impact, and change construct provides an opportunity for a leader to make an explicit connection between strategies, resources, and results (in other words, if we pursue these strategies, supported by financial resources allocated in these ways, then we believe we can show the following results). Similarly, a logic model framework, which many sponsors and philanthropic organizations commonly use, might enable leaders to show the relationships among inputs (including financial resources), processes and activities, outputs, outcomes, and impact.

Using these or other models can help superintendents and their leadership teams foster a more nuanced and in-depth understanding of strategic resource allocation. Such an approach also provides an opportunity to examine "what works" and "what does not work" among a school district's many programs and initiatives and can serve as a potential basis for re-allocation of financial resources. Not surprisingly, an increased focus on results and outcomes, especially on showing improvement in student achievement, has forced superintendents and their leadership teams to grapple with this question in more explicit ways. And although the complexity of assessments and metrics mandated by No Child Left Behind and state education authorities can present challenges in this regard, linking resources and results is a key element of strategic resource allocation.

3. *How does the district deal with declining or constrained financial resources, and how can one make the case for continued investment in public education?*

In many states and districts, the annual budget process has actually turned into the annual budget-cutting process. "Doing more with less" is the mantra for many school leaders as they engage their district's constituents and stakeholders in budget deliberations. In some cases, the budget reductions are of such a magnitude as to require leaders to develop strategies for closing schools on a large scale (recent examples from Kansas City and Detroit come to mind). In other instances, difficult choices about what to do, what not to do, and how to do "new work" present budget makers with complex resource re-allocation dilemmas. These decisions become particularly challenging when a series of budget cuts need to be made over several fiscal years, which is a common occurrence in many states, cities, and districts.

My sense is that two important types of strategic financial leadership must be exercised in these instances: (1) superintendents and their leadership teams must clearly establish and communicate the parameters and the criteria for budget cuts, and (2) superintendents and their leadership teams must develop a plan for continued and future investment in public education. The first form of financial leadership is especially crucial if budget cuts are necessary over multiple fiscal years. Failure to base budget reduction decisions on thoughtful criteria puts a district at risk of not providing resources to fulfill key planning goals and priorities. Similarly, an inability to develop and communicate a thoughtful and convincing "investment plan" may leave a district in a position of having to make never-ending budget cuts.

COMMON THEMES AND APPROACHES FROM STRATEGIC RESOURCE ALLOCATION CASE EXAMPLES

The following sections of this chapter describe the strategic resource allocation and re-allocation work of Arlene Ackerman, the chief executive officer of the School District of Philadelphia, and Christine Johns, the superintendent of Utica Community Schools in Michigan. Both of these case examples illustrate some common themes and provide a glimpse of the key elements of strategic resource allocation that are required to address the challenges inherent in the three guiding questions posed above. The following are among the common characteristics of and approaches to strategic resource allocation undertaken by these two superintendents and their leadership teams.

Articulating Core Educational Values to Guide Resource Allocation, Reallocate Decisions, and Inform Budget-Cutting Choices

Both superintendents appear to have developed a deep and strongly held set of personal and professional core beliefs and values about education, teaching and learning, and instructional improvement. We see both superintendents communicating their core beliefs and values widely and frequently and using them as the basis for guiding and framing decisions about planning priorities and financial resources. Both case examples affirm the importance of setting forth a clear set of foundational ideas about education and instruction and attempting to translate them into action. Furthermore, we see the significance of a leader's communicating what she or he "stands for" as an element of effective strategic financial leadership, especially in resource-constrained contexts.

Assessing the Overall Financial Condition of the District and the Impact of Federal, State, and Local Financial Challenges on the District's Budget

Although we see two somewhat different approaches in each superintendent's transition and entry (one external and one internal), having an accurate and in-depth assessment of the district's financial condition is critical in developing an overall district reform and improvement strategy and a resource allocation plan for supporting that strategy. Understanding the impact on a district's budget of federal, state, and local financial challenges is also important, especially given the current economic crisis. Translating and communicating the district's financial condition to internal and external constituents and stakeholders is another common theme running through both case examples.

Developing an Instructional Plan to Drive Resource Allocation and Re-Allocation Decisions

The development of a district-wide instructional plan is an essential aspect of strategic resource allocation and re-allocation. Such plans can provide the basis for both the allocation and re-allocation of existing financial resources and for the identification and receipt of new public and private funds. Both case examples illustrate the centrality of this idea, reflecting each superintendent's significant investment of time and energy to develop a comprehensive, district-wide strategic plan and instructional strategy. In my view, such an approach provides superintendents and their leadership teams with the framework and "narrative" for guiding budget and budget cutback decisions.

Communicating Effectively About the District's Strategy, Resources, and Outcomes

Both case examples underscore the fact that superintendents are the primary communicators of their districts' strategies, resource allocation decisions, and results. Superintendents must convey messages about all of these things to both internal and external audiences. It is crucial that a leader knows and can communicate effectively (using factual evidence) narratives on these three aspects of a district's work.

Leading and Supporting District-Wide and School-Level Change and Transformation

Just about any public school district's strategic plan, instructional strategy, budget presentation, or other document is likely to reflect a commitment to some form of district or school reform, improvement, and renewal. The work of strategic resource allocation in public schools is clearly not "status quo" work. In nearly all cases there are significant external and internal pressures for change, reform, and renewal, including shifting how the district allocates and uses financial resources. Both case examples show superintendents attempting to position their districts to meet a wide range of emerging challenges and demands—and in both instances, there is a palpable sense of urgency for embracing new ways of doing and funding the work of public education.

FUTURE TRENDS AND CHALLENGES

Public education is clearly at a pivotal moment. Superintendents and their leadership teams will need a combination of insight, persistence, wisdom, and courage to address the emerging financial challenges public school districts will probably face in the coming years. Superintendent Johns notes in her section of this chapter that school districts in her state appear to be trying to "cut their way to prosperity" as they grapple with such challenges as structural deficits, facilities needs, and other financial dilemmas. My sense is that this approach will probably not be viable or optimal for public school districts, especially over the long term. The two case examples presented in this chapter instead suggest that superintendents and their leadership teams must increasingly be prepared to "make the case" for financial resources to support public education.

The focus on results and outcomes (in other words, improved student achievement for all students) will heighten the importance of this aspect of strategic resource allocation. Public education funders at all levels; the federal government, states, and cities and towns; as well as private philanthropic organizations appear to be presenting school district leaders with both significant challenges and significant opportunities. At their best, superintendents and their leadership teams should focus on the latter. Through the articulation of fundamental core beliefs and values, the development of a comprehensive strategic instructional plan, and a well-thought-out resource allocation strategy, district leaders can and should "make the case" for public education's value and promise. Meeting the many financial challenges that lie ahead will require a leader's best work. The two case examples in this chapter provide helpful insights into what this work looks like.

Arlene Ackerman, School District of Philadelphia: The Quest for Educational Equity

Leslie Boozer and Laura Kelley

Sitting at her desk at Columbia University's Teachers College, Arlene Ackerman prepared a PowerPoint presentation of her five core beliefs for her transition team. Comprising thirty-six Philadelphians and national educational experts, the team needed to understand Ackerman's vision and priorities for the School District of Philadelphia—how she wanted to act with urgency to accelerate academic achievement for all students, channel resources to support teaching and learning, and engage the community to become partners in this work. Although her team's expertise varied from finances to school reform to community partnerships, they would represent her as they embarked on a "listening symposium," soliciting input from parents, students, teachers, principals, central office personnel, educational advocates, and community groups. This process had to be quick because Ackerman had only about a month before becoming the CEO of the district in June 2008. Contemplating her challenge, Ackerman realized she must harness the expertise of the team to boost her learning curve in Philadelphia if she was going to implement substantial reform efforts swiftly and efficiently.

Knowing that the transition team's work would set the agenda for systemic change in Philadelphia, Ackerman had already begun asking herself what the district needed to improve learning outcomes for all kids. She immediately recognized the inconsistent student achievement across the district, the high dropout rates, and the persistent incidents of violence. She had anecdotal evidence that some schools had access to more resources than others, yet she had not been able to secure accurate school-level budget information. She had visited schools and spoken with principals and teachers, hearing firsthand about the disparities across the system. But she still needed more data to understand the challenges the district faced. How were teachers and principals supported in focusing on the instructional core? Were the central office and regional offices organized to support teaching and learning? What accountability systems were in place for the adults in the system? And, most important to Ackerman, what would be required to shift the allocation of resources in a more equitable and transparent manner so all students could achieve at high levels? Ackerman picked up her papers and headed out to take a train to Philadelphia to speak for the first time to her entire transition team. She had ideas of what the team would discover about the district, but she knew one thing for certain—things were going to change in Philadelphia.

GETTING TO KNOW PHILADELPHIA

With over 163,000 students, 25,000 employees; and 10,000 teachers in the 2007–2008 school year, the School District of Philadelphia, or simply "the district," was the eighth largest in the nation and the largest in Pennsylvania. However, the district's total enrollment had declined by over 8 percent in the last decade. The remaining student body was 76 percent economically disadvantaged but diverse, with 61 percent African American, 18 percent Hispanic, 13 percent white, and 6 percent Asian students, and 2 percent other nonwhite minorities. In addition to the 256 district-operated schools, 31,300 students (1 out of 6 public school students) attended 61 charter schools or Education Management Organization schools (see Exhibit 7.1 on the CD). Approximately seven percent of total students were classified as English language learners (ELLs), speaking 113 native languages. These students represented 25 percent of all ELLs in the Commonwealth of Pennsylvania. Special education students represented 15 percent of the student body, whereas only 3.13 percent of the district's students were classified as gifted and talented.

Despite some pockets of excellent achievement, an analysis of the district revealed inconsistent instruction of the core curriculum and some alarming racial disparities. African American and Latino students scored about 24 percentage points behind white students and about 30 points behind Asian students on the state's achievement test in reading and math. Moreover, African Americans were overidentified in special education, making up 76 percent of students enrolled in emotional support programs (59 percent boys and 17 percent girls). Suspension rates were higher for African Americans and Latinos across the district. Of those students suspended in the 2007–2008 school year, seventy-six out of one hundred were African Americans, fifteen were Latinos, seven were white, and one was Asian. Meanwhile, one in ten white students versus three in one hundred African American students were identified as gifted. White students were also proportionally overrepresented in magnet schools and gifted programs. For example, although making up only 12 percent of the high school population, white students made up 28 percent of the magnet school population.

The district had long struggled to use its fiscal and human resources to meet the needs of the student body. After years of poor academic achievement, chronic underfunding, and a looming $200 million operating deficit, the Pennsylvania governor and the city's mayor entered an agreement to take control of the district in December 2001. They established a new five-member governing body, the School Reform Commission (SRC), with the governor responsible for appointing three members and the mayor appointing the other two. The SRC operated similarly to many elected school boards but was granted some extraordinary powers under Act 46 of the Pennsylvania School Code. Members not only were responsible for hiring the system's leader and monitoring finances for the district but also had the power to privatize schools in the district and incur debts.

With a new governance structure in place, the SRC looked to a different type of leader for Philadelphia. Given an overshadowing 2001 deficit, the SRC sought a leader with a strong business background. Changing the leader's title from superintendent to chief executive officer, they expected this new leader to help the failing system meet its financial obligations, restructure the supports to schools, and end the longtime fighting with the unions. The search for a CEO ended in July 2002 with the selection of Paul Vallas, the former head of the Chicago Public Schools.

The district incrementally improved the number of students scoring at or above grade level on the state achievement exam. The percentage of students performing at grade level in reading increased from 24 percent to 45 percent, and from 20 percent to 49 percent in math across all grade levels district-wide from 2002 to 2008 (see Exhibit 7.2 on the CD for sample student achievement results in grades 5 and 8). Notwithstanding this progress, African American and Latino students continued to score significantly below their white and Asian counterparts. In fact, Ackerman's transition team determined that if Philadelphia students continued the same incremental growth as they had over the six years prior to Ackerman's tenure, it would take between fifty to sixty years to close the achievement gap. The situation was even more bleak for students classified as ELLs or special education.

District finances did not fare much better. Prior to Ackerman's tenure, the CEO tried to stretch resources by enacting a series of one-time revenue enhancements, such as selling district property and refinancing existing debts on favorable terms (see Exhibit 7.3 on the CD). Additional fiscal woes stemmed from overspending for construction and repairs and rising costs for special education and employee benefits. Although the budget was balanced for the first time in seven years in the 2003–2004 school year, this progress was not sustained. Despite average annual increases of 7 percent in state funding and 5 percent in city funding over the preceding five years, in 2007 the system was left with a deficit upwards of $73 million. As the SRC prepared to select its new CEO in winter 2008, the district's spending deficit was forecast to be anywhere from $181 to $192 million for fiscal year 2007–2008, highlighting the inconsistent record keeping in the district.

THE NEW CEO

On February 19, 2008, the SRC unanimously selected Arlene Ackerman as the next CEO of the School District of Philadelphia. Ackerman had the experience the SRC was seeking. SRC chair Sandra Dungee Glenn said of their choice,

> [Ackerman's] passion for children in urban schools, as well as her track record and priorities of putting resources back into the classrooms fits with the goals the Commission has established for our students. Dr. Ackerman's proven record of raising student achievement and building effective partnerships with diverse communities makes her an excellent fit for Philadelphia. We are confident she will continue her academic accomplishments with Philadelphia's students. [School District of Philadelphia, 2008a, paragraph 2]

This proven track record included Ackerman's forty-plus years of experience working to put children first. A former teacher, principal, and central office administrator, she had previously served as the superintendent of District of Columbia Public Schools from 1998 to 2000 and of the San Francisco Unified School District from 2000 to 2006.

In 2006 Ackerman left her post in San Francisco and became a professor at Columbia's Teachers College. When she heard the story of the School District of Philadelphia, she knew it was time to come out of retirement and lead a district once more. As Ackerman explained,

> [I] believe I can make a contribution to students in Philadelphia. I am coming back to active leadership because I have missed my passion — the on the ground battle for our children who attend urban public schools. I believe I still have more to give in this important fight for social justice. [School District of Philadelphia, 2008a, paragraph 3]

Early in her career, Ackerman vowed to radically redefine public school systems, and she has demonstrated her commitment to social justice by continually striving for equity. In every district Ackerman has led, she heavily publicized her five core beliefs:

1. Children come first.
2. Parents are our partners.
3. Victory is in the classroom and is facilitated by a strong instructional leader.
4. Leadership and accountability are the keys to success.
5. It takes the engagement of the entire community to ensure the success of its public schools.

For Ackerman, sharing her core beliefs is her way of not only expressing who she is but also rallying together the school system in which she works. As she described,

> I share my core beliefs because I actually am trying to get people to buy into them. I tell people, "I don't change these. This is who I am." It's like Arlene is my name; these core beliefs are mine. I say to them early on, "I hope that you will embrace them and they'll become yours," and every place I've gone, that's what happened.

Ackerman's passion stems from her personal educational experience. Having attended segregated schools, she knows firsthand what it means to be denied an equitable education. Enduring long bus rides across town, she attended schools that did not have the same resources, the same curriculum, or the same opportunities as other schools in the city. During the 1960s she witnessed African Americans fighting for such basic civil rights as the ability to vote and access to public accommodations.

Ackerman sees it as her personal responsibility to fight what she classifies as the new civil rights movement, in which all young people have access to a quality education. Explaining the depth of her conviction in testimony provided to the Philadelphia City Council on May 12, 2009, Ackerman said,

> Public education is a civil right. To deny a child the right to learn, to deny the right to equal educational opportunity, is a civil rights violation — and we are accountable. Children fail because systems have broken down and adults have either failed to care or refused to notice. We are responsible for the educational well-being of all our children, as well as for the costs of repair. [personal communication]

EFFORTS TO REFORM PHILADELPHIA'S SCHOOLS

Ackerman desired a purposeful entry to the district that would provide her with data to start making immediate improvements to the system. Her initial research and anecdotal evidence suggested that an external review was necessary to answer her probing questions. When negotiating her superintendent's contract, she solicited the SRC for $100,000 to bring in a transition team of national education experts and local stakeholders to assess the instructional, managerial, and political situation prior to her start date in June 2008 (see Exhibit 7.4 on the CD for the makeup of the transition team). Knowing it would be critical for her to make informed decisions based on the data and culture of Philadelphia, Ackerman saw this collaboration as a necessary first step. Furthermore, having successfully used this method in Washington DC and San Francisco, she was confident the transition team's report would supply her with a blueprint for how to prioritize work in the first thirty, sixty, and ninety days of her superintendency, thereby allowing her to make substantial changes early on in her first year.

Based on her initial research of the district and her discussions with the SRC, Ackerman identified her top priorities for the team to explore the month before her start date. She gave the experts a clear purpose—to provide the data necessary to propel student achievement forward. Divided into subcommittees, the transition team began identifying information related to Ackerman's six areas of concern: (1) teaching and learning, (2) safety, (3) public engagement, (4) resource allocation, (5) capacity building, and (6) diverse providers.

The members spent April and early May combing through reports, audits, and district data to answer their charge. One thing in particular became immediately clear—the current fiscal instability was a serious impediment to improving teaching and learning across the district. Known for her financial acumen, Ackerman realized that no matter what the transition team recommended, her hands would be tied until the district improved its record keeping and balanced its budget.

Thus, before even taking office, one of her first hiring decisions was to bring former SRC member and secretary of the budget for the Commonwealth of Pennsylvania Michael Masch on board as the chief financial officer. Together, Ackerman and Masch lobbied for increased financial support from the state and the City of Philadelphia. Their efforts resulted in an additional $36.5 million (approximately) each from the state and the city, which allowed the district to reduce its deficit to approximately $40 million. Working closely with Masch prior to her official start date on June 2nd, Ackerman was able to tighten spending, particularly in the central office, and enter the district with a nearly balanced budget.

Meanwhile, the transition team spent the remainder of May conducting multiple school site visits and countless meetings with parents and community members. No one was prepared for the anger the parents expressed or the volume of people showing up to community forums—it quickly became standing room only. People needed time to vent. Many lamented how they had never been asked their opinions before, and parents began showing up in the hundreds to have their voices heard. They expressed how they felt betrayed by the school system, frustrated over the inequalities among schools, and left out of the decision-making process. One concerned citizen explained how he had been treated by previous administrations:

> You come to us, conduct these focus groups, gather information, and then we never hear from you again. You pick our brains, but we're not at the table when the real decision making takes place. We want to be included in the planning process, not just informed of the final decision.

Ackerman took these words to heart. As the audits were conducted, the teams shared their findings with Ackerman, her cabinet, the SRC, and the community at large. Ackerman commissioned the transition team to draft a final written report to share their collective findings and thoughts. In this report, the team penned Ackerman's challenge to the district—"to create a school system where stories of success are not limited by divisions of race, gender, age, economic status, program, or neighborhood" (Peterkin & McGuire, 2008, p. 21).

In early June 2008 Ackerman began assessing how she could maintain a balanced budget and still implement significant reforms to propel student achievement. The necessity of reform weighed heavily on Ackerman as she states, "There's a sense of urgency that's driving me like nothing else has driven me before. This is my last stand for kids" (Graham, 2009, paragraph 3). Disturbed by the reports of inequities, the low number of teacher and principal dismissals despite unsatisfactory test scores, and the persistent achievement gaps, Ackerman realized that she needed to take immediate action.

Based on her understanding of the symbolic power of leadership, one of Ackerman's early decisions was to change her title from CEO to superintendent of schools. She wanted to signal to the entire school community that she was more than just a business leader; she was an instructional leader. As Ackerman explains,

> I'm proud of my roots and the fact that I know what it looks like, what it smells like, what it feels like in a classroom. I'm proud that I know what it looks like, what it smells like, what it feels like in a principal's office. I'm proud that I've come up through the ranks, because I understand all aspects of this business.

Now that she had redefined her work, she was primed to redefine the role of the central office.

Armed with the data the transition team had gathered from April to June 2008, Ackerman embarked on a mission to change the way resources were used in Philadelphia. An analysis with chief financial officer Masch of the inherited 2008 budget confirmed that the funding shortfalls would not allow the hiring of many new personnel. To complicate matters, there was a dearth of data when it came to reviewing the school-site budgets. Masch explained their process for understanding how resources were being distributed:

> We are redoing the budget to make it clear how money is allocated out to the schools and how it gets spent. We are also doing a top-to-bottom analysis of how we spend grant funds, and what we contract for—but that work is just commencing. [personal communication]

A thorough budget analysis was going to take some time.

While Masch and Ackerman developed plans to improve the current budget's transparency and worked to create a strategy to make fiscal planning clear and aligned with long-term goals, Ackerman faced a real-time dilemma. She wondered how she could maintain current reform strategies that were working while increasing the focus on the instructional improvement necessary to close the achievement gap—all without flexible funding. Ackerman and her cabinet decided their best option was to rethink current staffing issues to better align personnel to the district's new vision focused on equity and excellence. This work during summer 2008 would include eliminating positions, creating some new ones, restructuring the regional offices, changing job responsibilities, and making initial cosmetic improvements to facilities.

Rethinking Human Resources in the Central Office

The community and parents' forums had one clear message—better customer service is needed. Hearing numerous parents' complaints of never being able to speak with a live person when calling the central office, Ackerman quickly embarked on an "enhanced customer service initiative." The goal was to ensure that members of the district's internal community, such as school sites, as well as the external community at large, felt welcomed to participate in the school system. Ackerman clarified,

> As service providers of educational services, our parents and students are our clients. We must begin doing a much better job as a District of meeting their needs by creating a more welcoming, customer-friendly business environment through extended business hours, friendlier faces, and other customer services improvements. [School District of Philadelphia, 2008b, paragraph 2]

Beginning June 16, 2008, a mere two weeks into her tenure, Ackerman restructured central office policies and procedures. She staggered central office staffing shifts to create a longer workday, meaning that a parent could interact with a live person either before or after work, with personnel starting at 7:30 A.M. and ending at 6:00 P.M. The district also enacted a new "no voice mail" phone policy. Ackerman wanted parents and community members to be greeted by a friendly, live district employee who could properly respond to their concerns. With approximately eighty departmental main numbers ready to receive calls and provide services, as well as a fully staffed district call center, callers were now only directed to voice mail at their request or outside of the newly established business hours.

Despite these early changes, Ackerman recognized that more feedback was needed. Ackerman ensured that customer service surveys, translated in eight languages, and comment drop boxes were placed within all central office departments and regional offices. Her team surveyed school employees to learn how central office could better support their work in the field. As a result of what she learned, Ackerman launched a 24/7 hotline for emergency school closings and other alerts. The new system resulted in the resolution of over sixty thousand parent concerns over the phone and in person, over five hundred e-mail concerns, and the registration of over one hundred new immigrant families that had previously struggled to obtain translation services, all within a few short months.

Reorganizing Instructional Resources

Meanwhile, Ackerman was examining the instructional resources in the central office. She found the curriculum and instruction department to be vast and unorganized. Absent a chief academic officer, Ackerman decided to serve in the position herself until she found the right person for the job. She reorganized the department, streamlined its purpose, and changed its name to the Department of Teaching and Learning. Having learned from the transition team audits that the district did not have the data systems in place to support a focus on instruction, Ackerman created a new department of accountability and data to oversee all aspects of testing and data analysis and management. Ackerman also hired a new deputy superintendent for accountability, David Weiner, a graduate of Columbia's Teachers College and a former principal in San Francisco, to create an accountability system for the district that would hold all adults in the system accountable for contributing to higher levels of student achievement.

During the reorganization, Ackerman learned that the district spent about $15 million during the past year on academic coaches, yet the job descriptions and responsibilities for the coaches were inconsistent, with no performance criteria to assess their effectiveness. Just one month into her superintendency, Ackerman decided to eliminate 218 coaches, leaving only 11 new teacher coaches and 53 reading coaches in place in the district. Not everyone agreed with these severe cuts. However, Ackerman unapologetically made it clear that this move was consistent with her mission to realign resources to focus on schools.

Restructuring the Regional Offices

In late July 2008 Ackerman began to rethink the regional offices. She and her leadership team determined that the eight existing regions were too large to allow regional superintendents the time and resources to provide intensive instructional support to all schools. Many regional superintendents felt that they were overtaxed with completing business functions, which diverted attention from focusing on the instructional core. Ackerman met frequently with the regional superintendents with a goal to reconfigure the district so each region would be smaller and the schools in each region would be connected by feeder patterns. Ackerman and her leadership team increased the total number of regions from eight to eleven, and reduced the number of schools each region oversaw from approximately forty schools to closer to thirty to allow regional superintendents to provide more time, attention, and resources to each school.

The collaboration among senior leadership also revealed that the structure in place forced each region to operate as a district unto itself with facilities management, staffing, information technology, and other compliance-oriented positions housed in each region. This led to inconsistent practices across the district, resulting in varying quality and quantity of resources and supports. After many meetings, Ackerman and her leadership team determined that these positions could be moved out of regional offices and managed centrally, eliminating many managerial tasks from the regional superintendents' responsibilities and allowing them to focus on instruction.

Improving Facilities

With the start of the 2008–2009 school year quickly approaching, Ackerman worked to diminish some of the visible inequities that existed among schools. Ackerman was stunned after visiting two schools. The first was Overbrook High School, a 1,700-student, eighty-four-year-old school in West Philadelphia. Ackerman marched into a girls' bathroom to find peeling plaster and many necessities missing; there was no mirror, soap, stall doors, or even hot water. She also saw exposed wires throughout the school, a paucity of art and after-school programs, and inadequate sporting equipment and practice fields. Despite a lack of capital funds, Ackerman vowed to make changes immediately.

Overbrook was starkly different from the high-achieving neighborhood elementary school, Fox Chase Academics Plus, which she visited next on the northeast side of town. As she toured this school, Ackerman observed well-stocked, working bathrooms; a state-of-the-art computer lab; and a wealth of art programs, including choir and instrumental music. As Ackerman explained to a reporter, "It was important to me to see the contrast as I begin to address equity issues. There are great students across this city, but we don't always treat them equally" (Graham, 2008, paragraph 7).

After these early visits, it became a priority for Ackerman to repair the schools before they opened again in the fall. Schools in need were repainted, floors cleaned, bathrooms repaired, and new light bulbs installed. What seemed to be minor changes improved student morale and parent confidence in the system. As regional superintendent Francisco Duran explained, "I had parents and students arriving at the schools, looking around and exclaiming, 'Wow.' We had only made the light bulbs brighter and added a fresh coat of paint, but they saw it as a huge difference."

While these changes were put into effect, Ackerman began long-term planning, which she insisted should include the opinions of all stakeholders. She began a series of community meetings conducted in multiple languages and held them throughout the city. The goal of these meetings was not only to share what the district had learned from its transition team and its early work but also to gather the experiences and recommendations from parents, students, and community leaders as the leadership team began planning for the future.

Ackerman's priorities began to drive how the district was spending its money. Some of these priorities included focusing more resources back into the schools, using $15.4 million for reducing class sizes; providing arts and music experiences for every student; and installing a qualified librarian, a counselor or counselors, and a nurse in every school. Ackerman had moved at a quick pace—it was only the third month into her superintendency, and she was insisting on accountability for expenditures. If an expense could not be linked to her core values or one of the newly established goals identified in the transition team's report, it was cut.

Ackerman was pleased with the changes she had made. However, strengthening the instructional program in the system remained an intractable problem for the district. She needed to implement a strategy targeted at raising the academic rigor in the district's most underperforming schools. Ackerman knew just the person with whom she needed to plan—Eloise Brooks, her former chief academic officer in the San Francisco Unified School District (SFUSD) and member of Ackerman's Philadelphia transition team.

ACKERMAN'S THEORY OF ACTION

While superintendent of the SFUSD, Ackerman had faced a significant achievement gap, similar to Philadelphia's, between African American and Latino students and their white and Asian counterparts. To combat these inequities, Ackerman and Brooks created and implemented a comprehensive reform strategy focused on raising academic achievement for all students. The plan required the district to provide numerous instructional supports, equitably redistribute district resources, and hold people accountable for results. Under Ackerman's leadership, the district implemented a weighted student formula, attaching a variable dollar amount to every district child based on his or her learning needs. The district also created Students and Teachers Achieving Results (STAR) schools and gave parents a choice in what schools their children attended. To provide strategic instructional and social support, Ackerman added new positions to consistently struggling STAR schools, including an instructional reform facilitator, a permanent long-term substitute, a parent liaison, an adviser in elementary and middle schools, and a learning support consultant.

This holistic approach to school reform encapsulated Ackerman's core beliefs. Decades of experience working in urban schools had informed

Ackerman's theory of systemic change: if a district provides academic, fiscal, and social supports to meet the documented needs of individual students in schools while holding all stakeholders accountable for student achievement, then all students will achieve at high levels.

Ackerman's theory of action resulted in San Francisco's experiencing five consecutive years of improved achievement while narrowing its achievement gaps (see Exhibit 7.5 on the CD). The STAR model proved particularly successful, with 86 percent of the district's underperforming schools making progress. Ackerman furthered the STAR initiative by introducing the reconstituted Dream Schools, which were designed to offer greater support structures to the most severely underperforming students in the district. The rising test scores resulted in San Francisco's becoming the highest-performing large urban school district in the state of California for the last two years of Ackerman's tenure. More important for Ackerman, *all* students made progress on the state exams—including special education, ELL, and gifted students. This documented decrease in achievement gaps and overall increase in test scores were exactly what Philadelphia needed to see.

EMPOWERMENT SCHOOLS MODEL

The transition team identified eighty-five elementary, middle, and high schools that were underperforming; underresourced; poorly staffed; and failing "academically, socially, and morally." Having encountered a similar situation in San Francisco, Ackerman and Brooks knew that no single intervention strategy would address the multitude of challenges facing these schools. Although they were confident they could tailor the STAR model to work in Philadelphia, they discussed how improving the district would require bringing their former strategy to scale and fitting it to Philadelphia's unique needs. In Philadelphia there were more than twice as many schools as in San Francisco that were in dire need of intervention, and Ackerman had limited funds to make a Philadelphia-based STAR program successful. She began to plan how she would accomplish the same feat: specifically, determining where she would get the funds and personnel necessary to make the new strategy a success.

Building the Plan

Beginning in August, Ackerman, her cabinet, and the regional superintendents worked together to devise a new approach to instruction. With 256 schools, the team wanted clear criteria to use for identifying schools in need of strategic intervention. They decided to focus on schools that had not achieved adequate yearly progress (AYP) targets under the No Child

Left Behind guidelines and were identified in Corrective Action Level II (CA-II). The team named their program the "Empowerment Schools Model."

Ackerman brought in Darienne Driver to lead the effort, a former reading teacher who was working as the coordinator of strategic management and accountability in another district. With extensive experience in curriculum development and district-wide strategic planning, Driver joined the Philadelphia leadership team as the new deputy chief of the Empowerment Schools. As Driver described,

> Dr. Ackerman's vision was to create a system specially designed for Philadelphia with supports in instruction, student and family services, operations, and leadership. What sold me was her affirmation that these are our most vulnerable kids and we can't experiment on them. We were going to use proven best practices to raise the level of instruction. I jumped at the challenge of leading this new initiative. I knew we could design a system of supports that would make a difference to the students, teachers, and staff of Philadelphia's most struggling schools.

After reviewing the school data and current research on failing schools, the leadership team agreed that chronically underperforming schools in Philadelphia shared many common characteristics—poor student achievement, lack of rigor in instruction and curriculum, high turnover and absenteeism of teachers, high numbers of inexperienced teachers, little to no shared planning time for teachers, and an inability to retain substitutes. Ackerman and her team set a specific goal for such schools, such as increasing achievement by providing targeted interventions at school sites, addressing systemic barriers that interfere with the process of teaching and learning, and devising support strategies tailored to the needs of these schools.

Two-Tiered Approach to Reform

Recognizing gross inequities in the school system and so many chronically underserved schools in need of assistance, Ackerman and her team knew that they would need to redirect financial and nonfinancial resources. They decided on a two-tiered approach for intervention and support. The most severely struggling twenty-three schools, labeled Empowerment I schools, would receive the most intensive resources. The second tier would consist of sixty-two schools, or Empowerment II schools, which would receive more limited but targeted resources.

The first step was to provide multiple personnel changes. Each Empowerment I school would receive support from an Empowerment School response team (ESRT), a social services liaison, a parent ombudsman, a student advisor, instructional specialists, a full-time auxiliary teacher, and principal mentor. Some of these resources would be full-time, on-site positions. However, limited funding meant some personnel would be shared between two or more Empowerment Schools, an important distinction from her STAR model in San Francisco. Ackerman did not have the resources to house all positions at every Empowerment School. Instead, most of the newly created positions, such as the ESRTs, were based at the regional or central offices. To lessen miscommunication, the new personnel were assigned specific days to spend at each school site. However, it remained a concern to Ackerman and Driver whether the traveling teams would be as effective as were the teams under the STAR model.

The Empowerment II schools would receive two full-time staff additions, a parent ombudsman and a student advisor, as well as support from an ESRT. Regardless of the tier in which a school was placed, all positions were designed to support student achievement. According to Anthony Irvin, the principal of an Empowerment School,

> Dr. Ackerman's approach starts in the classroom. It starts with the students. The focus is on teaching and learning, and there is an emphasis on professional development and also addressing some of the variables that impact our students in the urban setting — poverty, lack of resources in the schools, facilities.

The following new positions were used to ignite Ackerman's focus on teaching and learning. Together, they provided the supports for the once struggling Empowerment Schools.

EMPOWERMENT SCHOOL RESPONSE TEAM (ESRT). ESRTs supported all Empowerment Schools. These teams were created to provide school-based services to enhance teacher quality through learning walks, demonstration lessons, on-site professional development, site-specific and targeted interventions, and data analysis. Each team comprised a generalist, who worked mainly with the content area teachers; a data specialist, who not only analyzed data but also helped the teachers and the staff use data to guide their instruction; and finally a special services case manager, who focused on differentiated instruction.

Although Ackerman would have preferred to have an ESRT housed at each school site, there were instead fifteen ESRTs for all eighty-five Empowerment Schools. Ten teams were assigned to regions to focus on the sixty-two Empowerment II schools, while five ESRTs focused solely on the twenty-three Empowerment I schools. There were also two ELL specialists serving all eighty-five schools, but Ackerman gave priority to schools with the highest language needs. The district wanted to hire additional personnel to support ELLs, but only two qualified candidates applied for the newly created position. After a few months, a third candidate was recruited to complete coursework and training on the job.

INSTRUCTIONAL SPECIALISTS. The district placed instructional specialists at the Empowerment I schools, with one specialist typically being shared between two schools. Often teachers on special assignments, the specialists were responsible for one-on-one work with teachers and instructional leadership teams. As one Empowerment School principal noted, these supports were particularly important for new teachers:

> Forty-seven percent of my staff is new this year, so I've seen a difference as teachers learn about tiered activities and how to differentiate instruction. The ESRTs and instructional specialists have also been helping out with classroom management tips, so I see things getting better in those areas.

SOCIAL SERVICES LIAISON. Philadelphia schools generally did not have on-site social workers. However, many of the students attending the Empowerment Schools needed social services support. The social services liaisons worked with the school's leadership and counselors to increase the effectiveness of social services programs. They assisted families with accessing insurance; navigating child-serving systems (such as juvenile justice, child welfare, behavioral health, and the district); as well as transitioning during residential crises. Continuing Ackerman's customer service initiative, the liaison often met with parents and students in their homes.

FULL-TIME AUXILIARY TEACHER. The Empowerment Schools suffered from high teacher turnover, high absenteeism, and an inadequate number of highly qualified teachers. The schools also often had difficulty securing highly qualified daily substitutes because many teachers were reluctant to work in neighborhoods where the schools were located. To curb this problem, Ackerman hired an auxiliary teacher for each Empowerment School. This individual provided class coverage during professional development exercises, filled in when a substitute could not be located, and provided instructional support for struggling teachers.

PRINCIPAL MENTOR. Several Empowerment School principals were new to either Philadelphia or the principalship. Others seemed overwhelmed by the multitude of challenges they faced when leading these underperforming schools. To fight the isolation of this leadership position, Ackerman recruited successful retired principals to serve as part-time mentors. These mentors provided professional development, one-on-one coaching on instructional leadership, and guidance on school-site budgeting to the Empowerment School principals.

PARENT OMBUDSMAN. Many Philadelphia parents felt frustrated when navigating the bureaucracy of the system. Although Ackerman had already worked to improve customer service relations, she wanted a friendly, knowledgeable person to serve on-site as a liaison between schools and parents. This parent ombudsman served as an advocate for parents by gathering information and then connecting them with the principal, dean, or other personnel to resolve students' academic or behavioral issues. The ombudsman also educated parents on how to assist their children so they could reach their full potential in school.

STUDENT ADVISOR. Empowerment schools also suffered from high truancy and dropout rates. Student advisors worked with students and their families by focusing on attendance and truancy in the schools. Coupled with the parent ombudsman, the advisor worked with students and families to solve problems and make the school experience a positive one. Together they also eased the work burden of principals so they were not focusing on discipline and behavioral issues. As regional superintendent Duran described,

> Given those extra resources, a principal has the opportunity to focus on instruction, and just like we at the regional level need to be in the schools more, they also need to be in the classrooms more, and giving them these supports is definitely a plus.

Funding the Empowerment Schools

Ackerman realized early on that she did not have the additional resources to fund the Empowerment Schools unless the district made budget cuts and reallocated funds. After eliminating most of the academic coach positions, Ackerman was left with approximately $12 million in Title I Accountability grant funding (see Exhibit 7.6 on the CD, which shows a summary of reforms for the 2008–2009 school year's revised budget). Because many of the new Empowerment School positions served coaching functions, she quickly realized this elimination of coaching positions was the best way to shift these resources and clearly define performance criteria for the new positions. Meanwhile, Ackerman procured funding from some additional grants to reduce class sizes in grades K through 3 and in grades 6, 8, and 9 at all Empowerment Schools. Although these funds allowed the district to make changes, the resources available were still finite, and staffing was quickly becoming an issue.

The size of the initiative, coupled with the limited capacity of the district to fill these critical positions, hindered full implementation. To complicate matters, some positions, such as the student advisors and parent ombudsmen, were already starting to turn over in the first few months of implementation. Low pay, with average salaries between $33,000 and $35,000, and the tremendous need for support and attention overwhelmed some early candidates for the jobs.

Implementing the Empowerment Schools

To kick off the effort, Ackerman and Driver designed an Empowerment School Boot Camp, which was held from September 2 through October 10, 2008. While many team members were still being hired, this blitzkrieg of professional development focused on team building and effective leadership, cognitive coaching, the core curriculum and response to intervention, understanding data, differentiated teaching practices, and giving performance feedback.

As new members were hired, Driver worked with the regional superintendents to design professional development for all Empowerment Schools, including monthly instructional walk-throughs and a data-reporting system. The new system enabled the ESRTs to design a thirty-day action plan, which they then implemented and modified as necessary as new data were collected. Meanwhile, ongoing, targeted professional development on school-site budgeting, instructional leadership, and differentiation occurred at all levels for teachers, principals, ESRTs, regional superintendents, and central office staff.

Driver worked to establish a system for maintaining and analyzing the data that had begun to stream in. To monitor progress and make adjustments as needed, the ESRTs met regularly with the principals and regional superintendents to discuss classroom observations and review the data books collected for each school. The regional superintendents were responsible for creating recommendations based on these conversations for school-level instructional teams, and for coordinating with the central office to provide targeted interventions for the schools.

Accountability

While Driver's office was working on implementing the model, chief accountability officer Weiner was working to establish an accountability model to ensure results. Philadelphia had a history of little to no accountability for results, with no system of clearly defined roles or criteria for success. As Weiner described, "The two major beliefs of the Empowerment Schools Model are the concepts of equity and accountability. We created performance targets for individual schools, [and] the regional offices, and are in the process of developing targets for the central office." To demonstrate to the public how the district's schools were making progress, Weiner's office developed individual "school annual reports." The office first established baseline data, and then generated targets for numerous indicators, such as student achievement, school operations, community satisfaction, and school-selected indicators (see Exhibit 7.7 on the CD for an example from 2009). As Weiner explained,

> Our goal was to view data in a holistic manner. We believed this would provide a more comprehensive view of the school's progress. It wasn't just about test score data; it was also about decreasing school violence, improving parent relations, and teacher retention.

LOOKING AHEAD

Ackerman was aware that many schools were clamoring for the additional services and supports being provided to the Empowerment Schools. However, the district had been hard-pressed to find the necessary personnel and funds to staff the support for only eighty-five schools. As her team prepared to enter the strategic planning process at the end of 2008, Ackerman knew they would have to make many decisions and critical choices. Should the district implement a weighted student formula to further sustain the equitable re-allocation of resources? What shifts in resources would be necessary if the Empowerment Schools did not make expected progress? Should support be continued for Empowerment Schools that make AYP? How would the district continue to fund changes in instructional improvement and build on what the Empowerment Schools had started?

It was 6:00 P.M. one late-December evening as Ackerman walked into her next strategic planning meeting with determination and optimism. Teachers, staff, parents, and community members were charting ideas for the district's new strategic plan. As the working group struggled to redesign the district's evaluation system, Ackerman stopped to listen. With one hand on regional superintendent Pam Brown's shoulder, she encouraged the group to keep working by reminding them, "These are our kids. We can't wait on an invitation."

REFERENCES

Dean, M. M. (2008, July 2). Academic-coach jobs axed in district shake-up. *Philadelphia Daily News*. Retrieved from www.philly.com/dailynews.

Graham, K. A. (2008, June 3). District chief's first day a study in contrasts. *Philadelphia Inquirer*. Retrieved from www.philly.com/inquirer/.

Graham, K. A. (2009, June 4). Ackerman vows tighter teacher standards. *Philadelphia Inquirer*. Retrieved from www.philly.com/inquirer/.

Peterkin, R., & McGuire, K. (2008). *The School District of Philadelphia transition team report: An agenda for systemic reform*. Philadelphia: School District of Philadelphia.

School District of Philadelphia. (2008a). The Philadelphia school reform commission selects new CEO. Retrieved April 18, 2010, from www.phila.k12.pa.us/announcements/ackerman.html.

School District of Philadelphia. (2008b). Welcome to the new customer-friendly school district of Philadelphia. Retrieved April 19, 2010, from www.phila.k12.pa.us/announcements/releases/customer_service.html.

The Equity Fight in Utica, Michigan

Christine M. Johns

Utica Community Schools (UCS) is approximately one-fifth the size of the Philadelphia school district. It encompasses six municipalities that are situated in the heart of the automotive and manufacturing industry, eight miles north of Detroit. With twenty-nine thousand students in forty schools, UCS is Michigan's second-largest public school district. The student population is 90 percent white, 4 percent African American, 3 percent Asian, and 1.8 percent Hispanic students, and 1.2 percent other nonwhite minorities. Over 24 percent of the students are eligible for free or reduced-price meals, and 13 percent receive special education services. Approximately 3 percent of the students are ELLs, representing forty-seven languages spoken. Over nine hundred students attend the district through Michigan's schools of choice program, which permits districts to recruit students from neighboring districts.

My background and experiences growing up in western Pennsylvania and my undergraduate education in Pittsburgh during the collapse of the steel industry drove me to focus on my core educational values while addressing UCS's budget problem. With a clear understanding that *all* children must be equipped with the knowledge and skills necessary for postsecondary education, I had to balance the preservation of the core academic program with the necessary budget reductions.

Upon entering UCS in 2006, I recognized that the community held the district in high esteem and that the staff was proud. With a history of a stable board of education and superintendent, UCS enjoyed a reputation for conservative fiscal management and good stewardship of physical facilities. Strong public support for the district was evidenced by passage of multiple bond issues, and parents cited the district's reputation as the reason they chose public schools.

Like many public school districts, Michigan school districts are funded with a combination of federal, state, and local money. However, Michigan has an extremely high reliance on state funding for public education. Because school funding is directly linked to property values and sales tax, the effects of an economic downturn took its toll, as the state was reliant on automobile sales taxes. Thus the state's structural deficit problem had influenced district operations well before I entered the superintendency. The district had reduced the length of the secondary school day, offered early retirement incentives, eliminated central office positions, and begun implementing schools of choice in selected schools to save money.

The dependence on state revenue has forced districts into a vicious cycle of annual budget reductions. In Utica these budget reductions totaled $46 million from 2003 to 2010. While revenues are significantly declining, graduation requirements and accountability measures are increasing to address Michigan's need for a more educated workforce to compete in a global economy. This challenge is further compounded by the fact that school district enrollments are declining across the state due to an aging population and rising health care, and retirement costs are depleting the state school aid fund.

I knew during my tenure as superintendent that school funding would be a challenge, but the catastrophic collapse of the Michigan economy in 2009 and the national recession rapidly accelerated the pace of budget cuts and placed even greater pressure on school districts to balance their budgets in accordance with state law. With a state election on the horizon for a term-limited governor and a majority of the legislative seats open, most in the educational community knew assistance from the state capital of Lansing was unlikely, and the financial realities for schools would be devastating.

THE FIRST TWO YEARS

After careful consideration of the historical, political, educational, and financial landscape of the district, I decided to be my own transition person. My board of education for the first time had gone outside Michigan for a superintendent. I respected previous superintendents' long tenures and the district's solid, competent internal capacity while recognizing the district was somewhat insular. I knew that as an outsider I had to quickly build trust with the board of education, community, parents, students, staff, and policymakers if I was going to propel the district forward. Therefore, I presented a written transition plan to the board that focused on five goals and promised results in my first ninety days. The five areas included the following: (1) ensuring effective governance through positive and productive board-superintendent relations; (2) accelerating student achievement by building on the work of the district to improve educational outcomes; (3) establishing public trust and confidence through open, honest communication and positive relationships among stakeholder groups; (4) establishing a supportive, positive district climate and culture; and (5) examining the current organizational structure and functions to increase effectiveness and efficiencies.

Based on my research and assessment of the district, and with the board's support, I commissioned an external report that disaggregated student achievement data by demographics (race and ethnicity, gender, socioeconomic status, special education status, and so on); course enrollment; and comparison districts. The report acknowledged, in the aggregate, that UCS was performing well; however, there was much opportunity for future achievement growth within and among groups of students. I leveraged the achievement report and my research findings to establish an Accountability Advisory Committee, which comprised parents, teachers, district administration, and union leadership. Simply stated, their charge was to define accountability principles and to recommend the architecture of the new accountability system.

In August 2007 the board adopted *Indicators of Excellence: Our Plan to Improve Student Achievement*. The organizational structure was then realigned to the district's indicators of excellence, which included our core values, vision, mission, and district goals, along with specific measures of student progress. The goal of the organizational design was to establish linkages and connections to create a seamless K–12 education for all students, while implementing a system structure that provided a framework for data-driven decision making in schools and the central office. We loosely organized school clusters (vertical teams, learning communities, or school families) around school feeder patterns to improve coordination and communication among all grade levels. The cluster concept was designed to ensure that the curriculum in all subject areas was aligned, both vertically and horizontally, across schools and grades to maximize the ability of students to meet the state's rigorous high school graduation requirements, and to be well prepared to succeed in postsecondary schooling.

LEVERAGING PARTNERSHIPS AND RESOURCES

Driven by a strong belief that all students must be prepared for postsecondary education and that the responsibility for student progress rests with the adults, I continued to build on the successes of the district while leveraging opportunities. For example, the district had a history of being autonomous from the state; however, we had to rethink teaching and learning with the changes brought about by the new Michigan Merit Curriculum. I forged a partnership with the College Board to increase advanced placement (AP) course offerings and student enrollment in these classes. One of the initial challenges was convincing parents, teachers, and students that all students can succeed in more rigorous courses, not just those who are already enrolled.

As we implemented algebra II, physics, and chemistry courses in accordance with the new graduation requirements, along with additional AP courses, teachers and parents raised concerns that too many students were not prepared for the rigor, AP class sizes were too large, and not all students were going to college. By this logic, all students did not need to learn algebra II, chemistry, or physics. I consistently employed a strategy of communicating the new graduation requirements, what knowledge and skills jobs of the future would require, the importance of algebra and AP courses as predictors of college success, and repeatedly cited examples of current UCS student successes.

We continue to set high expectations, to provide teachers with appropriate staff development, and to conduct thoughtful data analysis in regard to student achievement, and we administered the PSAT (the Preliminary SAT) and EXPLORE (the ACT college readiness test) assessments to match students to appropriate courses and monitor their college readiness. The equity issues we had to address between and among the four high schools were the number and type of AP courses offered, how teachers were assigned to courses and students, and who participated in professional development. In addition, we had to determine why so many students were succeeding in the AP classes but not taking the AP tests. What we discovered was that some were not taking the tests for financial reasons, and others did not connect passing the tests with receiving college credit.

Although enrollment in AP courses doubled and student success on exams increased by 45 percent, further analysis of the data revealed that not all groups of students were appropriately represented. Working with the College Board and the secondary administrative teams, we conducted a review of every student. The focus of this discussion was to determine why students of equal ability from different groups were not enrolled in AP courses. The school personnel had to come to terms with what strategies they had to employ with individual students and their parents to enroll students and support their success. Further, we had to address the course-taking patterns of our junior high students. This is an area in which we must continue to improve if we are going to assist all students in reaching our goals.

SCHOOLS OF CHOICE

The Michigan schools of choice option is a provision of the state School Aid Act that permits districts to recruit and accept students from neighboring districts, whereby the student foundation allowance follows the student. Simply stated, districts participating in schools of choice receive a foundation allowance of the lesser amount of either the new district or the district of residence, and transportation is not required for choice students because it is not a mandatory public school service. Yet most districts traditionally provided it to their resident students. However, other districts have recently reduced or eliminated transportation to save money due to the budget crisis.

Having extensive experience with schools of choice programs, particularly magnet schools, on both the East and West Coasts, I found the Michigan choice model most interesting. The driving force for offering choice appeared to be money (the student foundation allowance) and not necessarily the improvement of the instructional program resulting from the increased competition. Although lawmakers and others argue that parents, who are taxpayers, should be able to choose on behalf of their children, in reality not all students have equal access. The main barrier to equal opportunity and access is free transportation. Therefore, families without the means may not be able to participate.

Within the provisions of the School Aid Act, however, there are opportunities for creative solutions structured around educational programs. One such approach was to pursue the federal Voluntary Schools of Choice Program (VSCP) grant to enable the district to offer specialized educational programs within a consortium. Although UCS had the requisite number of students to create the programs, the district's demographics would not have met the grant requirements. The goals of the grant did, however, encourage multidistrict partnerships, which allowed UCS to invite other districts within the county to apply.

Superintendents in the county have historically been very cautious about implementing schools of choice because of the fear of losing students to other districts, which would result in a reduction of state aid. In addition, there is concern about accepting students from one district and sending students to another district due to the possible complications arising from the socioeconomic or language differences of the students. In reality, the transportation limitation results in the majority of the nonresident students' being, in many cases, from middle-class families and, in other cases, people fleeing from one school system to another.

After numerous and extensive discussions pertaining to specialty programs, program location, student assignment, transportation, teacher contracts, length of the school day and year, grant administration, funding and expenses, as well as federal audit and reporting requirements, I and a neighboring superintendent opted to participate in the VSCP grant application. Together we were able to address the needs of a diverse student population and consider the possibilities for implementing theme-based instructional programs.

Several months later the partnership received a five-year, $12 million grant. This grant award allowed us to implement such specialty programs as the International Baccalaureate Programme, the Center for Science and Industry, the Academy of Arts and Sciences, and various career academies. Each of the partnership districts benefited from student-centered programs, professional development, personnel, national consultants, and equipment that it could not have afforded without the federal grant. Further, UCS leveraged the VSCP grant and a partnership with Michigan State University to apply for a Foreign Language Assistance Program (FLAP) grant. The result was a federal award of $1.5 million to implement an elementary Mandarin Chinese language immersion program, which is a feeder for the International Baccalaureate Programme, currently housed in a declining enrollment building serving a diverse student population.

THE BOND CAMPAIGN

In early 2009 Michigan's economy was suffering the worst recession in the country, experiencing high unemployment in excess of 15 percent, and with the combination of the banking crisis and collapse of real estate values the foreclosure rate skyrocketed. These factors contributed to a rapid decline in support for school bond issues at a time when the shrinking general fund could not absorb the costs of roof replacements, boilers, buses, or instructional technology.

Therefore, the decision of whether or not to seek voter approval of a $112.5 million bond issue had to be carefully considered. Several stakeholders proffered arguments as to why the district should not pursue approval of a bond issue, which included (1) the district in a failing economy should not extend the debt obligation when property values were dropping; (2) capital expenditures should be reduced because enrollment projections were declining; (3) school closures seemed imminent; (4) people did not have the money to support the debt because of the high unemployment rate; (5) there was lack of support for a bond issue among the growing senior population; and (6) there was a powerful anti-tax, anti-government constituency. Arguments in favor of a bond issue centered on the following: (1) equity among facilities and equal access to technology; (2) a history of conservative fiscal management; (3) commitment to preventative maintenance, safety, and security; (4) the district's reputation for delivering on promised projects; and (5) a clear understanding that the financial resources necessary to correct deteriorating facilities and the technology infrastructure would never be available if lost now.

Working with the board of education, we believed the decision to proceed with the bond issue was one of a moral obligation to current and future students and a commitment to allowing the voters to decide. I understood we had to effectively communicate that this bond was conservatively constructed to support infrastructure needs and provide equitable facilities for all children. In order to meet the challenges created by changes in absentee voter laws and the misperception that district voters' tax dollars were being used to support nonresident students, we had to educate the parents with facts, continue to discuss academic performance, and encourage them to aggressively pursue votes in favor of the bond. After nine months of persistent, face-to-face engagement with parents, community members, and business leaders, we successfully passed the bond with twenty-one votes to spare. The anti-tax, anti-government coalition attacked the election in an effort to reverse the outcome; however, the parents organized to monitor the recount. It became obvious to the anti-tax, anti-government group that the challenge was baseless, and during the recount they conceded that the voters had successfully passed the bond issue.

THE FUTURE—HOLDING ON TO THE ACADEMIC CORE

The reality in Michigan is that school districts are being required to cut their way to prosperity. The legislature has not addressed the persistent structural deficit problem and in the failing economy is unable to raise taxes to provide more revenue. At the beginning of the 2009–2010 school year the state informed Utica of a reduction in current year school aid that totaled $4.8 million. The requirement to reduce expenditures to compensate for the loss of $4.8 million and the impending severe reductions in the foundation allowance for the next fiscal year made it apparent that UCS would be fiscally bankrupt. I therefore launched an aggressive information campaign to create a deeper understanding of the severity of the crisis, clarify how schools are funded, and demonstrate how to contact state and city legislators and advocate for adequate school funding.

The current reductions in revenues have dwarfed all of the UCS cuts, restructuring efforts, strategic management of fund equity, and innovations to date. Over the past seven years the district has cut $46 million, and for the upcoming fiscal year UCS will need to reduce expenditures by approximately $33 million in a time when Michigan needs to increase its number of college graduates. Concurrent with preparing for the $33 million reduction for fiscal year 2010–2011, the district implemented midyear reductions of $4.3 million for noninstructional personnel. In addition, for the first time the district employed furlough days to lower current year expenditures.

The greatest challenge to budget cuts in UCS is that an overwhelming majority of people do not accept the proposition that the district does not have sufficient money to provide all of the services and activities they demand. One of the most time-consuming challenges is managing the complex interrelationships among all of the competing groups seeking to protect their jobs or programs at the expense of other groups. An additional challenge is creating individual understanding that meaningful structural changes must occur to solve these financial problems and that structural changes will affect everyone.

In an effort to protect the core academic program, UCS will need wage and health care concessions from teachers, administrators, and others. We may have to implement the provisions of the law that permit the contracting or privatization of noninstructional components, such as custodial work, skilled trades, maintenance, transportation, and food service. All of these actions are detrimental to the vitality of the school district because so many of these individuals live in the district, and their children attend our schools. These individuals along with our parents are the voters who pass bond issues and provide a sense of community. Although these decisions are extremely difficult, the financial realities of expenditures outpacing revenues demand hard choices in order to maintain the academic core.

In another effort to save general funds, I have been searching for expenses that are not the district's fiscal responsibility. For example, school crossing guards are statutorily the responsibility of the local law enforcement agencies. Working with the municipal authorities and local police chiefs, I commissioned a study to determine the appropriate distribution of crossing guards to ensure the safety of students. UCS, in partnership with the municipalities, will be transitioning the responsibility for crossing guards to law enforcement. The district will reallocate the money to support teaching and learning.

Based on an ongoing analysis of school capacity versus enrollment, the need for school closings is apparent. Early this school year I established a Facilities Study Team (FST) consisting of parents, teachers, and community members to evaluate the viability of school closures in order to consolidate costs while still providing a quality education. The charge to the committee was to review demographics, building usage and capacity, and finances to determine which, if any, school buildings could be closed. The administration provides input on program placement (including special education, English as a second language, and so on); student composition (including race and ethnicity, socioeconomic status, and so on); transportation and feeder patterns; community and neighborhood impact; and teacher assignment to provide quality schooling and minimize the concentration or isolation of poverty or special populations. School closings are heart-wrenching decisions in any community because they have a direct impact on students and their families.

The state's structural deficit problem will continue to influence district operations and will severely affect the academic core unless there is a willingness of the public, governor, legislature, and educational community to have a thoughtful dialogue that results in addressing the diversity and educational needs of the student population, the public education system necessary for a knowledge-based economy, and adequate and equitable school funding.

CHAPTER 8

Community Engagement

Why Family and Community Partnerships Are Important to District Reform

Karen L. Mapp

In 2002 my colleague Anne Henderson and I wrote and published *A New Wave of Evidence: The Impact of School, Family, and Community Connections on Student Achievement*. The book summarized the findings of fifty-one studies focusing on the influence of family and community engagement on student academic achievement and other outcomes. We discovered that, taken together, these studies made a strong case that when home and school partner to support each child's learning, children are more likely to earn higher grades and test scores, be promoted on time and pass their classes, attend school regularly, and graduate and go on to postsecondary education. When schools and community organizations partner, there are positive effects on student achievement, upgrades to school facilities, the implementation of higher-quality learning programs for students, increases in funding for extended day and after-school programming for children and families, and a boost to the civic and political capacity of the participating community members (Henderson & Mapp, 2002).

The research continues to grow and build an ever-strengthening case that school, family, and community partnerships have positive effects on children's learning and development. We know that family involvement is one of the strongest predictors of children's school success, and that families play pivotal roles in their children's cognitive, social, and emotional development, from birth through adolescence (Weiss, Bouffard, Bridglall, & Gordon, 2009). Further, a recent study by the Annenberg Institute for School Reform found that schools partnering with community organizing groups had higher student educational outcomes and stronger school-community relationships (Mediratta, Shah, & McAlister, 2009).

Perhaps the most groundbreaking research on the importance of school, family, and community partnerships appears in the new book *Organizing for School Improvement: Lessons from Chicago* (Bryk, Sebring, Allensworth, Luppescu, & Easton, 2010), in which the authors identify five essential supports for school improvement: leadership, parent-community ties, professional capacity, a student-centered learning climate, and instructional guidance. The authors argue that the process of school improvement is akin to baking a cake, whereby the school leader operates as the head chef while the other four supports serve as essential ingredients. The authors state, "Should a core ingredient be absent, it is just not a cake. By the same token, if there is material weakness in any core organizational support, *school improvement won't happen*" (Bryk et al., 2010, p. 203). At the Symposium on Organizing Schools for Improvement, one of the authors, Stuart Luppescu, commented on the strength of the findings of the study: "Taken as a whole, the analyses are so robust that it makes it very hard for us to imagine an urban school improvement effort succeeding without these five essential supports" (personal communication, January 14, 2010).

This new research, therefore, challenges school districts to elevate family and community engagement from its current not-taken-too-seriously, "when we have time for it" status to being an intentional and high-priority systemic component of any district improvement strategy.

MOVING TO A SYSTEMIC VIEW OF FAMILY AND COMMUNITY ENGAGEMENT

How can districts move from engaging in add-on, "random acts" of family and community engagement to a more systemic and comprehensive approach? I offer four research-based recommendations to serve as a guiding framework and diagnostic tool for districts preparing themselves for systemic work in this area.

Adopt a Systemic Lens for the Work

What do we actually mean by systemic family and community engagement? Much of what I have found is influenced by the work of Richard Elmore, Philip Schlechty, and my colleagues from the Public Education Leadership Project at Harvard.

A systemic family and community engagement initiative

- Is focused, either directly or indirectly, on improving the core enterprise; in this case, improving educational outcomes for all children. The initiative has an impact on improving the instructional core—the relationship between the teacher and the student in the presence of content. In other words, the initiative is "linked to learning" (Henderson, Mapp, Johnson, & Davies, 2007).
- Is aligned and coherent with the overall goals of the organization. For example, an initiative that builds the capacity of parents and school staff to work as shared partners and connects to student learning and development meets this criterion.
- Spans various stakeholders in the sector and mobilizes many people in the organization to contribute (shared responsibility).
- Is not a discreet "stand alone" or "boutique" project operating in a few settings, but connects to the work across various settings and has the possibility of going to scale.
- Attempts to change social structures and the culture in which these structures are embedded. For example, an initiative that enhances the social and political capital of families and *shifts the balance of power* between institutions and communities fits this criterion.

Embrace a More Comprehensive Definition of Family and Community Engagement

In recent years there has been an attempt to shift the language used to describe the role that families and the community play in children's learning and development. Many have argued for the use of the term family and community *engagement* rather than *involvement*. Dennis Shirley (1997, p. 73) discusses the important difference in the terminology:

> Parental *involvement* — as practiced in most schools and reflected in the research literature — avoids issues of power and assigns parents a passive role in the maintenance of school culture. Parent *engagement* designates parents as citizens in the fullest sense — change agents who can transform urban schools and neighborhoods.

The National Family, School, and Community Engagement Working Group has created a new, more comprehensive definition of family engagement (I have adapted their definition slightly for this introduction to include community engagement) that broadens the role of families and community members from fundraisers, homework helpers, and volunteers to *effective agents of change* who work with schools to support children's learning from "cradle to career."

Family and community engagement is

- A shared responsibility—schools, families, and communities support each other and work together to actively support children's learning and development.
- Continuous across a child's life span. It begins in early childhood and continues throughout college and career development.
- Carried out everywhere that children learn—at home and in the community.

This new definition suggests that families and community members must be seen as full partners in the work of improving schools. As such, they must be engaged in planning and governance at the front end of initiatives, not merely acting as consultants or reactors to decisions school officials have already made.

Create Infrastructures to Coordinate and Sustain Systemic Family and Community Initiatives

Many urban school districts, notably New York City, Boston, Denver, Hartford, Baltimore, and Philadelphia, have created senior-level positions responsible for the planning, coordination, and implementation of family and community partnership initiatives, and have placed parent and family coordinators in schools. Creating an infrastructure at the district and school levels helps ensure that the family and community engagement work is integrated into the overall reform work of the district.

Provide Information and Support to Engage in Partnerships to Support Learning

Families, school personnel, and community members need training in how to partner to support children's learning. Districts can collaborate with various community-based organizations, colleges and universities, businesses, and faith-based institutions to create learning, professional development, and technical assistance opportunities to enhance the ability of all stakeholders to be effective partners.

THE WORK AHEAD

The accumulated research in the area of school, family, and community partnerships appears to be having an impact on discourse, policy, and practice. On the federal front, President Barack Obama has called for a

> new era of mutual responsibility in education, one where we all come together for the sake of our children's success. An era where each of us does our part to make that success a reality: parents and teachers, leaders in Washington and citizens all across America. [Obama, 2008, remarks to the 80th Convention of the American Federation of Teachers given in Chicago via satellite while he was in San Diego on July 13, 2008]

The current secretary of education, Arne Duncan, has discussed the important role that school, family, and community partnerships play in ensuring the success of all children. Several family advocacy groups, such as the National PTA and Parents for Public Schools, have joined forces with researchers and practitioners to lobby Congress to insert more robust language on family and community engagement into the reauthorization of the Elementary and Secondary Education Act, commonly referred to as No Child Left Behind. Several states across the nation have enacted laws directing school districts, school boards, or schools to implement family engagement policies.

The Atlanta case and the Boston response in this chapter provide us with narratives from two districts attempting to embrace family and community engagement as an essential component of whole-district reform. Although the approaches are different, both reveal the attention paid to local context and include attempts to broaden the role of families and communities. I encourage you to use this introduction as a tool to examine and discuss the initiatives of both districts and to assess your own local efforts to cultivate and sustain systemic family and community partnership initiatives.

REFERENCES

Bryk, A. S, Sebring, P. B., Allensworth, E., Luppescu, S., & Easton, J. (2010). *Organizing for school improvement: Lessons from Chicago*. Chicago: University of Chicago Press.

Henderson, A. T., & Mapp, K. L. (2002). *A new wave of evidence: The impact of school, family, and community connections on student achievement*. Austin, TX: Southwest Education Development Laboratory.

Henderson, A. T., Mapp, K. L., Johnson, V. R., & Davies, D. (2007). *Beyond the bake sale: The essential guide to family-school partnerships*. New York: New Press.

Mediratta, K., Shah, S., & McAlister, S. (2009). *Community organizing for stronger schools: Strategies and successes.* Cambridge, MA: Harvard Education Press.

Obama, B. (2008, May 28). Full text of Obama's education speech. *Denver Post.* Retrieved from www.denverpost.com.

Shirley, D. (1997). *Community organizing for urban school reform.* Austin, TX: University of Texas Press.

Weiss, H. B., Bouffard, S. M., Bridglall, B. L., & Gordon, E. W. (2009). *Reframing family involvement in education: Supporting families to support educational equity.* New York: Teachers College, Columbia University. Retrieved November 11, 2010, from www.hfrp.org/publications-resources/browse-our-publications/reframing-family-involvement-in-education-supporting-families-to-support-educational-equity.

Beverly Hall, Atlanta Public Schools: From the Living Room to the Boardroom

Laura Kelley, Leslie Boozer, and Drew Echelson

It was early fall 1999 and Beverly Hall, the newly appointed superintendent of Atlanta Public Schools (APS), returned to her office angry. She made it a habit to refrain from raising her voice, but her demeanor gave her true feelings away—her dissatisfaction was palpable. The central office was on edge as their new leader walked by. Hall had just come from visiting Carver High School, and it was not what she had expected. In fact, her assistant remarked, "She left the car excited to see a school with a rich history of change and returned so livid that she couldn't speak. Our car ride, for the first time, was silent."

On the way to her desk, Hall ran into Kathy Augustine, her executive director of high schools (and later deputy superintendent) and said, "Bring me whatever data you have gathered on Carver High School. I also want a school-by-school report on all of our high schools put together by the end of the week." Hall returned to her office and shut her door. With a heavy sigh, she looked through her bookcase in her freshly settled office and pulled out a copy of Sara Lawrence Lightfoot's *The Good High School* (1983), flipping to the first chapter. She began to read aloud, her slight Jamaican accent seemingly out of place in Atlanta,

> Three years ago, [Alonso] Crim [the Superintendent of APS] was getting ready to close Carver High School. It was an ugly reminder of the deterioration, chaos and unrest that plagues many big-city schools. When the community got wind of Crim's intention to close the school, they rose up to defend it. "It's not much, but it is ours!" [p. 31]

Lawrence Lightfoot's chapter chronicles the leadership of Carver High School principal Norris Hogans, the charismatic school leader who was appointed to "save Carver from its demise." As Hall continued to reread the story, she remembered Hogans's two-pronged strategy for improving the school near collapse: (1) develop and implement a comprehensive curriculum that included the three realms of general, vocational, and academic training, and (2) connect Carver to the larger Atlanta community.

Hogans envisioned a school that prepared students to be productive members of the community with which he partnered. Hall finished by reading Lawrence Lightfoot's conclusions that Hogans's work made significant improvements to the structure and management of Carver. But other than in a few classrooms of outstanding, rigorous instruction, the focus in most classrooms was on rules and procedures rather than on rigor and concepts.

Twenty years later, Hall observed that Hogans's initial start to reform the school had never reached fruition. Sadly, the school had reverted. Walking through classrooms, Hall observed virtually no rigorous instruction. She observed students packed in cosmetology and automotive classes in which the academic expectations were so low that students lacked the basic skills to read or complete functional math. Chaos replaced the structure Hogans had worked so hard to implement. Graffiti covered the walls. Students skipped classes. Disrespect oozed from teachers and students. Low expectations and fights were the norm. Carver had returned back to the early days of Crim's tenure. Only about fifty-one to fifty-four students out of a class of two hundred or so entering freshmen actually graduated from Carver with a high school diploma (see Exhibit 8.1 on the CD). Soon Hall would learn that Carver was not the only school that faced such dire circumstances.

CONTEXT OF ATLANTA PUBLIC SCHOOLS

When Hall was appointed superintendent on July 1, 1999, she inherited a fifty-nine-thousand-student school system in despair, with spiraling teacher morale, decreasing student achievement, and dropping enrollment. Students in fourth grade lagged behind their peers statewide in reading and mathematics by nearly 20 percentage points, and the district had over seven hundred teaching vacancies to fill. Thirty-three percent of elementary school students, 45 percent of middle school students, and more than 60 percent of high school students were chronically absent (ten or more days) from the city's schools. Expectations for Atlanta students were so low that nine out of ten teachers said they didn't believe their students would finish high school.

Unstable leadership also plagued the city's schools. Hall was the fifth superintendent APS had hired in a decade. At times the school board was paying three superintendents at once. The school board itself had a hard time maintaining order, with members regularly yelling at each other, stalling over decision making, and representing dysfunctional leadership. Longtime board member Emmett Johnson recalled the city's frustration with the school system's governing body in the mid-1990s:

> When all the citizens were fed up, the chamber, various religious organizations, civic associations all came together, and they had a slogan called "Erase the Board." They wanted everybody gone, "Let's start over." Actually, the process was quite successful, as they were trying to get rid of those board members that were causing the most problems.

Frustration with APS and the board spurred action to find reliable leadership. Shortly after the 1996 Olympic Games in Atlanta, the business community and other community leaders galvanized around improving and supporting the city. They had successfully worked together to organize a worldwide event, and there was no reason they couldn't use the same coordinated effort to improve the public school system after the games. They banded together to play a role in the appointment of the next superintendent of schools. Hall was recruited from Newark, New Jersey, in large part because leaders in Atlanta believed she could deliver results.

Reflecting on her experience interviewing for the position of superintendent of APS, Hall commented,

> The business community played a major role in recruiting me to come to Atlanta. The chancellor of the university system was on the screening committee as an appointee of the governor. The presidents of the UPS foundation and Coca-Cola served as well. You had representatives from entities like the 100 Black Men of Atlanta on the committee. And altogether, they were there to say to the candidates that the transformation of the public education system in Atlanta was critical to them.

Hall heard the message loud and clear: the city wanted a new image for APS, and they wanted a "world-class education system" for their students. Moreover, the business and civic community pledged to remain engaged and supportive of Hall during her tenure. Hall knew that she would need their help to achieve the student learning outcomes she and they envisioned. Her strategy for improvement included rich and robust partnerships not only with the businesses and civic organizations but also with APS families and faculty and staff. The success of her tenure, Hall believed, would be tied to her ability to continuously engage these constituents in this important work.

In fact, communicating her beliefs about community engagement was the most compelling factor to the screening committee. One member of the committee spoke at length about Hall's answers to questions about working with the community,

> Dr. Hall expressed the belief that the school system belonged to the larger community. She understood that her role as superintendent was to ensure the community paid attention to APS; that the community supported the mission of the schools; and that the district ensured transparency of APS work, results, and expenditures. Dr. Hall understood that she needed the community to provide political support for the school board and the school administration. We chose Dr. Hall because we believed that she actually knew *how* to engage an entire community in the improvement and success of the school system.

BEVERLY HALL—ATLANTA'S NEW LEADER

Jamaican-born Hall immigrated to the United States after graduating from her competitive girls' high school. The rich and high-quality educational experience she had is what she aspires to provide for every child under her watch.

Upon graduation from Brooklyn College in 1970, Hall wanted to make a difference in the world, and she chose teaching as the career in which to make her mark. She began teaching English in a underperforming New York City middle school, where she quickly learned the value of an engaging lesson. "I was struggling at first. But I soon noticed the teachers who had the most thoughtful lessons had the best control of their students," Hall remembered.

After six years in the classroom, Hall decided to enter district administration—first as an elementary school principal in Brooklyn. It was during this experience that she learned the benefits of collaboration and creative thinking. Hall wanted to build on the strengths of the community, which had a mostly Latino population. Because most of her students were fluent in Spanish, she implemented a bilingual kindergarten and partnered with the teachers to revamp the school's curriculum. This was the support the teachers, families, and students needed, and the school experienced steady gains under her leadership.

While she was earning her doctorate in education at Fordham University, Hall was tapped to take over a struggling middle school. Quickly learning the value of cultivating outside partners, she helped her school become the first in New York to be adopted by a major corporation, Chemical Bank. This partnership gave her extra funds to work with teachers, and soon the school experienced a radical turnaround and was awarded an "A School That Works" designation by the New York Department of Education in 1990.

Recognizing her leadership potential, the racially divided Community District 27 in Queens appointed Hall as superintendent in 1992, following the removal of the entire school board for corruption. In 1994 she was promoted to deputy chancellor for instruction, the second-highest-ranking position in New York City, under Ramon Cortines. He selected Hall for her instructional leadership, confident she could overhaul the math and reading programs for the country's largest school system.

In 1995 Hall was named the state-appointed superintendent of Newark Public Schools, the largest school district in the state of New Jersey. Facing down corruption and schools in disrepair, Hall dramatically improved Newark's schools. Although she started first with an overhaul of the schools' physical appearance, she also partnered with parents to increase student attendance, raise graduation rates, and take control of the once-violent schools.

Throughout her early experiences, Hall deepened her conviction that "all children can learn" regardless of race, socioeconomic status, or family struggles. In Atlanta she consistently argued that by working together and setting high expectations, change would happen, student achievement would rise, and APS could become a model urban school system.

COLLABORATION WITH THE BUSINESS COMMUNITY

Hall stood delivering her introductory speech before over a hundred executives in the metro Atlanta region. Just one other woman had entered the meeting halfway through the speech, and Hall noticed just a handful of black men in the sea of expectant faces. Excited but curious about how these long-standing executives might receive her, Hall acknowledged how different she was—from them and from previous superintendents. Using the parlance of business and industry, she described explicit, measurable goals for the district that were grounded in her transition team report, and she expressed confidence that she could lead the system to greater achievement.

After several polite questions from the audience, Pete Correll, the CEO of Georgia Pacific, posed an angry one. Hall recalled him saying something like,

> You've outlined an incredible vision for APS, but I think you're going to do what every superintendent who comes here does — run as soon as things start to improve. I'm sick and tired of you hotshot superintendents waltzing into our city, with all your promises and plans, leaving us in the dust for more lucrative

> offers, with nothing to show for your time other than a few fancy educational words. What are you going to do differently than the others? Just tell us. What can we do to get you to stay long enough to do something?

Hall knew this was a critical moment in her superintendency, despite being just days into her tenure. She thought for a moment, took a deep breath, and began to speak calmly and deliberately:

> Mr. Correll, I understand your frustration. You want the best for APS, and I share your sentiments. In order to deliver on the results I am promising for APS, I need *you,* the captains of your respective industries. I need your intellectual capital and the intellectual capital of your colleagues in this room who can help me think through the complex problems we face.

Members of the audience were shocked. Many later commented to Hall that this was the first time they could remember a sitting superintendent asking them, or any member of the business alliance, for something tangible other than money. Hall wanted regular meetings with the city's top business leaders, forming what would be called Hall's "Kitchen Cabinet." Correll responded to her plea by asking for volunteers then and there, choosing ten CEOs from the sea of raised hands, and decided on a host and location for the first meeting.

Eager to draw Correll and the other CEOs into the work, Hall made concrete plans to convene this small group of business leaders who would troubleshoot with her to solve some of the long-standing district problems. Her only requirement was that the content of the discussions remain private. She promised not to bring her staff, and she asked them not to bring theirs. The reputation of APS was already fragile, and she didn't want anyone using the problem-solving conversations to beat up the system even further. Hall described the structure of the Kitchen Cabinet:

> Leaders of the major companies met with me on an ongoing basis quarterly for about four years. They were private meetings. There was no press, no need to do an open records request. You could be candid and talk about what needed to happen without expecting it to be the headlines in the next day's paper, which was quite helpful to me.

The Kitchen Cabinet began by tackling the problem of improving operations in APS. Leaders of the major businesses in Atlanta, such as Home Depot, Coca-Cola, General Electric, and the Arthur Blank Foundation had a level of unmatched expertise in streamlining business. The CEOs made concrete suggestions on improving an antiquated human resources department by developing new strategies for recruiting and retaining highly effective teachers and principals. BellSouth provided an executive who worked for a year conducting and coding a human resources survey, offering suggestions for improved recruitment, hiring, and placement practices in the school district.

The Kitchen Cabinet also supported Hall in thinking about more transparent structures and protocols for communicating the district's budget, and they recommended areas in which the organization could reduce central office positions. Finally, they suggested dramatic improvement in the way the central office operated by transforming and realigning practices, which would result in a customer-service-orientated organization that better served schools and families. Thanks to the various suggestions, APS became a more streamlined and strategic organization. Hall commented,

> While I took a hit in the press once the recommendations came forward, the fact that the community knew I had the blessing and support of the top business minds in Atlanta reassured the public that APS was making great strides to improve the business side.

Hall had the expertise and knowledge to lead the Kitchen Cabinet in discussions on teaching and learning. As she worked to grasp and apply the language of the business world, the business leaders in the Kitchen Cabinet attempted to understand the complexity of the educational issues at play. One such example included the challenge APS faced with improving math and science when so many math and science college graduates were not opting to become teachers. Although test scores indicated something needed to be "fixed" in regard to student learning, the larger and more complicated issue was the effectiveness of math and science instruction and teacher recruitment. In a Kitchen Cabinet meeting, the CEOs began to think through how they could allow some of BellSouth's employees to participate in a pilot program to work with APS teachers. Corporate employees would know the content, APS teachers would know the pedagogy, and the partnership would be one of sharing practices and knowledge to better educate APS teachers and students.

Georgia Tech also got involved in helping facilitate the relationship, ultimately creating externships for math and science teachers interested in working during the summers. The externships helped teachers understand more about applying their knowledge to real-world situations and the relevance of their work, and kept them updated in their content areas, all while allowing them to earn a part-time living in other businesses. Said Hall of the partnership,

> For me, the success wasn't just that pilot. It was getting these leaders to truly understand that it's more than an edict, more than setting a goal, that there are contributing factors that the school system has little control over. Later, APS got a $22 million grant from the GE Foundation to improve the teaching of math and science. I believe that those preliminary discussions — understanding

> the pilot, my consistent report to them that while we were showing dramatic gains in reading, English language arts, the gains in math and science were minimal — led to the GE grant.

The conversations and troubleshooting that took place in the quarterly Kitchen Cabinet meetings laid the groundwork for long-lasting professional support. CEO of Georgia Power Michael Garrett commented,

> She built a relationship with the CEOs around that table that went far beyond just those meetings that we had. She built relationships that, when we had issues, she could pick up the phone and call us, on a first-name basis, and we could do the same thing with her.

While Hall was working to build relationships and support with partners outside of the school system, she was struggling with pressures inside the organization. She would now have to call on the business community to assist with one of her immediate challenges inside APS: her partnership with her board.

PROBLEMS WITH THE BOARD

The business community learned very quickly that Hall was the right leader for APS, and they were intent on keeping her in charge. Not just the Kitchen Cabinet but also Governor Roy Barnes and the Metro Atlanta Chamber of Commerce intervened when Hall announced that a contentious board relationship and politics were interfering with her ability to lead. Recognizing the board's tendency to overstep its role, Barnes worked with the chamber of commerce to facilitate the definition of roles and responsibilities for the board. They secured the help of EduPac, a community organization dedicated to promoting quality school board leadership, to help board members understand their roles and responsibilities.

Sadly, the micromanagement and poor behavior that the "Erase the Board" initiative had tried to address had not been resolved. Early in Hall's tenure, the board seemed willing to work together with the new superintendent. But after about six months Hall noticed board members were up to their previous antics, with infighting and inappropriate involvement in day-to-day school district operations. Facing a difficult situation, she was reminded of the promise the business community had made to her:

> They said during my interview that if I were to come to Atlanta . . . they would remain engaged and supportive and wouldn't just walk away and leave things up to chance. They were instrumental in convincing me in particular that if I came to Atlanta, there'd be additional support for me and for the system in order to get what was then a daunting job done.

Hall reminded the community members of their promise, and Atlanta business leaders stepped up to the plate. They began by recruiting and supporting candidates for school board candidacy who had the leadership knowledge and the business skills required to lead for change. With help from the chamber, Don McAdams from the Center for School Reform in Houston came to talk to all the board candidates about board governance. After their election in Hall's second year, professional development for the board was expanded to include training at the Broad Institute. Eli Broad funded twenty-three newly elected school board members from various school districts to be flown to Colorado to go through a weeklong study on board governance. McAdams facilitated that work and brought in Harvard professors and others to help elected board members understand their new roles.

Under the leadership of the chamber, the business community supported a legislation change of the district's charter in 2002 that gave Hall more supervisory authority. With the general counsel and the chief financial officer reporting directly to Hall instead of the board, Hall could make stronger and more effective management decisions. This authority aligned with her assumption of accountability, which was evident in the district's balanced scorecard and in Hall's annual evaluation. Even annual bonuses for Hall, the central office staff, and eventually school-site leaders were all tied to the measures outlined in the district's scorecard.

Still, some members of the board remained unhappy with the change in charter years afterward. But the improved operations, student achievement, and financial stability of the district were evidence for those supportive of the change that Hall's strategies worked for the system. Even in her eleventh year in APS, Hall felt the danger of the board's returning to its former dysfunction. When three new board members were sworn in during January 2010, Hall continued to press for collaboration and training. "I take nothing for granted," she expressed. "Anything could change at any time, and we could always slip backward if we don't continuously work at it."

INVITING THE COMMUNITY INSIDE: THE PRINCIPAL FOR A DAY PROGRAM

While Hall was successfully partnering with organizations at the district level, she was also working to involve businesses, civic groups, and service organizations in each school. One of her trademark engagement activities stemmed from her work in Newark: Principal for a Day. Organized by the chamber of commerce, the program invited various community members to gather for a group breakfast and then spend a school day shadowing principals. At the end of the day, the leaders would reunite to debrief the day's events.

Evander Holyfield, Julian Bond, Atlanta mayor Andrew Young, and Atlanta attorney Mike Trotter were some of the high-profile participants in Atlanta's first Principal for a Day in February 2000. As Trotter, who had been a vocal critic of the school district, described the experience, "I feel better about the schools than I did before I got here. I am impressed by the competency and dedication of the staff and how well-behaved the children are" (Carter, 2000, paragraph 19). Hall was thrilled about the exposure, but she was even happier with the public's growing understanding of the complexity of public education's challenges, their changing opinions of APS, and the partnerships that began to develop as a result of the event.

When the program first started, APS had a hard time finding just one volunteer per school site. In 2009, some principals had as many as three community leaders working alongside them for the special day. The partnerships that developed from Principal for a Day have often resulted in financial donations, increased volunteer time with students, or school "adoption" opportunities through which a business or organization has entered into a long-term partnership with a school to support work in improving educational outcomes for students.

To support the growth of the program, Hall created the position of director of community engagement to help ensure that each school had at least one community partnership. This central office position helped principals market their schools to their local neighborhoods. According to an APS central office employee, marketing the value of a school was particularly important amid declining enrollment. As she explained, "You've got to market the good things about your school. You've got to reach out to your parents and try to hold them, because you don't want to begin to lose your children." By reaching out to parents with good news, principals laid the necessary groundwork to ask families to become involved. The process embodied the APS belief that "it takes a community to turn these schools around and make these schools better."

To assist with organizing the campaign, as well as to guide the school's instructional work, each school developed a balanced scorecard. Similar to the district scorecard, each school scorecard included goals and assessment measures delineating how each partnership improves student outcomes. For example, the Salvation Army worked with Gideons Elementary School, providing materials, clothing, and coats for children living in challenging environments. Georgia Pacific adopted M. Agnes Jones Elementary School, taking tutors by bus to the school each week and providing computers for classrooms. GE partnered with Maynard Jackson High School by offering mentoring, tutoring, SAT prep, and college exposure, with the end goal being to get more students eligible for and successful in college.

The program continued to gain more followers each year, and the chamber recognized the partnerships in an annual luncheon called the A+ Awards. Commented Rene Pennington, vice president of Atlanta Education for the Metro Atlanta Chamber,

> I think the takeaway from Principal for a Day is that a picture is worth a thousand words. When you come to the school, you put faces with what's going on. People realize ways they can help schools and students achieve in ways they might never have known otherwise.

SINGLE-GENDER ACADEMIES

As part of Atlanta's district-wide turnaround, Hall focused on a middle school transformation initiative. Two partnerships that developed as a result of community commitment have shown promise in sustaining middle school success. Drawing on her experience in Jamaica, Hall established two single-gender schools—the Coretta Scott King Young Women's Leadership Academy and the Benjamin S. Carson Honors Preparatory School—in 2007. The 100 Black Men of Atlanta and the Atlanta Cluster of The Links, a professional organization for women of color, have adopted the schools and provide mentoring, resources, and support services to the students and faculty. Hall reached out to both groups for this specialized support, asking specifically for what she envisioned for each school.

As she was developing the partnership with The Links and the 100 Black Men, Hall worked to prepare parents and community for their new school. Hall was determined that the new schools would support APS students with the greatest needs. Thus Hall carefully chose areas of the city that were riddled with economic and social challenges to study and target with the specialized schools. Before opening the schools, Hall embarked on an active campaign to teach the local communities why single-gender schools would be good for their children. According to Mary Bailey, retired APS employee and member of The Links,

> [Hall] was strategic in her planning, because APS had several meetings with parents prior to opening the schools so they could ask questions. She brought in experts in the field who were knowledgeable about the middle-aged child. They invited parents to all of these informational meetings.

Once the parents and community were on board, Hall continued to look to her partners for guidance in developing the schools' emerging culture. The Links assumed tremendous responsibility for the girls' school and were active in various aspects of its planning. Members not only raised funds to purchase uniforms for the entire first incoming class of girls but also served on the curriculum committee and the mission statement committee. Some even participated in the school's interview process when selecting the principal. With a strong commitment to serve as role models for the school's students, members of The Links were involved with the pinning of each girl at the summer inauguration of the school in 2007, and they promised to mentor each student.

In January 2010 the girls' school moved into its brand-new facility, an extensive campus built for the expansion of the middle school into a 6–12 academy. The Links was there to assist and celebrate, and with principal Melody Morgan and the School Reform Team district leader they crafted long-term plans for supporting the incoming cohorts of students. Hall and school leadership will continue to communicate ongoing plans to families through regular neighborhood meetings and community "chats," a format with which the city has become accustomed.

COLLABORATING WITH FAMILIES

When Hall first came to Atlanta, she was a stranger to the southern city. Most families had no knowledge of who she was as a leader, what she valued, or her vision for APS. For Hall, this was problematic:

> I wanted people to get to know me, particularly because I knew that in order to do the job well I would need to upset the status quo. As a result, there would be angry people who would have an interest in defining me in their terms.

Hall also realized that people living in different parts of the city had very different opinions of the school district. She determined that the best way to introduce herself and learn more about the different neighborhood communities of Atlanta would be to go directly to them. Hall described her decision:

> I decided that I'd say in one of my early interviews for the newspaper that if any citizen could get ten to twelve people together in either a living room or a community center, . . . I'd come and I'd spend an hour and a half listening to them. I said, "Let me go out there," and I introduced myself to them. I wanted to hear what people had to say. Persistent through it all was that parents felt that the school system didn't hear them. I wanted to change that perception.

This offer was particularly important because many families felt invisible to APS, as if their voices were unimportant. In addition, Hall noted a sense of apathy within the community:

> At that time the board was holding community meetings all across the district, and the same suspects showed up all the time unless there was a specific issue that would bring out a particular group. Once their issue was resolved or dealt with, they disappeared. This meant the majority of parents and community residents weren't engaged at all with the school district except in their individual schools.

It was important to Hall to create a sense of urgency with all families across the entire system.

To convey the comfortable, informal atmosphere for which she was striving, Hall dubbed these meetings "living room chats." Although she had several focus questions, such as What did you think of the issues? How do you view the school system? and What questions do you have for me? the time belonged to the community members and families to talk about issues that resonated with them. Hall vowed to answer any questions she could, and she promised to follow up on questions she could not immediately answer. Hall recounted one of her living room chats with APS families in Bankhead Court, one of the most impoverished Atlanta Housing Authority communities, which illustrated her goals and commitment to families:

> The first time I went, the parents in that community didn't even want to talk about the schools. Instead, they wanted to be heard on the state of their community. Drive-by shootings and drugs were all-too-common sightings for them and their children, and they demanded action from the management of the housing development. I promised them that I'd go back and contact both the police department and the housing authority. I spoke to the major at the police department, and he promised to take action. I invited the housing development executive director, Renee Glover, and we went back together. I knew when I said I'd come back, the families in Bankhead never expected to see me again. They were used to being made promises to and then being forgotten. I went back with her, and we listened to their concerns, and Renee changed the management company. Then I went back a third time. I said, "Now can we talk schooling?" At that point, they were ready to talk about their schools. There's no sense going to talk about the schools when people's lives are in jeopardy. It helped me to understand and be reminded of the realities that many families and their children were facing, even as we were trying to raise the bar in terms of their academic achievement.

Hall continued the living room chats, but scaled them back over time and developed a new structure for communicating with families—the "fireside chats." Meeting annually in each quadrant of the city, the fireside chats enabled each school to send family and community representatives to hear Hall present a "state of the system" address. The representatives from each school canvassed their community for questions and concerns to bring to the superintendent. During every fireside chat, Hall left ample time for questions and discussion. "Building relationships with families takes time," Hall reflected. "You have to go out into the community and build trust before they will be willing to follow you. The time I spent building relationships with the citizens of Atlanta profoundly affected my ability to lead this district."

Hall continued, "Along the way, I met so many interesting people who had valuable skill sets." Parent Katy Pattillo was one of those community members who sat in on a fireside chat, listening to Hall communicate her vision of APS, an experience that ultimately led her to decide to run for a seat on the board. "I remember first meeting Katy Pattillo, who eventually served as chair of the school board for two years, at a fireside chat," said Hall. "I think she would say she credited her attendance at the fireside chat as part of the impetus for her deciding to run for the board." Her clear understanding of Hall's vision and confidence in her own leadership enhanced Pattillo's eight years on the board.

Central office and school staff used the fireside chats as opportunities to learn more about curriculum decisions and facilities concerns. Meanwhile, parents received answers to their questions about whole-school reform initiatives. Hall took care to explain her core values, her reasoning, and why she continued to ask for more change. During the second half of Hall's tenure, she coupled the chats with a more concentrated effort to spread the good news about progress in APS. Board member Pattillo explained the importance of these efforts:

> People need to know that there are successes out there, and . . . we didn't have a story to tell for so long, but now we have all this information. People in our own city don't believe us. Nationally they know more about us than people here do!

IMPROVING INTERNAL COMMUNICATION

Hall spent the first five years of her tenure—more than most urban superintendents spend in any one district—working to establish rapport with the city of Atlanta and build a foundation for long-term community involvement while implementing systemic reform initiatives. Considering this community platform to be critical for any sustained improvement, Hall focused much of her attention on increasing the confidence and capacity of the greater community. Internally, however, APS was struggling.

Turnover at the school and central office executive team levels was both a challenge and an opportunity for APS. Hall saw at least 90 percent of the original team of principals in 1999 leave during her first six to seven years, some by choice and some not. There were a number of principals uninterested in making the dramatic change Hall was pitching to the community. Even though she asked them to "take a leap of faith" with her and "suspend their disbelief" that the change would produce positive results, many principals were angry about being asked to do even more work in the challenging environments in which they had already been serving. Two-thirds of the district's principal force were eligible for retirement, and many principals chose that option.

Although Hall realized it would take some time for principals to leave their anger behind in order to engage with her reform strategies, she also knew it would take time for her to find replacements for the school leaders who left the district. With this in mind, Hall decided in 1999 to reach out to another district partner—the Wallace Foundation—to fund and create the district's own two-year leadership development program called the Superintendent's Academy for Building Leaders in Education.

Meanwhile, Hall also had to focus on the district leadership. She hired and dismissed many senior cabinet employees in various positions—replacing some positions more than three times—in the first half of her tenure. Her focus on external team building and the struggling reputation of APS was not a recipe for attracting candidates who would ultimately be the best fit for the district. According to Hall,

> When I got to Atlanta, you must understand, it was very difficult to attract a senior team. Most people felt I wouldn't be there after two years; some felt not even a year. So it took me more than a few years to build a senior team, to convince competent people that they ought to apply.

Even once the senior leadership team was assembled with high-caliber, skilled staff, however, Hall noticed that her cabinet did not work together well. The "highly technical, very aggressive" reformers Hall had hired were incredibly capable in their own domains; but when she was not there to keep the peace, fighting erupted and the team fell apart. Hall decided to invest in developing the communication skills of her senior leaders by hiring consultant Barry Jentz from Leadership and Learning to spend time coaching the cabinet. For five years, Jentz helped the cabinet understand style and temperament as well as how to listen to one another and communicate clearly. The group set norms for engagement, and according to Hall, "Many of them have said it was probably the best professional development they've ever had."

The improvement APS has shown in terms of student achievement, securing outside grant funding, and collaborative community support has altered outsiders' perceptions of the district. Deputy superintendent Augustine commented that APS now gets applicants from "across the country . . . as far away as Los Angeles . . . because now people are beginning to hear that you can really have an impact in public schooling here in Atlanta Public Schools."

GETTING THE GOOD NEWS OUT

Since 2005, APS has worked to share the results of its transformation with the local Atlanta community. CEOs and civic leaders recognized the dramatic improvement of the entire system that had three-quarters of its schools making annual yearly progress (AYP) in 2009. Furthermore, results from the National Assessment of Education Progress (NAEP) Trial Urban District Assessment demonstrated that APS was the only one of the eleven large city districts that participated to show significant improvement in all grades and all test areas since the 2002–2003 school year (Hall, 2009; see Exhibit 8.2 on the CD). Despite the ongoing, rigorous campaign and the gains in student achievement, to engage families and organizations in the schools, many residents retained their pre-Hall perception of APS. Still, many parents were not ready to enroll their students in public schools.

Remembering many conversations with Coca-Cola and GE executives around the importance of branding, Hall knew she needed to create an APS brand. Hall again reached out to her collaborators for help. The chamber organized a national search in 2006 for a chief communications officer to craft a plan for telling the APS story. An experienced communications executive, Suzanne Yeager, was hired in 2007, and the school district began using multiple forms of media to spread the positive news of student success. The streamlined and focused communication plan was new for both Hall and district staff, in part because of Hall's hesitancy to share results she wasn't completely certain she could sustain. According to Hall,

> For the first couple of years, people kept saying, "You need to tell people what you're doing." For about four or five years, I didn't talk about the work in Atlanta. I kept saying, "Let's not talk about it until we have results and we know these results can be sustained over time." I could have been more aggressive on the front end because we began to see early gains, but I was extremely cautious and still am. I don't want to get ahead of myself. It wasn't until people like the Aspen Institute and others came to Atlanta and said, "What are you doing here?" that I began to feel more comfortable.

Atlanta residents have voted three times in nine years to pay an additional one-penny sales tax to fund APS's much-needed capital improvements campaign. Hall continues to remind the city what its money helped support. As she explained,

> Of course, we are very grateful to Atlanta's taxpayers. Over the past nine years we have completed new construction, renovations, or upgrades to sixty-six schools, and to gain operational efficiencies we have closed twenty schools. In all, we have invested $900 million through this tax in creating twenty-first-century learning environments for our students.

ATLANTA EDUCATION FUND

Over time the Kitchen Cabinet, providing leadership advice and support, morphed into a broad-based coalition of Atlanta leaders called the Atlanta Education Fund (AEF). Established in 2007, the AEF is what Hall called a "legacy fund," intended to sustain the improvement efforts that have been made no matter who is chosen as her successor. Members of the coalition include high-ranking officials in Fortune 500 companies, Mayor Shirley Franklin, and university presidents. Members of the faith-based community, major philanthropists, the PTA, the APS teacher of the year, and Augustine and Hall also sit on the coalition. The AEF was created as a way to unify community support for key APS reform strategies, including garnering additional external grants as needed. The mission of the AEF is to sustain and accelerate the student achievement of Atlanta students by enhancing the community's capacity to support and advocate for effective education reform.

Complementing the work of the AEF is a district partnership with the Panasonic Foundation. The goal of this partnership is to help create a permanent record of APS processes for purposes of sustainability. Board member Johnson argued,

> We've got to sustain what's happening, and if we can do this, Atlanta will be the model of how a school system should work. A lot of times when systems start getting good, the parents, the business community, the employees become complacent. We don't want to ever say, "No, it snuck back down again, and you've got to start over." The challenge here is sustainability, and we worry about it in Atlanta.

Keeping community and external support is of utmost importance to Hall as she moves toward taking the district to even greater achievement. For example, support from the Bill & Melinda Gates Foundation has been a financial anchor for APS's high school transformation. The foundation recently awarded the district $10 million to replicate the success APS has seen at Carver.

Carver has again become "the Good High School," and four new high schools were established on the Carver campus in 2005. Carver's 2002 graduation rate of 14.4 percent increased to a 2009 rate of 100 percent at two of the new small high schools based at the former Carver campus, a more dramatic increase than the 30-percentage-point gain in the district-wide graduation rate that occurred during the same time period (Hall, 2009; see Exhibit 8.1 on the CD). Student achievement on the Georgia High School Graduation Test at the four small schools at Carver also soared (see Exhibit 8.3 on the CD). Transformations like the one at Carver can only be sustained with the consistent support of all stakeholders working in conjunction with district leadership.

REFERENCES

Carter, R. (2000, February 24). Holyfield steps into education ring; Boxing champ joins other leaders to see Atlanta school realities in Principal for a Day role. *Atlanta Journal and Constitution (Atlanta, GA)*, p. 7D. Retrieved February 27, 2010, from Lexis-Nexis Universe/General News database.

Hall, B. L. (2009, November 18). A marathon, not a sprint: Ten years of reform and growth in Atlanta Public Schools. Retrieved April 6, 2010, from www.udel.edu/dasl/conferences/11_18_09_Beverly_Hall.pdf.

Lightfoot, S. L. (1983). *The good high school: Portraits of character and culture*. New York: Basic Books.

Hit the Ground Listening

Carol Johnson and Michele Brooks

Boston, the birthplace of our nation and the birthplace of public education, is a city of neighborhoods and families. These neighborhoods (whether Roxbury or South Boston, Charlestown or Chinatown), represent the traditional ethnic identities of the early growth of the city. Boston is old, traditional, and classic, and simultaneously new, renaissance, and revolutionary. It is these multiple identities that bring together diverse voices, and sometimes competing interests, in the common space of democratic town hall meetings.

The students who arrive in our classrooms reflect this diversity. Entering this context requires one to listen and to recognize that no single voice captures the community pulse, and silence is not always consent. In the early days of my arrival as superintendent, I was greeted by those who affirmed the city's reputation of academic excellence and those who wanted and expected the continuity of the status quo. Others were outraged at the reports of higher dropout rates, stagnant high school graduation numbers, and a sense that the achievement gaps for some were never going to close. These disparities in outcomes and perceptions are in part what make the work of creating an ongoing community dialogue complex and ambiguous. Excellence and equity must be connected and inseparable if success is to occur for all, not just some, of our children.

Every community wants leaders who listen to every citizen and are invested in the success of each child attending our schools. Educational leaders must understand the critical and integral link between the success of our nation's public schools and each community's economic and social well-being.

THE ROLE OF COLLABORATION

The work of collaboration is not only about the families we serve today but also about future families and the broader group of stakeholders who influence the policy decisions and resources that our schools need to thrive. Urban public schools live in an even larger court of public opinion because the messages about school and student performance are annually quantified, publicly compared, and showcased in reports about students' test scores. Incidents that compromise student safety are often magnified in today's complex media and communication networks, and within seconds both accurate and inaccurate information about a given school is transmitted.

Public education leaders who are successful in this work, like Atlanta superintendent Beverly Hall, comprehend the need to create forums for developing ongoing support and advocacy, and for putting the difficult challenges they have faced in understandable yet surmountable contexts. The diversity of community opinions and voices, coupled with the speed at which new information is transmitted, make it impossible to rely simply on newsletters carried home in backpacks to translate controversial decisions about changes in programs, accountability actions, fiscal challenges, school closings, or an incident that occurred after school.

THE IMPORTANCE OF BROAD RELATIONSHIPS

Relationships matter. The capacity to connect with the core group of business and community leaders and to develop long-term partnerships with them remains a critical lever for implementing any change agenda that disrupts and threatens the status quo. These opinion leaders are influential (whether appointed, elected, or relying on position status) and are an essential element of the school district's efforts to promote confidence in its work. However, school leaders would ultimately fail if they relied solely on the most powerful voices to construct the road to success. The neighborhoods, and the students and families in the neighborhoods at "ground zero," demand respect, and because they are the direct and primary recipients of the school district's efforts, they have the right to be heard. Without careful and strategic attention to their participation and involvement, engaging them cannot succeed. It should be noted that no single person could do this heavy lifting alone.

Urban public schools are large bureaucracies and small families. They are large and broad in constituent interests, but small and local in terms of the neighborhood conversations. It is as if we all still talked in the barbershop or across the fence. There is the common wisdom of one's individual experience (all too often negative), and that narrative gets retold over and over, becoming the basis for the community's notions about whether or not to trust and join with the district in the journey to educate our children.

In Atlanta, superintendent Hall understood that the narrative that existed when she arrived needed to change, and by inviting the community inside to talk, to share their untold story, she has worked to capture the community "buy-in" so essential to reshaping the vision for schools and moving students' achievement forward.

THE ROLE OF LEADERSHIP IN BUILDING COMMUNITY

Leadership matters. The journey to invite the community in to join the conversation requires a cheerful and bold spirit, a commitment to authenticating their participation and to persisting in the face of setbacks. It was clear that to achieve this new level of engagement in Boston required the expertise and wisdom of a leader who had the outsider's angst, passion, and vision for change, combined with the determination and deep faith to believe that things could be better for students and their families. My selection of Michele Brooks as assistant superintendent for family and student engagement in Boston indicated my intent to have in this pivotal leadership role a change agent who was willing to make the shift from being an outsider to transforming conditions while operating within the bureaucracy. A former director of the Boston Parent Organizing Network and a local parent activist, Brooks was appointed by Boston mayor Thomas Menino to serve on the Boston School Committee.

She clearly had established herself as a bold, and sometimes critical, voice among district parents, advocating for equitable access to quality education through partnerships with families and the community.

For Brooks, it was a difficult and soul-searching decision. Would she compromise her values by joining forces with Boston Public Schools (BPS), or was there actually the potential to make a huge and unprecedented difference for families, for all students and their learning? Her decision was ultimately influenced by our agreement that the work of family engagement had to be connected to the instructional core and not relegated to a vehicle for parent complaints, school fundraisers, or a symbolic presence without influence on budget or decision-making authority. Brooks was to be central to the my executive-level leadership team and participate in conversations before decisions were made.

ASSUMING LEADERSHIP

Upon assuming the role of assistant superintendent, the challenge for Brooks was to assess the state of engagement in the BPS. Having been a community activist and school committee member with a particular interest in partnering with families, Brooks began her new role with some insights in regard to existing family engagement efforts, including the successes and the challenges of the work. Meetings with parents, education activists and organizers, family engagement staff, and principals confirmed her assumptions that the effectiveness of family engagement efforts was inconsistent and most efforts were neither aligned nor connected to the schools' or the district's goals. School staff and principals were clear that the district expected family engagement, but there was less clarity about who was responsible and how to effectively implement a family engagement strategy. Some believed that supporting families was a responsibility belonging to central office departments. Even in schools that had designated family engagement staff, the engagement efforts generally lacked focus; there was little documentation about what strategies worked or did not work; and outreach efforts were inconsistent, making the task of systemically measuring results impossible.

WHY CONNECT FAMILY AND STUDENT ENGAGEMENT?

The restructuring of the Office of Family and Community Engagement into the Office of Family and Student Engagement provided an opportunity to align the work of student engagement with family engagement in a way that empowers both groups as influential partners with an impact on student learning and school improvement.

Boston has a rich history of student activism that predates desegregation. The Boston Student Advisory Council (BSAC) was established to cultivate student leadership, to give students the opportunity to be heard, and to help shape district-level policy and decisions. The success of BSAC in influencing school committee policy decisions provided the initial building blocks to transform schools and develop a peer culture that owns academic success. But BSAC needed to be positioned to actually achieve this vision of students' broader ownership of and engagement in their education.

Engaging students provides them with opportunities to play a pivotal role in shifting the culture of an institution that has a major impact on their lives and that had largely concerned itself with the interests of adults. There is a natural intersection between family and student engagement that educators have not previously leveraged. Students and their families are the most critical stakeholders in the education process, and the work has to not only build strong linkages with students and parents but also create the conditions for their engagement.

The central learning triangle involves the schools, the family, and the student. Despite the need to have commitments and accountability from all three partners, what has been traditionally undervalued is the need to develop school environments in which the voices of parents and students are heard and elevated so that the ownership for student success belongs to everyone. A typical district organizes family outreach activities in a department that combines family and community. The community advocates have a collective voice that is important to the school district's overall agenda; however, even with the best intentions, community leaders too often see their work as "speaking for" families and students, not necessarily as building the capacity for parents and students to develop the skills, knowledge, and confidence to speak for themselves. We have not always invested in the two groups most in need of the development of this leadership capacity. When these voices are empowered, they will demand that those of us who work in schools be more responsive to their needs. This can present an additional set of challenges unless we help students and families be constructive and results-oriented in their efforts to seek change and improvements.

Large, bureaucratic institutions have a difficult time acknowledging the need for families and students' active participation and believe a few community meetings to outline the budget and get feedback on school boundaries or closings suffice as evidence of family engagement and parents' voices being heard. In fact, these efforts are usually episodic, offer little in the way of long-term capacity building for the families and students, and fail in large part to have an impact on school communities. There is a power dynamic in our culture that positions the educators as the ultimate, all-knowing authority. This may be less evident in more affluent neighborhoods and private school settings than in neighborhoods with significant populations of poor students and students of color. In the former, the families assume that they are entitled to speak about, question, and influence school practices and decisions. In the latter, when students and families don't view themselves as owners of the enterprise, students see themselves as learners but not leaders, and parents feel less responsible for student academic outcomes so they tend to blame educators when things don't work out. They don't see themselves as part of the total equation.

BUILDING THE INFRASTRUCTURE

Designing an infrastructure to support the engagement of families is challenging within the bureaucracy as it currently exists in most urban public schools. Our culture has blamed parents for inadequate parenting, underestimated the benefit of their engagement, and made assumptions about whether they truly value education. This is sometimes more true in urban communities, where there is a disconnect between those who serve and educate the district's children and those who are served and educated. This disconnect is not solely about culture, race, or income; most often it is about whether or not a school and school district staff choose to welcome, respect, and honor the district's students and their families and see them as co-owners of schooling. School communities often collide with the students they have failed and the families who have had negative experiences in those schools. Without changing the conditions for dialogue, the mistrust will continue.

In Boston, the new district vision for this work required a paradigm shift to empower families and students. My guidance as superintendent and input from parents and school staff helped craft a common vision for this engagement. It was concise and direct: "Every school will welcome every family and every student, actively engaging them as partners in student learning and school improvement." It was accompanied by a set of core beliefs that affirmed the hopes and dreams that parents have for their children and their capacity to support their children's success. These core beliefs also placed the onus directly on schools for fostering engagement focused on learning and building trustful relationships among families, students, and teachers. Those in power have the greater responsibility for stepping up to the plate.

KEEPING OUR PROMISE TO FAMILIES

The BPS's newly crafted vision for families articulates a promise to welcome and engage them as partners. All parents have hopes and dreams for their children, and the district's role is to encourage and provide opportunities for their engagement that allow them to support their children's success. The persistence of the achievement gap that disproportionately affects students of color, low-income students, and those whose native languages are not English creates urgency for engaging and empowering these historically marginalized families to become active partners in educating their children.

Conversations with families affirmed the belief that all families have the capacity to become powerful advocates in support of student learning and for improving student outcomes. The keys to the development of families in this role are knowledge and opportunity. Information is powerful, and the opportunity to be actively involved in learning is more powerful.

We crafted our primary strategy for building the capacity of parents to become what Rudy Crew describes as "demand parents"—those who will advocate for their children—using the lessons we learned from successful models across the country, such as the Parent Academy model in Miami, and from BPS's experience in the mid-1990s with Parent Leadership Academy. The response to the new Parent University from BPS families has been overwhelming. Parents representing the diversity of the schools from across the city have convened to share, learn, and expand their capacity to support their children's development as learners and to influence school improvement. It is clear that parents want to learn, expect to be engaged, and do respond when given authentic opportunities to support their children's learning.

Although an infrastructure to support the embedding of family and student engagement is rapidly developing, resistance to this new model of engagement persists. The challenge is to continue to create opportunities for new experiences that yield positive results and to influence the shift in the existing mental model of family and student engagement for school and district leaders, school staff, families, and students.

THE FUTURE OF ENGAGEMENT IN BOSTON

Moving forward, BPS will continue to engage families, students, and the broader community in its efforts to improve outcomes for every student. Building the district's capacity to authentically engage stakeholders is an ambitious agenda, but one that is critical for its success.

If American public education is to succeed, schools must be led by those who understand how to bring the collective powers of teachers who teach well, students who own the road to excellence and put in the effort required to succeed, and families who bring their voices and demands to the table. What we must resolve is whether we are truly committed to a shared endeavor through which diverse voices and leaders emerge to move the students forward. Every district has the potential—not all will have courage—but as Oliver Wendell Holmes once said, "A mind stretched by a new idea never returns to the same shape." In our efforts to exact a new contract between families and schools, and schools and students, we will need to stretch our minds to new ideas for engaging those whose very lives and futures depend on our success.

CHAPTER 9

Scaling Up

Scaling Up: The Key to School Improvement

Robert S. Peterkin

Although this book is organized around themes of leadership—resource allocation, community engagement, sustainability, and so on—the common thread across the cases is the challenge for superintendents to bring instructional improvement and enhanced student outcomes to scale. That is, each superintendent faces the imperative of reducing, and ultimately eliminating, the underperforming schools in the district, increasing the number of schools meeting state and federal standards of "proficiency" while maintaining and enhancing the "islands of excellence" that exist in even the most dysfunctional school districts. The superintendents represented here, as epitomized in this chapter's case on Rudy Crew and reflection by Amalia Cudeiro, came to this challenge from a defined framework of equity, recognizing the mandate to educate *all* children at high levels. Larry Leverett, former superintendent of the Plainfield Public Schools in New Jersey and current executive director of the Panasonic Foundation, articulates it best in the foundation's mission statement—"All Means All" (Panasonic Foundation, 2009).

The leaders featured in these chapters embrace the twin goals of equity and excellence as essential to their vision of creating challenging and rigorous environments for their students. They were not satisfied with simply providing the opportunity for all students to attend school, a goal that was part of the unfinished civil rights agenda of another era. The goal for them now, our goal for *this* era, is to improve student outcomes for those who were left behind *and* those who leapt ahead academically. Some called it "raising the floor and lifting the ceiling," with the ultimate target being the elimination of the achievement gap between (primarily) African American, Latino, American Indian, and low-income students and their middle- and upper-middle-class white and Asian counterparts. For these leaders, no longer were the islands of excellence to be accepted as examples of what the districts could do for their most privileged students, while other students languished in underfunded and academically less challenging schools. Over time, these leaders will come to be known as "equity warriors."

THE DEMAND TO ACCELERATE THE PACE OF CHANGE

The No Child Left Behind legislation accelerated and memorialized a movement for equity and excellence that started with the U.S. Supreme Court's *Brown* v. *Board of Education* decisions of 1954 and 1955, increased during the passages of Elementary and Secondary Education Act legislation from the 1960s forward, was hastened with the publication of the report *A Nation at Risk* in 1984, and was propelled by the standards movement of the 1990s. For many of the leaders depicted in this volume, the twin goals—the inseparable goals—of equity and excellence grew in the soil of the school effectiveness movement of the 1970s and 1980s, embodied in the work and research of Ronald Edmonds. Edmonds, who studied the reasons that some schools were more efficacious than others (the school effectiveness factors), famously issued the clarion call for equity and excellence:

> We can, whenever and wherever we choose, successfully teach all children whose schooling is of interest to us. . . . We already know more than we need to do that. . . . Whether or not we do it must finally depend on how we feel about the fact that we haven't so far. [Edmonds, 1979, p. 23]

Some educators initially saw scaling up as "a rising tide that lifts all boats." This approach was an initial reaction to—and a rejection of—the islands of excellence approach in which only some students were expected to prosper. Although an improvement, the "rising tide" ignored the fact that some boats were larger than others and rode higher in the metaphorical waves. Yet some saw this as being "fair," disadvantaging none. What they ignored was that fair is not the same as equitable. Fair called for the application of the same resources and approaches for all children. What was ignored in these first stages of scaling up was that students have different backgrounds and needs for learning, and educators must provide resources (teachers, academic supports, special education services, and so on) according to those needs. An equal distribution of educational resources to all students will, of necessity, not be equitable in regard to the needs of all students.

As we increasingly recognize the need to scale up throughout our country, the situation in our urban school districts approaches crisis. The sheer number of underperforming schools in urban districts seems to overwhelm the remedies state and federal authorities are seeking. That is largely because government entities fail to appreciate the importance of local context in fashioning the approaches to scaling up. Scaling up, at its simplest, is tackling the task of creating and sustaining instructional improvement in all schools in a district. An understanding of the instructional core—the interaction of the teacher and the student engaged with rigorous content—is central to this work (City, Elmore, Fiarman, & Teitel, 2009; Cohen & Ball, 2001). Leaders must recognize the idiosyncratic work at the classroom level, which is based on the needs of students, the abilities of teachers, and the content provided, in the execution of district-wide instructional improvement.

The superintendents depicted herein recognize the centrality of the instructional core to scaling up instructional improvement in their districts. Those who are part of the Harvard Graduate School of Education's Urban Superintendents Program (USP) embrace the mission: "Making good teaching happen for every child, every day, in every classroom, is the single most important means by which public schools can deliver on their promise to enable all children to learn and achieve at high levels."

They also recognize that scaling up involves all schools, with recognition of a special responsibility to underperforming schools and the ill-served students who attend them. Therefore, although their work may seem "top down" to the casual observer, it reveals that these leaders possess a deep knowledge of teaching and learning at the center of their work. They also recognize that there are many dimensions of leadership, but that the dimensions of politics and management serve the exercise of educational leadership.

In USP we emphasize three key dimensions of leadership: political, managerial, and educational (Johnson, 1996). As profiled in this chapter's case study, Crew found that political leadership (acquiring the authority to set the educational agenda) and managerial leadership (changing instructional leadership where needed) had to precede his schedule for bringing instructional improvement to scale. Beverly Hall, whose work is examined in Chapter Eight, also found that the exercise of political and managerial leadership laid the foundation for scaling up instructional improvement. Her solicitation and engagement of the business and parent communities, her commitment to make changes in governance, and her use of managerial tools borrowed from the business community provided the basis for a superintendency that has improved instructional outcomes for Atlanta's students. Finally, Cudeiro, whose reflections close this chapter, chose yet another approach based on her local context in Bellevue, Washington. Given the relatively small number of schools in her district in comparison to Miami-Dade and Atlanta, she chose to take her instructional improvement and equity efforts to scale at all of Bellevue's schools at the same time. The persistent inequities in the district, coupled with her mandate from the school board for change, propelled her efforts early in her tenure.

A FALSE DICHOTOMY—RADICAL CHANGE VERSUS INCREMENTALISM

In regard to scaling up for instructional improvement, an apparent dichotomy is currently up for debate. On one side, some educational reformers, at least those who are observers of the urban superintendency, identify what has come to be known as *incrementalism*. This position maintains that it takes years to create a culture that is deeply committed to instructional improvement and enhanced student outcomes; five to ten years is the current estimate. In this scenario, a superintendent would initiate school reform slowly and carefully, building consensus, or buy-in, for necessary changes at the school and classroom levels. Student performance would improve incrementally, with large student test score gains coming years after these foundational efforts took root.

The other pole in this dichotomy is *urgency*. In this scenario, the superintendent would take a more radical approach to instructional improvement at scale and institute far-reaching change at a rapid pace with little attention to consensus or buy-in. The introduction of school reform models, mandatory professional development for district and school staff, frequent monitoring of student data, and principal and teacher dismissal and replacement, if rapid student growth is not forthcoming, would be central to this approach.

From my experience in working in urban school districts and my observation of the practices of the superintendents in this book, I find the perception that a dichotomy exists at all to be false. The superintendents represented herein all express an urgency to make the requisite changes for instructional improvement to provide excellence and equity for all of their students. As previously mentioned, the new leader must examine the context and history of the district if she wants to effect deep, positive change. In this book we argue that the superintendent should undertake an entry plan to obtain information on what direction to take, and to determine who is available, and with what resources, to initiate change at the district level (Jentz, 1982).

THE NEED FOR A THEORY OF ACTION

Using such information the superintendent ideally can develop, with the appropriate team of insiders and outsiders, a theory of action for the school district that defines the causal relationship between the district's approach to instructional improvement and significantly better student outcomes. This theory of action for all schools in the district would be accompanied by a problem of practice that describes the major impediment to instructional effectiveness. Each district school would then develop its own theory of action and problem of practice consonant with those of the district, ensuring instructional coherence and accountability.

In the case in this chapter we could arguably see Crew as a radical change agent with an urgent agenda. Indeed, that is his national reputation, based on his work in New York City and Miami-Dade. We should discard this facile description along with the above-mentioned false dichotomy. The case reveals Crew's accurate and careful analysis of the impotent state of school governance at the level of the chancellor and the board of education. Crew fought for changes in the governance structure of New York City schools that restored "control" to the central board for the first time in a generation. Recognizing the political necessity of governance change and creating a new organizational structure for underperforming schools (the Chancellor's District) gave him authority and accountability unparalleled in the modern history of the district. Crew recognized that such a strong response was needed to combat the culture of failure that had been created around these children and their schools. In addition, he recognized that the launch of the Chancellor's District could serve as a catalyst for system-wide change. If New York City, with 1.1 million students and hundreds of underperforming schools, could successfully educate all of its students at high levels, what excuses could hold up for the lack of similar results in other urban school districts?

In the case study we also get to see Crew's theory of action in another context. Given 350,000 students and a greater percentage (approximately

13 percent) of underperforming schools in Miami-Dade, Crew recognized the need for the same careful yet urgent response to ill-served students. His theory of action, much like the one he employed in New York City—focusing on the instructional core, directing resources to the students and schools with the greatest academic and socioeconomic needs, frequently reviewing the data, and strategically appointing teaching and administrative personnel—supported the creation and implementation of the School Improvement Zone in Miami-Dade within the first six months of his superintendency.

Finally, we witness the growth in Crew's theory of action for undertaking instructional improvement at scale in the largest districts in our country. In Miami-Dade, Crew sought out community partnerships to support the School Improvement Zone. Parents became a particular emphasis with the creation of the Parent Academy, whose sole purpose was to create "demand parents," building social capital in parent populations that traditionally had no voices or roles in their children's education. The concept of earning autonomy as student outcomes improve adds another dimension to scaling up, with each school shedding its underperforming status and having an opportunity to play a leadership role in the education of its students.

Scaling up student academic success in our large urban districts is the present challenge of providing high-quality education to every child, in every classroom, every day. All Means All. By accepting the centrality of the instructional core to creating instructional excellence and rejecting the facile observations and definitions of school reform observers, superintendents can use the tools and resources at their disposal in the political and managerial realms of their work to create systems of equitable and excellent education for all of their students.

REFERENCES

City, E. A., Elmore, R. F., Fiarman, S., & Teitel, L. (2009). *Instructional rounds in education: A network approach to improving teaching and learning*. Cambridge, MA: Harvard Education Press.

Cohen, D. K., & Ball, D. L. (2001). Making change: Instruction and its improvement. *Phi Delta Kappan, 83*, 73.

Edmonds, R. (1979). Effective schools for the urban poor. *Educational Leadership, 37*(1), 15–24.

Jentz, B. C. (1982). *Entry: The hiring, start-up, and supervision of administrators.* New York: McGraw-Hill.

Johnson, S. M. (1996). *Leading to change: The challenge of the new superintendency*. San Francisco: Jossey-Bass.

Panasonic Foundation. (2009). What is the Panasonic Foundation's mission? *Panasonic: Ideas for life.* Retrieved April 29, 2009, from www.panasonic.com/meca/foundation/mission.asp.

Rudy Crew, New York City Public Schools: Instilling Success in Every School

Laura Kelley and Leslie Boozer

Rudy Crew walked the length of his new office in Miami-Dade. It had been just one week since Crew assumed the role of superintendent in Miami-Dade County, Florida, and he looked at the folders of student achievement data of the schools with concern. The school board had hired him to dramatically turn around the district—and quickly—but some of the schools lagging behind would require a completely different instructional approach than others. It would take more than simply additional professional development, for instance, to change the day-to-day practices in the district's three hundred schools. It would take a multifaceted approach, including implementing new structures and supports to improve the academic achievement of Miami-Dade's poor children and students of color.

A knock at the door interrupted Crew's pacing. "Come in," he called out, shuffling some papers before him. A tall man walked into his office and handed Crew a folder of data he had requested on Miami-Dade's most underperforming schools. The data associate lingered for a minute, sitting down in one of the chairs in front of Crew's desk. "The data are clear," he said. "We have some schools that are in real trouble, schools performing far behind the others. But this is why you're here, right? To turn these schools and system around as easily as you did in New York?"

Crew looked at his new employee and pondered his question. Despite the size of New York City (NYC), one of his most successful school improvement strategies actually began quite small, with just a few schools. He had changed the way people viewed what was possible for large-scale reform and what the role of the superintendent could be in systemic change for poor, minority, and disadvantaged students. "It wasn't easy," Crew recalled as he leaned back in his chair. "Even getting the necessary authority to change practice and scale up improvement proved to be tremendously difficult."

As he faced the same challenge in Miami-Dade, Crew thought back to his work in New York and one of his most powerful strategies for instructional improvement: the Chancellor's District.

THE LEADER

Hard work and perseverance were integral parts of Rudy Crew's upbringing in Poughkeepsie, New York. After the death of his mother when Crew was just two, Crew's single father Eugene worked multiple jobs and long hours to maintain the family household. Despite obtaining only a grade school education himself, Eugene Crew prioritized his children's education above all else, serving as a model for Crew's later mantra of doing "whatever it took to get results."

As a child, Crew found it hard to take an interest in and excel at reading. Given his poor reading performance, a counselor later told his father in no uncertain terms that Crew was not "college material." Determined to ensure that his son did not fall through the cracks and was not boxed into failure, Eugene took on another job and enlisted the help of a young woman to tutor Crew. She used nontraditional reading strategies and techniques to unlock Crew's interest in books. "I learned then," Crew said, "that not all kids need the same things and that we should look at what *we* have done, and never tell a child that *he* can't."

Crew's efforts to overcome his academic struggles and his father's persistence to make sure he had the resources to do so paid off. Crew graduated from high school and become the first male member of his family to get accepted to and enroll in college. One of the first African American students to attend Babson College, Crew studied economics and accounting. Although he transitioned into teaching, his economics major would be the source of his innovative educational strategies for years to come. Crew worked as a teacher, principal, and assistant superintendent, becoming a deputy superintendent in Boston and then superintendent in Sacramento, California, and Tacoma, Washington. When he was tapped to lead the New York City Department of Education (NYCDOE) as chancellor in 1995, he was entering his third superintendency before he was forty-five years old. His unwavering commitment to all students under his watch and his decisive and confident leadership made him New York's top choice after a dozen years of turnover.

Crew continues to put his convictions about differentiation, high expectations, and unlimited potential, along with perseverance and hard work, into practice. In all of his superintendencies, his leadership staff members have frequently heard him say, "Plain and simple, we must expect more from our children. Settling for less is treasonous." Crew knows for certain that with support and attention to results, anything for anyone is possible. He has lived it.

THE CHARGE: LEADING THE NEW YORK CITY BOARD OF EDUCATION

At the end of Crew's first week in New York, he emerged from a fifty-minute meeting with leading NYC decision makers and political power brokers smiling. He had already discussed the scope of what he planned to undertake—instilling success in struggling schools and bringing strong practice to scale in every single NYC school—and no one had tried to dissuade him. A few raised eyebrows and skeptical glances shot around the room, but people seemed willing to give him a chance. Exhausted but confident, he knew that his upbringing and his experiences in Tacoma and Sacramento had prepared him to lead the nation's largest school district. Yet even with his confidence, Crew was under no illusions about what he had inherited.

NYCDOE was unlike any other school system in the country. With over 1.1 million students taught in over 1,600 schools, the NYCDOE had more teachers on its roster than Crew had students when he was superintendent of Tacoma, Washington.

When Crew arrived, the large majority of New York City public schools were the most underperforming schools in New York State. Only some schools on the Upper East Side of Manhattan, the selective Bronx High School of Science, a few other schools in the Bronx and Brooklyn, and Stuyvesant in lower Manhattan were notable top achievers. One of the most diverse cities in the United States, NYC housed a large percentage of students whose home languages were not English, with one-third of all New Yorkers being born in another country. To address this challenge, the NYCDOE was required to translate report cards, registration forms, and other important documents into Spanish, German, French, Arabic, Urdu, Persian, Hindi, Korean, and more than nine other languages and dialects. Thirty-seven percent of students identified as Latino, 34.7 percent black, 14.2 percent white, and 14.3 percent Asian. Even though they represented the smallest portion of the student population, white and Asian students tended to disproportionately attend the city's prestigious and specialized schools.

The gaps in academic achievement spread across income levels, race, and English language proficiency. When it came to serving all children, the New York City Public Schools were not making the grade. Although the district saw some modest gains in their 1995 performance results in comparison to previous years, there was certainly room for improvement. On the 1995 state math exam, more than half of New York City's third through eighth graders, 53.3 percent, scored at or above grade level, an increase of 3.4 percentage points from the previous year. In reading, just 47.5 percent of students in third through eighth grade scored at or above grade level, an increase of almost 2 percentage points (Toy, 1995). At the high school level, in the 1994–1995 school year only 21 percent of New York City students received a Regents diploma, compared to 40 percent statewide (Berger, 1996). (NYC results on the state test from 1995 to 1998 are available in Exhibit 9.1 on the CD.)

Compounding the need for improvements in student achievement, several New York City schools were in great need of physical repair. "We expect many children to fail and deliver that message by letting schools collapse physically around the children's heads," Crew noted upon his arrival. He couldn't believe the conditions in which some New York City students and teachers were working. Bricks fell inside buildings, toilets were inoperable, and several schools had dangerously exposed electrical systems. In addition, school violence was running rampant, and police presence in schools was not unusual.

The state, the mayor and board, parents, and the press were all looking to the new chancellor to see how, or even if, he would tackle these challenges.

SETTING THE STAGE TO SCALE UP REFORM

"When I was in New York, it became clear to me that I was going to educate these children in spite of how damnable the system was," Crew recounted as he thought about the structure and corruption in the New York City school system. "I had to operate on the basis that there are some fights you want to take on, and the fight for accountability seemed logical to me." He continued, "The challenge was to establish and utilize centralized authority while supporting local districts and schools to improve their outcomes for kids."

In 1969 then-mayor John Lindsay relinquished control of public schools, and the New York City school system was organized into thirty-two geographically demarcated community school districts; six high school superintendencies; and District 75, a citywide special education district. Community superintendents, who reported to local elected community school boards, ran the quasi-independent community districts. Although the chancellor had responsibility akin to those of a chief state school officer, he was held directly accountable for every school, despite lacking the authority to hire, fire, or evaluate the community superintendents or principals.

The community school districts, once intended to protect and attend to the disparate needs of communities that composed the large city system, instead paved a pathway for corruption, particularly in the city's poorest neighborhoods and communities of color. The community school boards appointed the district superintendents, yet New York City had never seen a turnout for board elections that reached above 10 percent of the voters. Because of the low voter turnouts, corrupt or ineffective board members were often reelected.

The Bronx County district attorney's office investigated school board members for accusations of applying pressure to school employees to make donations to their campaigns or risk losing promotions or even their jobs. As a result, the city established a small, independent unit that spent its full time investigating the administration. This unit, staffed with over forty people, was charged with uncovering the corruption and illegal doings inside the NYCDOE. Their findings were frequently publicized, and, not surprisingly, the credibility of the New York City Public School system was at an all-time low.

Compounding this complex and partially corrupt system, the chancellor also had to contend with the opinions of the mayor, the governor, city and state assemblies, parents, and the teachers union, and the school system's own 3,700-member bureaucracy. The teachers union in New York, the United Federation of Teachers (UFT), was considered to be one of the best-organized political organizations in the state of New York. The UFT wielded exceptional political power with the New York legislature and would frequently bring its agendas to the state courts, returning with winning verdicts.

And there were numerous other organizational constraints to reform. School principals had tenure after five years on the job, making it difficult to remove even the low-performing ones. Social promotion of students was the norm, and the mayor publicly expressed his desire to have the police take over security in public schools. There also was stress between the NYCDOE and the New York State Education Department (NYSED). A move toward recentralization began in 1989 when the state commissioner of education created "schools under registration review," or "SURR," a status for persistently underperforming schools, many of which were in low-income sections of NYC. The state threatened to take over those schools and districts that were not able to decrease their number of SURR schools.

With so many structural impediments to the chancellor's leadership, Crew knew his line of direct authority would require radical changes in order to hold others accountable for improving achievement in every school:

> This school system, like almost all others, has operated as if it believed we should expect less of certain students and schools because of who they are, where they come from and where they live. We have become, perhaps unwittingly, an organization that tolerates — arguably even supports — different expectations for different students. [Steinberg, 1996, p. 2]

Crew expressed to millions of New Yorkers his desire to build a system that assumes every child can learn.

NEW LEGISLATION—REDISTRIBUTING AUTHORITY AND ACCOUNTABILITY

Crew, as chancellor in New York City in 1996, found that his hands were tied without the ability to make a swift and permanent change: bringing success to scale would be impossible without the authority to disrupt the culture of corruption and underperformance. And Crew was willing to accept the responsibility for change along with the authority. Impatient and unwilling to accept NYC schools' status quo, he began shaking up the system, removing adults who were not delivering results or acting in the best interests of students, such as in District 12 in the Bronx.

The state justice department initially blocked Crew's suspension of the corrupt community school board for District 12, deciding that Crew's actions essentially denied the district's voters, who were predominantly black and Latino, the ability to choose their local school board members. Crew asked the justice department to reconsider, submitting a revised plan for the district that included giving parents a greater say in the appointment of trustees for the district. Deval Patrick, then the assistant U.S. attorney general for the civil rights division of the justice department, said the move violated federal law. Still, Crew hired security guards to bar elected officials in District 12 from school district offices, citing "chronic education failures."

The blatant corruption and Crew's bold leadership sparked action among NYC's political leaders. In late 1996 Crew and Rudy Giuliani, a Republican, along with Democratic board president Bill Thompson, lobbied in Albany and convinced the Republican governor, George Pataki, and the state legislature to reconsider earlier decisions that Crew was overstepping his authority and thus violating Section 5 of the Voting Rights Act of 1965. The justice department reversed its position and allowed Crew to take over District 12. The U.S. Department of Justice had to approve this recentralization of power, and Crew traveled to Washington, DC, to meet with Attorney General Janet Reno. She approved the legislative changes in the chancellor's authority, noting that the law did not have a discriminatory purpose or effect, at the same time twenty-six of the thirty-two community superintendents' contracts were up for renewal.

Democratic UFT president Sandra Feldman was a strong backer of the new bill, supporting a change from the patronage politics that existed in some communities. She was eager to see students and teachers achieve, and she saw in Crew someone who was willing to work *with* teachers, not in spite of them. She saw Crew's vision of scaling up instructional improvement as imperative for her membership. For the first time in decades, this new authority gave the chancellor room to hold school leaders responsible and accountable for improvement, beginning with himself.

The law rescinded the authority of locally elected community school boards to manage and operate district schools and programs; to hire and assign personnel; to run instructional, social, recreational, and other programs; to determine instructional matters, including selection of textbooks; and to submit capital proposals, transferring these responsibilities to the community superintendents. Boards were now responsible only for employing community superintendents, whom the chancellor selected from groups of candidates after a publicly inclusive vetting process. Community superintendents were authorized to appoint principals after a screening by committees of parents and school personnel. Superintendents could also transfer or remove principals for "persistent educational failure" and evaluate principal performance at least once a year.

The law gave the chancellor authority to select community superintendents and to supersede and even remove community school board members and superintendents for cause. He could reject principal candidates selected by community superintendents and transfer or remove principals for persistent educational failure, ethics violations, and conflicts of interest. He could also intervene in, supersede, or take control of any school or community district that was persistently failing and establish training programs for employees. He was further empowered to develop a school-based planning process involving parents, teachers, school staff, and, when appropriate, students. As part of this process, the chancellor's office would put in place a comprehensive system of school-based budgeting and public budget reporting. The chancellor's central office finally had control over all schools in the NYC school system for the first time in more than twenty-five years.

With this new law in place, business as usual dramatically changed in New York City. Although the school system's central administration had possessed the authority to remove failing schools from their community districts since 1969, no one had exercised that power prior to Chancellor Crew. His assertion to personally assume control of some of the most underperforming schools on the SURR list marked a historic departure from centralized authority.

CRAFTING THE REFORM APPROACH

Crew's newly sanctioned authority clarified the chain of command and lines of accountability in NYC. As Crew described,

> This is a system that was a loose confederation of schools. It wasn't bound together by a common vision. A clearer line of supervision over superintendents is exactly what we need to [ensure] there will be strong, vibrant leadership at the school level. [Hendrie, 1997]

Crew considered all of the theories about "ungovernable" large bureaucracies that are "impervious to reform." He focused on leadership, explaining:

> People look at large urbans as monoliths, and they almost don't give themselves the benefit of thinking that the practice they can use, the strategies they can use there, are not different from the strategies you'd use in a classroom of thirty-two kids. When it comes right down to it, average size of a class in New York City was thirty kids. You can actually be a pretty good teacher in a class of thirty kids. There were thirty-two superintendents. I could be a pretty good teacher to a class of thirty-two superintendents. It's all how you understand the proportions of this. Yeah, it's a great big city, but it really boils down to thirty-two superintendents.

Crew called each superintendent into his office for information-gathering meetings during fall 1995. After meeting with community superintendents and examining the available school- and district-level data, his preliminary inclinations about how to improve the system were confirmed—he would need to change the quality of instruction. Decades of corruption, poverty, and unstable leadership and instruction had left some NYC students in danger of not graduating. "We don't have a lot of time, which is why I feel this incredible urgency," Crew told the *New York Times* (Mosle, 1997, paragraph 17).

Then the chancellor met with Barbara Byrd-Bennett, community superintendent of the Crown Heights district. Byrd-Bennett and her deputy had followed instructions: "Come prepared," Crew told them. "I expect to hear what is going on in your district and what you are doing about it." Byrd-Bennett carried a black binder with her strategic plan and district assessment data neatly organized and labeled inside. She wanted his support in her efforts to turn around her struggling district.

"I'll talk you through it piece by piece," she said confidently, and began to outline the situation in Crown Heights. She discussed her plans and strategies for coherent improvement. Crew's deputies fired questions at Byrd-Bennett, and each time she patiently directed them to a tab in her carefully designed book when answering. As the meeting concluded, Crew tipped back in his chair with surprise and satisfaction, realizing he saw in Byrd-Bennett the leadership needed to turn around some of the most struggling schools on the SURR list.

CREATING A NEW DISTRICT

Faced with numerous challenges, Crew opted to focus his attention and targeted resources on his most underperforming schools on the SURR list. To help turn around those schools and focus the system on student achievement, he applied an economics theory of differentiation and his experience as an educational leader to bring about change.

Crew analyzed the problem of NYC schools as one of a system sending the same messages—the same communication, the same expectations, and the same budget—to schools that were extraordinarily different in terms of need and performance. This struggling subset of SURR schools, in Crew's mind, met a market niche entirely different from those of other schools in the system. Different markets respond to different stimuli, and they comprise incredibly diverse variables. Crew wondered,

> How does central office talk to these schools? Do we just include their name on the memo and send the memo out? How do we talk to the principals? How do we talk to the teachers here? How do we talk to the parents?

In order to reconstruct a system that supported all school "markets," the chancellor talked to his leadership team about his plans to create a new structure for his most struggling schools. Crew used the pressure from the New York State Education Department as leverage for creating this new structure, which consisted of a new subdistrict of geographically noncontiguous schools that Crew dubbed "the Chancellor's District." He asked Byrd-Bennett to transition to central office so that she could support the new district with all of the resources NYC schools had to offer. Byrd-Bennett recalled,

> My personnel office became [the central] personnel office. My budget office became the central budget office. All of the operational end of the district that sits in a local school district [shifted to] the central headquarters, and I navigated these offices to do what needed to be done for those schools.

But owning the most underperforming schools wasn't enough for Crew. When he described his vision of the Chancellor's District to Byrd-Bennett, he also identified evidence indicating they would have difficulty sustaining improvement over time. Districts with inconsistent achievement and heavy concentrations of high-poverty schools received extra attention from Crew via Byrd-Bennett. Some of the other community superintendents were less than pleased with the extra attention and support, feeling their authority and competency were in question. Taking schools away from some community superintendents was quite painful for them, and Crew met with each of his regional leaders to explain his thinking:

> I told them the truth about what I thought about their capacity to do it. This was the same kind of conversation that you have with children when you are trying to encourage them to rise above their last failure. It's an intimate, compelling, hard-hitting, but ultimately supportive conversation. It was a learning conversation, not a mean-spirited one.

Not all of the school leaders affected by the creation of the Chancellor's District felt supported, however. One principal of a Chancellor's District school said that learning her school was designated as failing felt "awful." She lamented,

> It was hard because it meant adjusting to some philosophical changes about top-down authority and accountability, which were against my beliefs as a leader. So I had to do a lot of soul-searching in trying to find a way to not leave my staff and abandon them, and [about] how do I take this on and make it work.

Some parents and communities were also less than pleased about being designated as "failing." According to Byrd-Bennett, some of the community conversations were very difficult:

> People just felt really bad. Essentially, being a Chancellor's District school said to them, "You're failing, you're bad, you're awful. You're so bad and awful you can't even remain a part of your own school district. We've got to take you out." And people didn't know me, and [there] was a new chancellor, and our schools were mostly in the communities that were disenfranchised, poor, second language learners, and low attendance. It was tough having conversations to say to somebody, "I know what's best for you, and so open wide and drink this."

But there were some parents who were happy someone was finally paying attention to their children. As one parent put it, "I don't know if this will work, but at least he's trying. It's about time someone cared about our kids."

Designing the Chancellor's District

Once the overall structure for the Chancellor's District was established, Crew and Byrd-Bennett began designing strategies for supporting the so-called "wounded environments" the Chancellor's District intended to help. The virtual district began with ten schools—six elementary schools, three middle schools, and one high school. Schools on the SURR list at the highest risk of continued failure were the first ones chosen for the Chancellor's District. Crew, deputy chancellor for operations Harry Spence, deputy chancellor for instruction Judith Rizzo, and Byrd-Bennett collectively agreed on which inputs could make a difference in the Chancellor's District schools.

Focusing on leadership was a priority for the cabinet, so the authority to identify, screen, and select principals was key. Once the legislation passed giving Crew the authority to hire and fire community superintendents and remove or appoint board members, the authority to remove and appoint principals followed. Next, Crew thoughtfully worked to increase authority over the composition of the teaching staff. Gaining the ability to move teachers to and from schools to provide highly skilled instruction in Chancellor's District schools required negotiation with NYC's United Federation of Teachers. For Crew, partnering with the UFT was one of his greatest successes in the Chancellor's District:

> When I proposed the Chancellor's District to [then-president] Sandy [Feldman], she just got this (snap!) that quickly. She helped me figure out how to renegotiate the contract that would allow people to be in these schools. The deal was made with Sandy and me before anybody else, before I did anything publicly. She knew exactly what I was going to do, she knew how many teachers in which schools I'd have to remove, she knew what she was going to say when they came to her and said, "Why are you allowing them to remove me?" She was just 100 percent present. There was no rollover in Sandy, but there was complete partnership. I never felt like this was just mine and I was doing it to the union. This was Sandy and me together.

Without Feldman's collaboration and insight, the Chancellor's District would have struggled to achieve its goals.

The negotiation provided for incentives for teachers to work in Chancellor's District schools, including offering certified and experienced private school teachers $10,000 bonuses to work in the Chancellor's District and additional compensation for NYC public school teachers willing to stay in or relocate to Chancellor's District schools. This design allowed for the manipulation of teaching time in Chancellor's District schools, and led to the implementation of an extended-day concept, with school starting earlier or ending later in the afternoon for an additional twenty minutes of instruction per day, as well as an extended school year. Developing after-school programs designed to enhance and extend the daily learning for all interested students in Chancellor's District schools further added to instructional time. Tutoring was also available for students in grades 3 through 5 who needed additional help in math or reading.

Changing Instruction

A key element of the Chancellor's District was the instructional program. The top-down approach included a mandated daily schedule and curriculum throughout the district. There was a heavy focus on literacy instruction. Elementary school schedules required two ninety-minute daily literacy blocks using Success for All and the Balanced Literacy program in each block. The mandatory sixty-minute daily math block used the Trailblazers math program, and an additional thirty-minute skills block alternated between math and literacy instruction each day. Science and social studies were each taught once per week in elementary schools.

Time for literacy and math in Chancellor's District middle schools was more balanced. Middle school schedules mandated one ninety-minute daily literacy block and two literacy skills blocks each week; ten forty-five-minute math periods using the Math in Context program; and one period each of science, social studies, technology, a second language, and physical education or art (see Exhibit 9.2 on the CD for a list of Chancellor's District characteristics).

Some principals and teachers did not appreciate the prescribed, mandated approach to curriculum and instruction. A principal complained,

> We were micromanaged tremendously. The instructional program was outlined from A to Z. I grew to understand that in a lot of these schools, there was no teaching going on. I learned you have to be able to give some structure to schools when there's nothing there, but my school was not in the same place.

The NYCDOE's commitment to changing what was happening in each and every Chancellor's District school was in large part dependent on its intensive professional development strategy. Globally, Byrd-Bennett wanted to engage principals and teachers around "the key elements of teaching and learning—particularly around literacy—how to look at data, how to self-reflect and change practice for the students."

The Chancellor's District also facilitated many opportunities for inter- and intra-district school visitation for schools to learn from each other. Each school was assigned a team of at least four instructional support specialists to assist with math, English language arts, technology, and Success for All. Embedded, on-site professional development and coaching were offered at each school's teacher center staffed by an instructional specialist. Byrd-Bennett's middle school instructional specialist Lori Bennett describes the support provided to Chancellor's District schools:

> The most striking difference I found, working in the Chancellor's district compared to work I had done before, was the amount of support that was provided for the schools. Teachers spent many more hours — which were built into the contract — of professional development time, which of course is crucial if you want to see teachers make any kind of change. Schools weren't left to their own devices to make changes. The idea of this kind of support was very important, and I think that was a big change for turning these schools around.

Another integral part of the Chancellor's District design was the emphasis on student assessment data and achievement. Assessments integrated and aligned with the Success for All and Trailblazers programs were designed to give frequent feedback to teachers about student progress. Educators used

New York City's Early Childhood Literacy Assessment System (ECLAS) for students in kindergarten through grade 3, and developed benchmark assessments for reading and math in grades 3 through 8.

Crew and his team reassigned numerous principals in Chancellor's District schools, and hired additional assistant principals to support the instructional program. Training for the new leadership teams focused on instructional improvement and providing stability within the schools. Chancellor's District schools were also given additional resources of up to $2,400 more per student than other SURR schools, but according to Crew, many schools were not sure how to make the most of the extra dollars:

> These schools had money in Title I, special education services, Title III. There was just no knowledge about what to do with it. In the first iteration I hadn't really developed this whole question about how to build new knowledge, but I knew that piece was important. I was investing an incredible amount of money and time in the folks working in these schools and couldn't afford to repeat the process. So I had to create a way of keeping them, which meant showing them they could be successful at turning these schools around as a virtue of becoming more skilled.

Byrd-Bennett's office provided some of this support by implementing additional school-based supervisory personnel and instructional help from the district's teaching and learning office. This often entailed "surprise" visits to schools to work with principals. As one principal noted,

> Instructional support teams would come in, and we'd walk through classrooms and talk about instruction. We had to speak about how we're supporting teachers, what were some next steps and observations. And we had a very good instructional superintendent who I learned a lot from, but she was very "bottom line." She was tough. It was good because it was about improving schools, and the visits were very focused. It was all data driven, a lot about classroom instruction, professional development, and the accountability for the principal.

Scaling Up the Work in Miami

Crew might have started with the Chancellor's District, but his aim was to focus on instructional improvement across NYC. Putting that same theory to work when he arrived in Miami-Dade, Crew created a School Improvement Zone of thirty-nine underperforming schools, which amounted to a greater percentage of the district and a larger number of schools to support than in NYC. Although the Chancellor's District started with ten schools, it grew over time. The School Improvement Zone, like the Chancellor's District, would be based on several stages of work.

"I see the work in three phases," says Crew. "The first phase is you actually have to pull apart the schools. In the second phase you put the schools back together again differently, and then in the third phase you start sharing what you know about all the various parts. It's more of a dissemination of new knowledge and the creation of new knowledge."

Scaling Up the Chancellor's District

Crew's belief that underperforming schools can change and that all students should be educated to the same level shifted the mindset of NYC. Adopting common standards across the district set the groundwork for extending those expectations to all schools, even those in the Chancellor's District. According to Spence,

> The Chancellor's District was Rudy saying, "We've got to do something about achievement in failing schools." The standards movement pushed for more. We said, "Okay. We're going to take the logic of that to the whole system. The entire system has to be focused on improvement." These two steps deeply redefined the work of the New York City school system.

For Crew, the Chancellor's District was just the beginning. "I knew that if you go put yourself out on the line and publicly declare that you're going to get *this* done, the system will take note." However, the recognition was not always positive, as Byrd-Bennett recalled: "The conversations with the local school communities were often tough, because at the time that Rudy started this, to go to the Chancellor's District was not the place to be. And so people went in kicking and screaming." Nevertheless, over time a shift in culture started to occur, resulting in some improvements in student achievement (see Exhibit 9.3 on the CD).

At the same time, some communities worried that the resources provided to their schools as a result of the Chancellor's District might be removed when those schools returned to their respective community districts. As Crew and Byrd-Bennett began to think about how to transition schools back to their community superintendents, they tried to establish conditions under which the schools should leave the Chancellor's District and how those schools might still be supported.

REFOCUSING THE ENTIRE SYSTEM

"Rudy wanted to reshape the whole system around the notion that student achievement was what we were all about, which had not been the case when we arrived in 1995," explained Spence. "The Chancellor's District was the very beginning of that, as an actualization of the adoption of standards for all students." The attention to and focus of the Chancellor's District sparked an emphasis on student achievement across the system, beginning with the community superintendents. With a finite amount of resources, educators began to channel their concerns and questions about who was receiving attention and support toward the goal of school improvement. The Chancellor's District was Crew's catalyst for system-wide change, with different schools and regions implementing various types of reform. As Crew recalled,

> The noise of people not just talking but listening, not just chattering but focusing, will cascade into the rest of the culture, but you just need time. I didn't need all thirty-two superintendents to join me, but I needed a critical mass. It all started around this Chancellor's District approach. At first it was loud because people balked at the idea of focusing a lot of resources on underperforming schools, because it takes the attention away from what other districts are doing. While we were focusing attention on certain schools, other districts in New York started catching that fire too, and they were working on their own improvement. Then the noise started to change. Their improvement just didn't look the same as it looks in the Chancellor's District.

The 1999–2000 school year marked a committed change in the Chancellor's District, with Crew adding thirty-seven more schools with systematized structures across the district. Crew's Model of Excellence plan formalized the procedures of support and accountability. The SURR schools added to the Chancellor's District were "somewhat smaller, much less white, considerably poorer, and had more special education students, but fewer immigrant students" than the average NYC school. Although Crew could not assume all SURR schools into the Chancellor's District, he provided tiered support to the remaining SURR schools, designated Category 2 and Category 3 schools (See Exhibit 9.4 on the CD).

Crew set aside an additional $20 million to implement the Model of Excellence across the expanded Chancellor's District, promising continued support to schools that worked their way out of the virtual district. Due to the intensity of instructional and administrative support for Chancellor's District schools, the NYCDOE increased per-student funding by one-third. Further, Crew reallocated additional dollars from the system budget to provide the tiered support to Chancellor's District, Category 2, and Category 3 schools. Part of that funding went toward additional incentives to recruit, train, and retain certified and experienced teachers, and part was for decreasing class sizes. Class sizes were reduced to a maximum of twenty students in kindergarten through grade 3, and twenty-five students in grades 4 through 8.

Community superintendents took notice of the changes and began attending to instructional improvement in their remaining schools. According to Spence, the change of focus was evident in leadership meetings:

> The core conversation between the chancellor and superintendents when we arrived wasn't about student achievement. It was about corruption issues. It was about budget issues. It was about political issues. It was about everything but student achievement. The Chancellor's District prompted people to say, "No, no. This dialogue is all about student achievement." Part of Rudy's goal was to switch from 80 percent politics and administration and 20 percent practice to 80 percent practice and 20 percent politics and administration. That happened over the five years that we were there. By the last two or three years, the conversation was constantly about instructional improvement. Constantly, constantly, constantly about instructional improvement.

After Crew left New York in 1999, the Chancellor's District continued. Over the duration of the Chancellor's District, the results were positive, and student achievement increases were exceeding those of SURR schools not in the Chancellor's District. The percentage of fourth-grade students in Chancellor's District schools meeting the state's reading standard increased considerably more than did the percentage of fourth-grade students in other SURR schools. Although the reading scores of Chancellor's District schools still lagged behind those of NYC schools overall, Chancellor's District schools showed an 18-percentage-point improvement compared to a 14-percentage-point gain in citywide scores. The Chancellor's District ultimately served fifty-eight failing schools before its end in 2003 and all schools returned to their designated regions; fifteen of these schools returned to their home districts, and eleven closed prior to 2003.

IMPLEMENTING THE SCHOOL IMPROVEMENT ZONE IN MIAMI-DADE

Four years after leaving New York, Crew had more advanced data systems, more knowledge about effective instructional reform models, and time for self-reflection to advance his thinking about tackling achievement gaps in Miami-Dade schools. Taking the lessons he learned from the Chancellor's District, Crew knew Byrd-Bennett was right when she said,

> You've got to be fearless with the people that you're working with and really be really clear about what the expectations are for output. You've got to have the courageous conversations with unions and be willing to be very clear and transparent about what you're doing.

As he formulated his comprehensive strategy for improvement in Miami-Dade County Public Schools, Crew felt even more urgency to move quickly and establish differentiated support as early as possible in his tenure:

> Thinking back, I think we had enough time to get New York through its first phase of the work, which was to stop the hemorrhaging and create the basis for a new culture. I don't think we created a new culture, I think [we] just created the conditions for a new culture to begin to get ripe, just to come in.

Crew and his leadership team set their sites on thirty-nine underperforming schools in Miami-Dade to serve in the to-be-created School Improvement Zone. Many of the same structures and initiatives used in New York, such as extended time and managed curricular programs, were also in place for the Zone. As Crew recalled,

> I learned a lot about this process of scaling up in New York. My takeaway from New York is that there are enormous pressures to get this right on the first go-around. Once you announce that you're going to do something like this, then skeptics stand back and attempt to watch you fail. Secondly, there are enormous opportunities for success, but you almost have to, early on, define sort of what that success is going to look like. You have to define what constitutes success and what constitutes failure. It can't be that you just let that lie fallow and assume that people will just get that the effort was a good effort and things began to happen. Finally, [what] I would say is to just simply understand that politics is the dog with which you will lie for some number of years, and expect to catch fleas. Expect it, don't be shocked by that fact, expect every aspect of it, so that your heart doesn't sink when you see it.

Six months into his tenure, in the 2004–2005 school year, Crew initiated the School Improvement Zone in Miami-Dade. He began leading the students, families, and educators in the system through the difficult process of change, determined to come out with significantly improved schools. He prepared to teach the entire system how to work together to support all of its students:

> The only thing that sees people through hard times is their underlying faith and belief that they're not alone. They're not doing this in isolation. To enable people to feel like a learner, and to be almost joyful about that, makes the struggle not just bearable but winnable.

REFERENCES

Berger, J. (1996, April 24). City faces big Regents-diploma hurdle. *New York Times,* section B, p. 8. Retrieved December 15, 2010, from Lexis-Nexis Universe/General News database.

Hendrie, C. (1997). Crew packs arsenal of new powers in N.Y.C. *Education Week, 16*(16), 1. Retrieved December 15, 2010, from www.edweek.org.

Mosle, S. (1997, August 31). The stealth chancellor. *New York Times*, section 6, p. 31. Retrieved December 15, 2010, from Lexis-Nexis Universe/General Newsdatabase.
Steinberg, J. (1996, January 25). Schools chief calls for loftier standards. *New York Times*, p. 5B. Retrieved December 15, 2010, from Lexis-Nexis Universe/General Newsdatabase.
Toy, V. S. (1995, June 13). In reversal, test scores rise at New York City's schools. *New York Times*, section A, p. 1. Retrieved December 15, 2010, from Lexis-Nexis Universe/General Newsdatabase.

Scaling Up Connections

Amalia Cudeiro

Rudy Crew's case study outlining his struggles and achievements in scaling up reform efforts in both New York City and Miami-Dade County, Florida, provides an accurate and vivid picture of the challenges facing all superintendents who are focused on improving the instructional fate of underserved and underchallenged poor and minority students in this country. As a new first-year superintendent in a district much smaller and with significantly different demographics and socioeconomic levels, I am surprised by the number of connections between his and my experiences, personal values, and beliefs.

VALUES AND BELIEFS

Key to Crew's legacy of turning around low-performing schools in New York City was his belief that it was possible. He knew that with hard work and perseverance he would be able to turn around a system in which adults had lost faith in their most needy students. He believed that it was possible because he had experienced his own struggle in school growing up and had overcome the challenges. My personal experience as a child of immigrant parents, in a country where diversity was not valued, forced me to develop a strong work ethic also. I understood early on that education was my only path to economic survival. Like Crew's father, my parents had high expectations for me and worked multiple jobs in order for me to graduate from high school and achieve a college education. The support and unrelenting pressure from my family to succeed in school were critical in my development and key to any accomplishments I may claim today and in the future.

The belief in the importance of high expectations for all students and in the value of hard work and perseverance continue to drive my efforts as superintendent in Bellevue, Washington. Despite amazing successes, such as having four high schools in *Newsweek*'s top 100, high percentages of students taking and passing advanced placement courses, and a robust high school graduation rate, we continue to fail one-third of our students by allowing them to perform below a basic level of proficiency. Most of these students are second language learners and often students of color. My first goal for the district is to eliminate the achievement gap; my second one is to further challenge students who are at or above grade level. Although I do not have nearly as many students in that bottom third as Crew had in New York City, we both still needed to begin our work by building a common belief that closing that gap is possible.

BACKGROUND AND PROFESSIONAL EXPERIENCES

Another connection, which may or may not be important to other leaders' approaches, is that Crew and I reached the superintendency following very similar and traditional career paths. Even though Crew began with a background in economics, we were both teachers and principals, and had a range of central office experiences. As a teacher I worked with poor minority students who spoke languages other than English at home, and yet I saw many students achieve at or above grade level. As a principal in East Los Angeles I was able to see how improving teacher practice could be scaled up across an entire school, and as a result we experienced significant increases in student learning. As deputy superintendent in Boston I had the privilege of watching superintendent Tom Payzant lead the entire system through multiple years of continuous improvement. Those experiences have had a profound effect on my beliefs, values, and commitment to the success of all students no matter how poor or how challenged in their ability to speak, read, and write English.

ACCOUNTABILITY

I have also learned that passion and values pertaining to the importance of a quality education and a strongly held belief that all students are capable of learning at high levels are—although essential—not sufficient for a superintendent to act on and implement a vision of quality teaching and learning for all students. We as superintendents must have the authority to hold ourselves and everyone else in the system accountable for results, and we must measure those results in terms of increased student learning. In order to do the work of educating all students at high levels, Crew had to first take control of the accountability structures in New York City. He had to change the structures controlling the authority over community superintendents and principals; address corrupt or ineffective board members; redirect the work of a bureaucratic central office; and reach out to one of the most entrenched, highly organized unions in the country.

Even in the best scenario, a superintendent must first address the accountability structure in the district in order to have the authority to implement changes that will have an impact on improving teaching and learning system-wide. My first challenge in the accountability arena in Bellevue was to make changes at the cabinet level. These changes in leadership were necessary in order to expand the system's focus from simply implementing a common curriculum for all to ensuring that all teachers provide quality, differentiated instruction in order to meet the diverse needs of our student population. The existing cabinet had been selected for their strength in developing a rigorous common curriculum, and they probably would not have the expertise and experience necessary for implementing the professional development needed either to address the learning gaps of our underperforming students or to further challenge students who met or exceeded standards. Each of the six current cabinet members is assigned a number of schools at which he or she serves as the instructional leadership coach to the principal of that school. A portion of each member's evaluation, including my own, is tied to the improvement of student learning at the schools in which they serve as coaches. Another critical change that I made to the accountability structure in Bellevue was to move supervision and evaluation of principals directly under my area of responsibility as a superintendent. In order for me to lead system-wide instructional improvement, principals needed to be directly accountable to me. Without a direct line of accountability between the superintendent and school leaders, these changes might not have been taken sufficiently seriously or implemented fully.

TRAINING AND SUPPORT

Crew understood that having area superintendents and principals directly accountable to him for improving underperforming schools was critical. However, changing the accountability structure alone would not yield the necessary change for the system to meet the instructional needs of the lowest performing students. Effective instructional change required that he provide the support and training his leaders would need to accomplish the task. He began this work by targeting resources on his most underperforming schools. In Bellevue, with only twenty-seven schools, I felt the urgency to focus our instructional change efforts on all of our schools. I knew that training principals to lead instructional change in their buildings would not on its own be sufficient. In order for instructional changes to take place at the classroom level, I needed to include teachers in leadership roles as well. My first task was to change the culture from one of isolation and privatization of practice to one of collaboration and trust, in which teachers share effective teaching strategies and develop processes and structures to challenge each other's practice in a collegial, nonevaluative manner. We have started to address this cultural change in Bellevue by training instructional leadership teams from every school. These teams comprise administrators from each building as well as teacher leaders, often selected by their peers. The purpose of the instructional leadership teams is to lead instructional efforts in their schools and facilitate true professional learning communities of practice. This year instructional leadership teams from each school have led their staff in analyzing student achievement data, targeting an instructional area for improvement, and developing a professional learning plan that will require teachers to receive training in research-based strategies relevant to the targeted instructional area. In order to ensure implementation happens, instructional leadership teams as well as other teacher teams in each building will engage in learning walks to identify how well and how consistently all staff members are implementing the instructional strategies they learned through the training.

SCALING UP

System-wide improvement results from scaling up the model and moving from small-scale implementation to whole-district implementation. Once the accountability structure was in place, Crew began his reform efforts by first addressing his lowest performing schools. His plan was to take what worked in his Chancellor's District with a small number of schools and apply the same strategy system-wide. In Bellevue my plan is to scale up the work by building instructional leadership in every school with a small number of teachers first, and then have that group—the instructional leadership team—along with building administrators lead and facilitate instructional improvement in every classroom. Scaling up in Bellevue will require that instructional expertise does not solely rest with the teachers in the instructional leadership teams. In order to have an impact on every classroom and every student, each member of an instructional leadership team will need to facilitate the process of improving instructional practice and creating a culture of shared accountability for student results with other grade-level teacher teams and with clusters or department teams.

EQUITY AND DIFFERENTIATION

Finally, eliminating the achievement gap and ensuring that all students are challenged regardless of their levels of performance in Bellevue will also require that we craft a new definition of equity. Currently, as in most districts, all schools in Bellevue receive funding allocations based on student numbers and programs. PTAs in our most affluent schools are able to raise considerable dollars to augment the schools' district allocations, creating inequitable conditions in some of our most needy schools. Improving student results in our five lowest performing schools, those serving most of our poor students and students of color, will require that we allocate district resources in an unequal but more equitable manner. This will be a difficult task to accomplish given our current economic environment of budget cuts and reduction of staffing. The other aspect of equitable versus equal with which we are dealing concerns instructional practice. Equal levels of resources, including staffing and instructional programs, and simply providing all students with the same common curriculum delivered in the same way, will not allow us to reach each and every student sufficiently to bring them all up to proficient and above. In order to eliminate our achievement gap we must provide differentiated levels of support and differentiated instructional strategies in every classroom, retaining the same high standards and expectations for all but adjusting the level of help according to need.

The changes I have initiated in Bellevue this year—new accountability structures for both central office and school leaders, the work with instructional leadership teams to minimize isolation and privatization of practice and maximize collaboration and transparency, as well as training on research-based instructional strategies—are helping us lay the necessary groundwork for true instructional change to take root at scale. We are at the early stages of implementation, and there is much more work to be done before we accomplish our goals of eliminating the achievement gap and further challenging all of our students. However, the changes we have implemented thus far have sent a clear message to everyone within the district and the community that "business as usual" is not acceptable, and that all of us, principals, teachers, and superintendent, will be held accountable for increasing student achievement results.

One big difference between the challenge facing Crew in New York City and my own work in Bellevue is that I am very fortunate to have an exemplary team of school board members who are committed to supporting these cultural and instructional improvements. It is because of this united team of leaders in the district that I hold such high hopes for accomplishing our goals.

CHAPTER 10

Sustaining Improvement over Time

Replicating the "Long Beach Way"

Carl A. Cohn

Last fall I was contacted by two young women from Dubai who are traveling the globe on behalf of McKinsey Consulting, interviewing leaders of school systems that have sustained improvement over the past decade and a half. They're updating their 2007 report, *How the World's Best-Performing School Systems Come Out On Top,* and they wanted to interview me, as the former Long Beach superintendent of ten years, because Long Beach is one of only three American school systems being studied in this new report.

So much of school reform is both simple and complex. In its 2007 report of global school improvement, McKinsey found that the best school systems worldwide get the right people to become teachers, develop them into effective instructors, and target support to make sure that every child receives excellent instruction. In so many ways, this is the "Long Beach way" and the story that you are about to read, but I would argue that every successful urban school system has a complex and nuanced backstory that is filled with the usual landmines of governance, labor relations, and local context that keep most urban school systems from sustaining success over time.

What makes Long Beach truly unique today on the American urban school reform scene is the specter of two back-to-back, long-term superintendencies in which consistency of purpose—as evidenced by a focus on student achievement—has prevailed. In 2012 Chris Steinhauser will have completed ten years as superintendent just as I did. Although my tenure was marked by the jaw-dropping statistic of four out of five school board members who hired me staying for all ten years, thus providing extraordinary stability in governance, Chris's tenure has seen considerable disruption in governance, labor relations, and fiscal support, making his and the school system's successes all the more remarkable.

BUILDING SLOWLY

As I have followed Long Beach's successes over the past eight years, I have been amazed at how some initiatives that started out small with a much more narrow focus have grown into major engines of system-wide improvement. The Baldrige process, an integrated framework for managing an organization based on a set of specific criteria, for example, grew out of our frustration with our payroll office's inability to pay teachers accurately in regard to their extra compensation checks. I thought it would serve as a clever vehicle for improving the customer service aspects of our central offices that weren't very customer or client centered if we actually went through the plan-do-study-act (PDSA) cycle. I was skeptical about its utility to drive improvement at schools until Kristi Kahl, as a newly appointed principal, successfully used it to transform one of the district's lowest-performing middle schools into a national Blue Ribbon award winner. Long Beach's culture of learning from the talented people who run the schools served us very well in this instance.

The same can be said about learning from the people who teach in Long Beach schools. I was always fond of saying that reform in Long Beach was going to be both top-down and bottom-up. It's a good applause line in any superintendent's speech, but it's sometimes short on specifics when it comes to the real world of urban school reform, in which educators often make harsh judgments about the need for a sense of urgency that doesn't include waiting for teachers to get it right. In this chapter's case study, you're going to read about one teacher who got it right when it came to math instruction (MAP2D), and about the school district's delivery on the promise that reform in Long Beach would be both top-down and bottom-up. Developments like this go a long way toward demonstrating that classroom teachers have much to offer when it comes to improving both schools and districts.

At a time when strategic management of human capital has emerged as an important part of the Obama administration's efforts to improve urban school systems, Long Beach's insistence on the development of homegrown talent stands in stark contrast to the powerful perception in some school reform circles that only the acquisition of outside expertise will rescue underperforming school systems. Both the Principal Apprentice Program and the Aspiring Assistant Principal Program are designed to develop Long Beach's own version of "new leaders," and to further develop the "bench strength" that has been an important characteristic of the district for the past two decades. I recall going to a meeting in Sacramento in the late 1990s at which I spoke with a state leader who had just returned from a meeting in Washington, DC, where one of our labor relations staffers had made a presentation. He turned to me and said, "Long Beach has amazing bench strength if that person is only at the director level." I replied that I agreed.

It is important to note, however, that the school system's outstanding development of student data and assessment systems has taken place since the mid-1990s under the exemplary leadership of two very talented research and evaluation experts—Lynn Winters and the late James Gulek. These two remarkable leaders brought their outside expertise and skills to a district filled with inside talent. Their visibility in the schools and their uncanny knack for making accountability both teacher- and principal-friendly have distinguished Long Beach's research and evaluation office from what you find in most urban school systems. More than number crunchers, both of them had people skills that reinforced the notion that collaborating with those who actually work in schools should be at the heart of a district's reform efforts.

THE IMPORTANCE OF PARTNERSHIPS

Another of the most gratifying developments I have observed in the eight years that I've been gone from Long Beach is the work of the school system's partnership with higher education—one that has grown into a "College Promise" that guarantees students a tuition-free first semester of higher education. When we first started this initiative in the early 1990s, I was very skeptical about education institutions' ability to work together on common purposes. Historically we in the K–12 system had so little confidence in California State University, Long Beach (CSULB), that we referred to it as "the mausoleum on the hill."

Enter Carl Cohn, new superintendent of schools, and Bob Maxson, new president of the university. Both of us were aware of how the usual finger-pointing and blaming goes in regard to K–12 and higher education: "You're sending us students not ready for college." "You're sending us teachers not ready to teach." We were determined not to follow that path of recrimination but instead to create a new opportunity for our people to work together, to find a way forward that would build on the strengths and talents of both institutions.

One of the usual refrains coming from institutions of higher education is that working with K–12 school systems is not a scholarly activity and does not improve *U.S. News & World Report* rankings, or whatever the current private sector measurement instrument is. President Maxson, to his credit, argued that improving the K–12 educational system is a university-wide responsibility—one that is not confined only to the School of Education.

Real-world problems and challenges, like incoming university freshmen failing writing and math entrance tests, were addressed by university English and math and science departments working with high school math and English teachers on issues of rigor and assessment. The result was a dramatic improvement in passing rates for our Long Beach students entering the California State University system.

Another challenge we addressed was better recruitment, induction, mentoring, and ongoing support of new teachers, thus leading to significant increases in retention of new teachers in urban schools—a commonsense reform that large urban school systems rarely achieve.

I'm delighted to acknowledge that initially I was completely wrong about what could be accomplished in the area of partnering with institutions of higher education, and that Long Beach's sustained success in student achievement over the past decade and a half owes much to higher education.

IT IS ALL ABOUT THE CONTEXT

As any student of urban school reform knows, the Long Beach story is more the exception than the rule. Most superintendents do, in fact, get tripped up by governance, labor relations, and the local context of reform in their efforts to sustain improvement over time. I wouldn't have known that firsthand, however, if I hadn't come out of retirement in 2005 to head the San Diego school district, the second-largest school district in California, a mere one hundred miles down the coast from Long Beach. In accepting that position, I reasoned that another Navy town with similar demographics couldn't possibly be that different from the one that I had led for ten years.

When I arrived as superintendent in San Diego in fall 2005, the list of active employee grievances ran to more than forty pages. Conflict on a wide variety of fronts had been pervasive throughout the district for the previous seven years. In addition, employees had received no raises for four years. The school district's enrollment was declining, and a robust charter school movement was capturing 10 percent of families. Even more astounding was the number of administrators who came to me seeking sanctuary and arguing the "Nuremberg defense" for their actions, indicating that higher-ups had ordered them to do things that they knew were wrong, but that they had gone ahead and done them out of fear of job loss.

One of the particularly disturbing admissions coming from an area instructional leader involved the involuntary transfer of an excellent elementary teacher from her inner-city school because she had exercised her free-speech rights in criticizing the top-down nature of the previous superintendent's "Blueprint for Student Success." In a development filled with irony, that teacher was elected president of the San Diego teachers union in 2006.

When I left the school system at the end of 2007, active grievances were down to a single page; employees had received three raises in eighteen months; the school district's enrollment had grown for the first time in six years (stunning our own demographer, who had predicted no change in the decline until 2015); and San Diego had become the only large urban school district in the state to meet adequate yearly progress (AYP) under No Child Left Behind two years in a row.

So with that kind of success, why am I not still working there? Simply put, I have to work for a school board that I respect and in which I have confidence. The hard work of sustaining improvement over time is not just about making AYP, it's also about closing the gap. And what we found out about San Diego is that there are local policies, fostered by the board of education, that make it very difficult to close the achievement gap there.

One such program for gifted students is called GATE Seminar or "GATE within GATE." If a youngster scores at the 99.9 percentile on a single test called the Raven, that student gets a class size of twenty in grades 4 through 12. The difficulty in closing the gap becomes readily apparent, in a program that enrolls 75 to 80 percent white and Asian students, when the most academically advantaged students get classes of twenty while African American and Latino students, who may be at or far below grade level, are in classes of thirty-five to one.

At one point we proposed not getting rid of GATE Seminar, but merely increasing class size from twenty to twenty-five to one. Our school board at that time refused on a 3-to-2 vote. For two years in a row we proposed raising the poverty threshold to 60 percent for schools receiving Title I funds so that we could concentrate more dollars at the schools with the poorest kids. Again, the same 3-to-2 board majority refused to go along.

We at the local school level are often quick to blame unions, state capitals, and Washington for why we can't do the job, but the San Diego case presents an example of a local school district that doesn't have the courage to take the necessary steps to improve student achievement for those youngsters who historically have been left behind.

Since I left San Diego at the end of 2007, yet another superintendent has come and gone in a tenure that lasted only eighteen months, which makes the Long Beach case that you are about to read all the more remarkable as an example of an urban school system sustaining success over time.

Chris Steinhauser, Long Beach Unified School District: Eluding the Allure of Quick Fixes

Leslie Boozer and Laura Kelley

As Long Beach Unified School District (LBUSD) superintendent Chris Steinhauser walked into the central office conference room, he ran numbers through his head. The district had already cut over $100 million dollars from its yearly budget in the past five years. Steinhauser was painfully aware that $50 million more would need to be cut before the 2011–2012 school year. He had called the executive staff together for its weekly meeting to discuss district planning and where they could make future cuts. As he considered his words, Steinhauser ran his fingers through his short blond hair and reflected on his past twenty-nine years as a district employee and his last eight as superintendent. The steady, significant progress of student achievement, the support of the community, the impact of business partnerships, generally supportive board members, and the dedication of the district's employees came to mind. As he took his seat at the head of the table next to his deputy superintendent, Chris Dominguez, he looked around at his leadership team:

> Despite the California budget crisis, our system hasn't changed. We must continue prioritizing our work. If we are going to be a district of continuous improvement, we must reexamine, redesign, and redeploy our resources. I know there have been a lot of painful cuts the last few years, and unfortunately we must make more. We are down to the core of Long Beach's work: high-quality instruction.

With over eighty-seven thousand students in ninety-three schools, Steinhauser and his team have worked to raise student achievement every year since he took the lead in 2002 (see Exhibit 10.1 on the CD). Building on the work of his predecessor Carl Cohn, the district was awarded the

Broad Prize for Urban Education in 2003 and has been a finalist every year it was eligible, for a total of five times. This is just one of many accolades bestowed upon the district.

Under Steinhauser's leadership, the district has redefined student outcomes through closing achievement gaps, increasing college access, and raising rigor by enrolling more students in advanced placement (AP) courses. In 2008 Long Beach's African American, Latino, and low-income students outscored similar students in the state in reading and math at all school levels. According to the state's accountability system, known as the Academic Performance Index (API), the district as a whole, as well as the African American, Latino, and low-income student subgroups, have shown achievement gains, often in double digits, every year since 2003. AP enrollment overall has increased by 65 percent under Steinhauser, with African American students' participation increasing by 85 percent and Latino students' by 90 percent. In 2009 *Newsweek* named six of the district's ten comprehensive high schools among the top 6 percent in the country, and Long Beach students earned a record $40 million in college scholarships, doubling the total from just two years before.

The job of pushing the work forward was not met without resistance. In addition to the state financial crisis, the teachers union questioned Steinhauser's leadership and launched an active campaign to win control of the five-member school board. They successfully won two seats in 2006, often leaving Steinhauser with a 3-to-2 split board. Despite the division, Steinhauser and his staff have focused on continuous improvement and shielded the classroom as much as possible from politics and fiscal losses. But with significant budget cuts ahead that are likely to have an impact on the classroom, Steinhauser and his staff must now answer the question: How can LBUSD continue to sustain its improvements and protect the instructional core?

HOMEGROWN LEADER

The continuous success of Steinhauser has often been credited to the "Long Beach way." As he enters his twenty-ninth year in the system, there is no denying that Steinhauser is a significant part of the Long Beach culture. He grew up in a working-class family in Long Beach and attended the public schools from kindergarten forward. After graduating from Wilson High School, Steinhauser attended Long Beach City College (LBCC) before transferring to California State University, Long Beach (CSULB). He has worked in multiple positions in every level of the school system, beginning his career as a teacher's aide at Signal Hill Elementary School. Years later he would return to transform the school that gave him his start in education.

In the 1990–1991 school year, Signal Hill was a school in crisis—facing serious discipline problems, low morale, and plummeting achievement scores. It was the second-lowest-performing elementary school in LBUSD, and many had written off the school and its students. With almost 100 percent of the student population being students of color and recipients of free and reduced-price lunches, many thought this population of learners could not perform at high levels. Steinhauser strongly disagreed. Even though he had never been a principal, Steinhauser was tapped to reform the school. He immediately began major instructional reforms, including mandating school uniforms and introducing a Reading Recovery program. He began working closely with parents to boost the PTA's enrollment and involvement in the school. As the school's instructional leader, Steinhauser, whose wife is an over-twenty-year veteran teacher in LBUSD, also transferred his two children from high-performing elementary schools and enrolled them in Signal Hill. It was important to Steinhauser to communicate to the entire community that this school was good enough for his own children. With a belief that "education is our generation's civil rights battle," Steinhauser became determined to give the children of Signal Hill the best education possible.

After four years with Steinhauser as principal, Signal Hill had turned around and become one of the highest performing elementary schools in the district. The school's new reputation for excellence, with virtually every student scoring proficient or above on the state's achievement test, resulted in a boom of attendance and a long waiting list. Then-superintendent Cohn pulled Steinhauser up to work in the central office and began grooming the district's next leader. Over the next decade, Steinhauser served as the district's director of special projects, as a liaison with the Office for Civil Rights, as the assistant superintendent of K–8 schools, and as deputy superintendent. As the district's deputy, Steinhauser set a new tone for personal accountability when he accepted responsibility for overseeing the system's nineteen lowest-performing schools.

Since becoming the superintendent in 2002, Steinhauser has kept his focus on instructional leadership. He remains connected to the classroom by periodically teaching summer school and serving as a district substitute five days out of every school year. The latter he also requires of all certificated central office personnel. This practice serves not only as a cost-saving measure but also as a way for staff to stay connected to the district's most important work—classroom instruction.

For Steinhauser, sustainability is about building on past successes. He has continued the curriculum work that Cohn began, such as adopting a standards-based curriculum, using data to guide the work, and requiring uniforms for all K–8 students. Steinhauser recalled, "When Carl took over in 1992, there was a conscious effort on building culture and having a focus on instruction." While that work continued, the district also began to focus on accountability and alignment. As Steinhauser explained, "We have streamlined our work—the superintendent goals, the board goals, and the school-site goals—for total alignment."

CREATING ALIGNMENT—THE BALDRIGE CRITERIA FOR PERFORMANCE EXCELLENCE

Beginning Steps

Under Cohn, LBUSD began using the Baldrige Criteria for Performance Excellence after receiving a grant from the Broad Foundation. This traditional business tool for continuous improvement was one of the district's first forays into using data to guide their work. Immediately upon his appointment as superintendent, Steinhauser worked to make this high-level system more applicable to education. After surveying principals and teachers, Steinhauser and his team learned some of the business jargon was halting communication instead of facilitating it. Steinhauser's team realized that the Baldrige terminology had to make sense to their school staff or they simply wouldn't use it. Thus they dropped the business terms and adapted Baldrige to fit the needs of a school system. To enhance this process, they switched to a trainer-of-trainers model that allowed key individuals from the school sites to be trained and then deployed back to their schools to disseminate the information in language they could understand that was tailored to the needs of LBUSD.

After the grant money ended in 2004, Steinhauser wanted to continue training school leaders in Baldrige strategies. However, he needed a way to make this work self-sustaining due to state budget shortfalls that had required the district to cut $57 million from its budget. Long Beach decided to share its knowledge of Baldrige—and how the school system tailored Baldrige to education—by becoming a training center for other Southern California districts. Under the leadership of Baldrige administrator Cindy Young, LBUSD began offering twenty-two classes on implementing a range of Baldrige strategies designed for multiple levels of the organization, from classroom teachers to central office administrators. The classes taught educators how to use data gathered through testing and leadership surveys to develop action plans for both the operational and instructional work of the district. This shift from learner to trainer allowed LBUSD to not only hone its practice of Baldrige strategies but also earn the necessary funds to continue internally training personnel at no cost to schools.

Moving from Baldrige to Strategic Planning

Although Baldrige had produced some positive results and increased the use of data in the system, the alignment piece was still missing. Perhaps it was the business language or the difficulty of managing data in the classroom setting, but Baldrige was never fully implemented in every classroom, in every school. Compounding this issue was the fact that the district still operated largely in silos. Administrators and teachers were not hearing the same message from all of district leadership. The school sites instead kept hearing, "You need to have mission statements. You need to have schoolwide goals and grade-level goals. Teachers need to have personal goals. Kids need to have goals"—yet none of this was modeled from the executive staff.

Thanks to the progress made under Cohn and continued during the early part of Steinhauser's tenure, the district was starting to receive a lot of attention, which brought new opportunities—universities, foundations, and nonprofits wanted to be a part of the district's touted success. Steinhauser and his executive staff immediately recognized that the district would need to turn down some opportunities, even if they were good, when they did not align with the vision they were working to create. As Steinhauser was discussing new opportunities with his colleagues, he was pleased to hear Dominguez, Young, and others consistently question alignment, asking, "How does this program align to what we are trying to do?"

The district needed a strategic vision to take its work to the next level. The "Long Beach way" had allowed the district to significantly increase student outcomes, but even with Baldrige in place the district lacked the overall focus required to make sustainable change. For instance, in 2003 the district learned that students of color and students of low socioeconomic status were not taking the Preliminary Scholastic Aptitude Test (PSAT). In fact, only 10 percent of all LBUSD students were taking this diagnostic test. To encourage all students to take more rigorous courses, Steinhauser decided to mandate that all sophomores take the test and used Title V funds to make the test free. The first year of the program, 6,600 students took the PSAT.

Still, the district struggled with a persistent achievement gap, and rigorous instruction was not the norm for all students. Steinhauser and his team realized they were putting out individual fires instead of creating a systemic plan for resolving pressing issues. For example, Steinhauser and Dominguez were concerned that AP enrollment did not reflect the district's population. Even though they made up only 16 percent of the population, white students were the majority of students taking AP courses and exams.

To facilitate desired changes, Steinhauser and his team developed the district's first strategic plan. To lead this process, Steinhauser looked to the Baldrige office. He added a new title to Young's tag line so she would also serve as the strategic planning administrator for LBUSD. Young confirmed the thinking behind this new strategy:

> A written, formalized strategic plan for our district was new. While we had always had a strategic vision that everyone knew in their head, how we operated and how we did business, . . . it was never really captured in the sense of this is specifically what we do, this is the "Long Beach way."

Implementing this new process of strategic planning was not a quick transition. Former middle school principal Kristi Kahl joined Young as a strategic planning administrator. Kahl, who focused on building support in the school community, noted the importance of this work:

> We went through a long process of committee work. While it might have seemed to take too long to some, there is a definite bonus to approaching the work this way—it makes us sustainable. It slows us down a bit, but I think it gives us an opportunity for change to take root. Chris and the board may have started the process, but there is a much larger group involved in the development of the plan. It allows us to own the result.

UNION DISAPPROVAL

Although Steinhauser was attempting to make strides to further improve the district, the union was not pleased with his leadership. They argued for increased transparency and re-allocation of resources. They felt less money should be spent on administration and more on the classroom. Desiring change they failed to see in the new strategic plan, the Teachers Association of Long Beach (TALB) decided to challenge the hallmark of Cohn and Steinhauser's tenure—the stable, supportive governance structure. They launched an aggressive campaign to win control of the five-member school board during the April 2006 election. As TALB-supported candidate Michael Ellis argued in his candidate's forum in the local newspaper, the *Long Beach Press-Telegram,*

> Long Beach School Board's priorities are wrong. While the school board and district bureaucrats enjoy a luxurious multimillion-dollar office building, thousands of our students study in crowded and old portable bungalows. They cut close to 400 teaching positions in the last two years and now class size averages are one of the highest in L.A. County. . . . Worst of all, our schools are not safe and too many children, and teachers, are scared of falling victim to crime and violence on our campuses. While the Long Beach police

> seem to be making in-roads into addressing our gang problems, I see no discernible, coordinated effort by the district. This is another problem that is either being ignored [or the result of] resources failing to be allocated. [Ellis, 2006, paragraph 7]

Ellis's campaign was successful, as was that of TALB-supported candidate David Barton. After winning two of three seats up for election, TALB almost got their wish and left Steinhauser with a tenuous 3-to-2 majority as he continued to push through new reform measures.

In large part due to over a year of committee work that included numerous union members, the school board unanimously approved the district's strategic plan on September 11, 2006. LBUSD identified five major district goals:

1. All students will attain proficiency in the core content areas.
2. All students will graduate from high school prepared for postsecondary and career options.
3. Ensure staff and student safety.
4. Improve the growth and development of the workforce.
5. Improve communication throughout the district.

The union and board worked to determine if they could support Steinhauser as he changed the system to ensure these goals were met.

THE WAY TO CONTINUOUS IMPROVEMENT—MEASURING STUDENT PROGRESS

With the development of the strategic plan in 2006, Steinhauser decided to bring on a new assistant superintendent of research, planning, and evaluation. He recruited James Gulek from a Northern California district to head up the research department consisting of four managers and six support staff.

Under Gulek's leadership, the district began collecting data in support of its newly identified strategic goals. Gulek was determined to make the system relevant and user-friendly—particularly to fill the void in places where Baldrige had failed to fit into the system. Much more than just the state required assessment data was necessary to gauge the district's progress. As Young explained,

> Often the focus is on getting that big data binder that you see so many principals carrying around in other districts. In Long Beach, it is about frequently using your site's authentic data to guide collaborative discussions with your

> teachers versus just looking at the state achievement data once a year. What we are trying to do is help people understand what the important data [are], because you can sit and look at a bunch of information, but it may not necessarily be the data that you need in order to know what your next step should be.

Steinhauser's executive team was constantly identifying new types of data to guide their work. Gulek worked with deputy superintendent Dominguez and her staff to provide locally created assessments for each of the subject areas across grade levels, starting in kindergarten. The office also developed benchmark assessments for the core subjects to be given every trimester at the elementary school level to measure growth and diagnose areas of weakness. The research office provided detailed, itemized analyses quickly following each test. As Gulek explained, "We provide reports where the teachers can actually pinpoint where the students are not meeting the standard so they know what to reteach and how to adjust their instruction going forward."

To provide more site-specific feedback connected to the district's first strategic goal, the data office organized school walk-throughs. Each school leadership team devised a school-site plan, which identified areas of instruction they wanted to focus on at their school. The elementary, middle and K–8, and high school offices then developed walk-through protocol (see Exhibit 10.2 on the CD). Tailored walk-through teams, comprising curriculum leaders, research specialists, special education and English language learner personnel, and assistant superintendents, would visit school sites to conduct three- to four-hour walk-throughs. Serving as "critical friends," the district personnel provided feedback on the school's specific goals, and they added the data collected to the site's arsenal for use when evaluating next steps.

Whether analyzing results from a written assessment or observational data, Gulek's team constantly worked to ensure they quickly returned good, clean data to the schools. This required the research department to grow from ten to over twenty people in just three years. Even in hard financial times when other department budgets were being cut, Steinhauser felt this investment was necessary. Explaining the importance of immediate feedback, Gulek noted,

> To provide access to the data . . . you have to think about turnaround time. You have to be prompt. Otherwise, people will be resistant to data-driven decision making. If you don't have the data quickly, it can't drive your school culture.

After receiving feedback from school principals and teachers, Gulek's office also realized that data needed to be accessible and simple to use. He worked to develop an online system for data reporting so teachers and principals had access to LBUSD's academic data browser, which works like a cumulative folder online. Teachers could access data and search for and examine groups of similar students, such as all English language learners, in a particular class. This search feature allowed classroom teachers to disaggregate their own data based on their needs. As Gulek described,

> It is completely customized, and all the information is right at their fingertips. Plus, we have a live person to answer all incoming calls to the research office. It doesn't matter if it is early or late in the day, research staff is staggered so any issue can be resolved immediately. It is all about ease of access for the school sites. We are here to serve our customers.

USING DATA TO IMPROVE INSTRUCTION

Full and open access was critical to sustaining improvement, particularly for LBUSD's high-performing schools. As Young, who, due to budget cuts, had a third tagline of *principal* added to her title in 2008, observed,

> When a school is high performing, it is a different challenge to grow. People will say that we are already good and we do everything right. Yes, but as principal I must say, there's still a gap — our students are not 100-percent advanced. There is room to improve. It's no longer what you do overall to raise student achievement; it's what you do individually for the children who are not there yet. You have to ask yourself, what am I going to do differently for this particular child? What am I going to do to maintain the students' growth? What am I going to do if the school slips backwards?

Recognizing the central office's responsibility to hold the adults within the system accountable, Steinhauser and his instructional leaders regularly combed through the data to see what was working well in the district and when schools were struggling. They used these data to design new interventions that were specifically tailored to meet the needs of LBUSD students. One area in need of improvement in 2007 was middle school math instruction. Over the first five years of Steinhauser's tenure, elementary students experienced a sharp increase in math performance, often outperforming the state average in grades two through five. This improvement was attributed to a locally designed math curriculum, called MAP2D, adapted from lessons created by one elementary school teacher. Dominguez and her team partnered with this teacher to learn about his instructional program. After designing the MAP2D curriculum, the math coaches started training other classroom teachers, and the district started piloting the technique in other elementary school classrooms.

What started as a small pilot quickly spread to other schools as teachers and parent groups heard about the incredible results, and the program expanded to over forty-five schools. Schools that were underperforming in math were approached by Steinhauser and strongly encouraged to start using the MAP2D program. "We try to balance a bottom-up and top-down approach. If a school is producing students who perform at high levels, we let them. But if students are struggling, we are going to step in," he explained.

After the results in the elementary schools, Steinhauser piloted MAP2D in the most underperforming middle schools. Exclaimed Steinhauser in the fall of 2007, "Your students are leaving our elementary schools proficient and advanced in math. In one year, we are seeing their proficiency drop, often by 20 points (see Exhibit 10.3 on the CD). Since we know that the MAP2D program works at the elementary level, help us design it to work equally as well for our middle schools." Over the following year, Dominguez and the math content experts met regularly with the pilot schools to examine the data and make changes to the middle school MAP2D curriculum. Use of these continuous feedback loops was a contributing reason to LBUSD's sustained instructional improvements.

MAJOR STUDENT REFORM INITIATIVES

Early in his tenure Steinhauser wanted to target the students who were struggling to finish high school. The data revealed that Latino and African American students had the highest dropout rates. With the overall dropout rate close to 15 percent in 2002, Steinhauser felt it was unacceptable to be losing these students.

To encourage students to return to the district, he started Project TEAM—Teaching and Encouraging Academic Minds, which was led jointly by two young, local counselors—one African American male and one Latino male. Steinhauser hoped students would see these young men as role models for staying in school. The counselors confirmed which "no show" students were actually dropouts, and they began the recovery effort by looking in statewide databases, local adult schools, and city colleges for missing LBUSD students. The counselors would make phone calls and home visits to talk with students and encourage them to continue their education in either LBUSD or one of the district's partners. As a result of Project TEAM's efforts, over 10 percent of students originally identified as "dropouts" have been removed from the district's list.

As the initiative started to see success, Project TEAM needed more counselors. Using funds from a state counseling grant, LBUSD decided to target resources to the district's lowest-performing students instead of reducing the student-counselor ratio for the district overall. Therefore, the district hired counselors to work with at-risk students, those scoring far below the basic level on the state achievement test. Managing two hundred students instead of the average of five hundred students per person, these counselors met with students on a monthly basis to monitor grades and attendance. Through this close working relationship with students and their families, counselors were able to not only discourage students from dropping out of high school but also encourage them to enroll in higher education.

The strategic plan put even greater emphasis on ensuring that all students were college-ready. As the initiative grew to include over thirty counselors at the middle and high school levels, the services they provided grew as well. Using categorical state funding, Project TEAM began holding group counseling sessions, taking the students on field trips, and providing other motivational activities. The support didn't stop upon graduation. The Project TEAM counselors also worked with local colleges and universities to monitor and support the students as they transitioned from high school to college.

The Male Academy

Project TEAM continued to show positive results, but two specific groups of students seemed to be particularly hard to reach—African American and Latino males. These students often failed to graduate, and many succumbed to gangs and criminal activity. Steinhauser wanted to transform these males into campus leaders and positive role models, and he started the LBUSD Male Academy in 2008 as the vehicle to achieve this change.

Tailored to address the physical, social, and emotional issues these young men face, the Male Academy began in six of the district's large comprehensive high schools. Ten leaders were identified at each school by school administration and teachers. These men were struggling academically but were perceived as the campus leaders, often because of their involvement in athletics or gangs. This group of ten students would then choose twenty additional perceived leaders to produce a core group of thirty participating males of color. According to Maggie Webster, assistant superintendent of high schools,

> It has been amazing to see the change in the Male Academy students. One young man said to me, "Just the fact that this district cares about what I can do makes me want to change." This young man had once identified himself as an instigator, causing some of the violence on campus. Now, it's just been a complete turnaround.

The Male Academy gave new hope to students and had an impact on entire campuses by reducing racial tensions and fights. LBUSD, by identifying males who were typically only given attention if suspended or implicated in on-campus violence, saw the results that can come from positive attention. Students connected with other positive male role models, such as the 100 Black Men of Los Angeles, and they participated in a wide variety of culture-building activities, including visits to the Museum of Tolerance, the African American Museum, and the Museum of Latin American Art. The students were shown a life outside of their gang-ridden communities by participating in off-campus, overnight retreats and attending sporting events at the University of Southern California and the University of California, Los Angeles. As one male student noted of such experiences, "I never thought anyone would see me as a leader. It has completely changed the way I see my future."

Developing New District Leaders

While members of Project TEAM and the Male Academies were building leaders in the schools, others were working to strengthen the professional development programs in the district. Because the work of administrators had shifted with the renewed focus on data collection and analysis, professional development also had to shift early on under Steinhauser's leadership. In district-led trainings, administrators and teachers learned how to use the multiple district data systems and support teachers in a data-driven environment.

A few years into the data work, the district began to experience a high turnover of principals due to retirement incentives by the state. Having risen from within the district's ranks, both Steinhauser and Dominguez valued cultivating leadership from within, just as they had been trained by Cohn. As Steinhauser explained the importance of developing a pool of potential leaders, "My goal as a superintendent is that you be two- to three-deep at all levels—ready to step in when a leadership position opens."

With this goal, Steinhauser's staff worked to make principal development a priority. As Kahl recalled,

> We realized the principal's job had changed so much with the use of data. The instructional leadership piece had grown for the principal, but the assistant principal's job hadn't changed much. The [assistant principal] was more concerned with school organization, discipline, and management. There was a huge disconnect between the two positions, and some new principals were struggling. We had to offer more support to ease the transition between the two positions.

Steinhauser and his staff recognized that schools couldn't lose years of momentum when new leaders were hired. Kahl and the professional development staff designed Change of Principal Workshops. These monthly support meetings were a safe place to share expectations and discuss data with the new leaders. Successful principals and central office administrators were assigned as mentors to provide ongoing support, including making school visits to discuss school-site issues. To further bolster this work, the district created performance power standards for administrators to guide their professional development. Continued follow-up proved critical to the transition. According to Kahl,

> When I was a new principal, for example, there wasn't any of this kind of support. I would go to a regular principal's meeting, and they'd start talking about transferring an assignment, let's say. All the principals would know exactly what the superintendent was talking about, the procedures and what was expected. I'm sitting there and I'm like, "Oh no — what are they talking about?" New principals have no way of knowing routine district procedures unless we teach them. This is one of the goals of the Change of Principal Workshops.

Even though this program worked well, Steinhauser wanted to be more proactive and support future leaders even before hiring them as principals. After receiving grant funding from the Broad Foundation in 2007, the district developed a Principal Apprentice Program that allowed future principals each to work side-by-side with a successful school leader as an apprentice for one year. By creating cohorts of future leaders, the district was ensuring that they had a steady stream of educators trained in the "Long Beach way" and ready to take the helm. The "Long Beach way" prioritized promoting from within the district before seeking outside hires. Although this maintained connectedness and consistency, some believed it also tempered radical change.

The district also started an Aspiring Assistant Principal Program to allow teacher leaders, coaches, and other coordinators to step forward and become school leaders. Similar to the Change of Principal Workshops, this program consisted of monthly training meetings that prepared teachers to transition to the position of assistant principal. Workshops on such topics as résumé writing and interviewing skills also supported them in their job search. This was particularly important because LBUSD conducted group interviews for all school leadership positions, with current principals, parents, teachers, and central office administrators as the interviewers.

Academic & Career Success Initiative

Steinhauser wanted to bring the public's focus back to improving instruction for every student, every day. In 2006 the district began a series of committee meetings to set specific academic metrics for the newly passed strategic plan, which only consisted of goals and subgoals without specific targets. The board of education identified this effort as its main academic reform strategy, naming it the Academic & Career Success (ACS) Initiative. To track progress, the ACS committee identified a series of academic growth indicators, such as fifth- and eighth-grade mathematics and English language arts proficiency, as well as the graduation rate. The board of education passed the ACS unanimously on September 11, 2007. This unwavering support was critical for Steinhauser:

> I felt strongly that the initiative had to be board-approved. I feared if the top of our organization did not sanction it, people might not think it is important. We promised to report publicly on our progress, and we do — three times per year at board workshops. Throughout the whole system — the board, the community, and the schools — people know our goals, and the work is directly related to them.

After the ACS's passage, the committee, which comprised a large group of central office administrators, principals, teachers, parents, community members, and students, identified targets for the district to achieve by 2013. Growth targets were based on 2006–2007 baseline data. For example, the committee realized that currently 38 percent of eight-grade students were proficient in English language arts. The ACS committee debated how hard they should push teachers and students by 2013. They questioned, Should we set a target of 50 percent, 60 percent, or 65 percent? In the end, the committee settled on a 2013 target of 55 percent of eighth-graders scoring proficient in English language arts.

BUILDING PARTNERSHIPS INSIDE LONG BEACH AND BEYOND

The CSULB-LBCC Agreements

Collaborative work produced an informal agreement that CSULB and LBCC would work together to ensure Long Beach students had access to higher education. LBUSD students received priority acceptance, and if a student chose to start at LBCC, CSULB would accept the credits earned. The three institutions worked together to set admission standards and reduce remediation, and many Long Beach students entering higher education attended one of the two postsecondary institutions.

Steinhauser formalized the agreement with the local colleges as one way of making higher education an attainable goal for every LBUSD student. On March 20, 2008, the three education institutions signed the College Promise, a ten-year commitment to LBUSD students and their families. As part of this pact, all incoming LBUSD students at LBCC were guaranteed a tuition-free first semester by 2011. Plus, CSULB promised admission to Long Beach students who complete minimum college preparatory requirements or minimum community college transfer requirements. LBUSD also committed to outreach efforts encouraging college completion to Long Beach families, beginning in the sixth grade.

The partnership produced rapid results. After the first year there was a 36 percent increase in the number of Long Beach students attending CSULB. For Steinhauser, this promise was about giving students and their families options:

> CSULB had 74,000 students apply in 2008, but they can only accept about 6,000. The College Promise is all about closing the achievement gap and giving our students access to higher education. Each of our subgroups has made huge gains in the number of students going to college. This is why we developed the partnership. This is why we increased AP access. It's all about gap closures.

The Fresno–Long Beach Learning Partnership

While developing partnerships inside the district, Steinhauser also started working to establish outside partnerships, most notably with Fresno Unified School District. The two districts were similar in size and composition, although LBUSD was performing higher on state tests. Having met at several state events to provide feedback on education issues, Steinhauser and the superintendent of Fresno, Michael Hanson, had begun sharing information in 2006. Soon personnel were traveling from Long Beach to Fresno to lead professional development activities. Fresno reciprocated by helping Long Beach develop the ACS targets approved in late 2007.

Hanson and Steinhauser also began sharing fiscal strategies and brainstormed how their respective districts could use funds differently if state restrictions were relaxed. In 2008 the two districts lobbied the state department of education to pilot a formal learning partnership. The goals of the partnership centered on structured collaboration of best instructional and operational practices. Steinhauser and Hanson asked the state for greater local control over categorical funds with increased accountability for student achievement. In order to maintain the flexibility in spending, both districts committed to meeting specific academic benchmarks that were aligned with the districts' existing goals (such as those of the ACS in Long Beach).

Because Long Beach had shown better student performance, Steinhauser asked for greater flexibility. For instance, the state granted LBUSD more leeway to use the Teaching as a Priority Block Grant (one of the state's many initiatives geared toward improving instruction) for any school, instead of reserving it for only the most underperforming schools.

POLITICAL AND FISCAL TENSION

With partnerships starting to develop outside of LBUSD, some long-standing relationships inside the district became increasingly strained. The union and the board of education were experiencing power struggles as opposing factions fought to gain control. Unhappy with Steinhauser, TALB leadership led a charge to gain control of the district's board of education in the April 2006 election. Out of three TALB-supported candidates running for seats, two were elected, splitting Steinhauser's board support.

In 2007 TALB's leadership was divided over allegations of fiscal mismanagement and controversy that resulted in a takeover by its parent union, the California Teachers Association (CTA). According to an article published in the *Long Beach Press-Telegram,* an audit initiated by CTA determined that the ousted TALB leadership might have spent close to $500,000 financing the 2006 campaign of LBUSD board candidates (Butler, 2008). The audit revealed that an additional $110,000 might have been spent from the union's general funds to finance the campaigns. With these public allegations and no clear direction for its work, the union was frustrated and angered over the politics of its divided leadership.

The union was not the only divided district group. The rift in the district's governing body equally affected teacher and administrator morale. The local media consistently highlighted how local school board member Ellis was rarely showing up for duty, and he frequently missed committee and board meetings (Mehta, 2009). In 2007 Ellis pleaded guilty to drunk-driving charges and was placed on probation. The probation was twice revoked for Ellis's refusal to complete a mandatory three-month alcohol program for first-time offenders. Many parents and community members were distraught over the coverage, fearing it was setting a poor model for students.

In an effort to put the focus back on education, the other board members decided to take action. In December 2007 three board members voted to urge Ellis to resign immediately (Mehta, 2009). The only opposing vote came from fellow TALB-supported candidate Barton. Following the vote and Ellis's refusal to step down, the Long Beach Area Chamber of Commerce announced in a board meeting that it would try to gather enough voter signatures to hold a recall election to remove Ellis from office. After not obtaining enough signatures, the chamber abandoned its efforts in April 2008. However, the board remained divided. When Steinhauser's contract was up for renewal in spring 2008, the vote was 3 to 2, with Ellis and Barton arguing that the district was not progressing as it should. The split board ended with Ellis finally resigning on September 1, 2009 (Butler, 2010).

STATE BUDGET CRISIS

The budget constraints in 2008 and 2009 tremendously affected Steinhauser's leadership. As he explained, "The central office has reduced by over 60 percent. My office has reduced by 50 percent. The research office will reduce by at least 25 percent in 2010." Although personnel positions were cut, productivity remained high. Steinhauser noted, "Despite the cuts, people are working harder than they've ever worked, and the output is actually greater than it has ever been."

Several cuts had to be justified to the school community. He had to eliminate the Principal Apprentice Program and the Aspiring Assistant Principal Program in 2009. Administrators as well as noncertified personnel were reduced at all levels. According to Kahl,

> [Steinhauser] has been very deliberate about not touching the classroom or professional development. He says, "Let's look at everything else; let's look at every other possibility. We're not going to touch this until we have to. This is the core of our work. It is the most important thing."

REFERENCES

Butler, K. (2008, August 8). TALB audit finds questionable political spending: Study shows Long Beach union expended $110,000 more on campaigns than leaders had authorized. *Long Beach Press-Telegram*. Retrieved on April 1, 2010, from www.presstelegram.com/archivesearch.

Butler, K. (2010, January 2). The aughts: Losses, scandals played parts in difficult Long Beach decade. *Long Beach Press-Telegram*. Retrieved on April 1, 2010, from www.presstelegram.com/ci_14113030.

Ellis, M. (2006, January 1). Candidate's forum: Michael Ellis. *Long Beach Press-Telegram*. Retrieved on April 1, 2010, from www.presstelegram.com/search/ci_3430110.

Mehta, S. (2009, September 2). Long Beach school trustees call for special election. *Los Angeles Times*. Retrieved on April 1, 2010, from http://latimesblogs.latimes.com/lanow/2009/09/long-beach-schools-trustees-call-for-special-election-to-fill-spot-vacated-by-controversial-board-me.html.

Building and Sustaining Improvement over Time: The Austin Story

Pascal D. Forgione Jr.

Reading the Long Beach case study reminded me of this Tolstoy line from the first chapter of *Anna Karenina*: "Happy families are all alike; every unhappy family is unhappy in its own way." Not that I believe urban public school districts are unhappy or even hopeless organisms. Quite the opposite: the urban public school district is our most important battleground and our greatest hope for the future of prosperity and democracy in this country. But to make sustained progress in an urban district, it is important to understand the particular context in which each district operates and to learn from the obstacles encountered in one's quest for educational excellence and equity for all students (Cuban, 2010, pp. 10–23).

As clearly described in the accompanying case, the Long Beach Unified School District has been a benchmark urban district in terms of its continuous academic performance and well-deserved recognition, especially the Broad Prize for Urban Education. The Austin Independent School District (AISD) has also demonstrated a positive trajectory of progress on a number of important education indicators over the past decade, including greater percentages of students in every student group passing the new, more rigorous Texas assessment, the Texas Assessment of Knowledge and Skills (TAKS), since its inauguration in 2003 (TEA, 2008); validated strong academic progress that earned a very high ranking of fourth among the thirty-seven big city districts studied (Loveless, 2009); academic performance at the top of the National Assessment of Educational Progress/Trial Urban District Assessment (NAEP/TUDA) results for mathematics, reading, and science (National Assessment Governing Board, 2005, 2007, 2009); strong levels of performance over expectations among NAEP/TUDA districts (National Assessment Governing Board, 2009); and Austin's high international standing exceeding the TIMSS and OECD averages (Phillips, 2008).

THE STRUGGLE TO MAINTAIN

However, unlike Long Beach, AISD has not been able to sustain the strong consistency of high performance across all levels and schools. For example, in 2009 all 78 AISD elementary schools met both federal and state accountability standards—a terrific accomplishment! But at the secondary level, as the accountability metrics continued to rise and more student group cells became active, a number of Austin's 32 middle and high school campuses missed one or both of the accountability standards. And although the district met state accountability standards each of the six years and the federal accountability standards in five of the six years of my tenure, AISD has been challenged by an unevenness in the performance across the 112 campuses for a number of student group cells, notably special education, as are most urban school districts throughout the country.

Now, to understand how we, as educational leaders, can make significant progress in environments facing compounding economic, social, and political challenges, we have to first understand the contexts in which we are operating—including our similarities and differences. Certainly, concentrating diminishing resources on developing, supporting, and retaining high-quality educators is a value that AISD—as well as many other urban districts—shares with Long Beach. At the same time, the fact that Long Beach has enjoyed nearly two decades of totally aligned leadership with board support is difficult to replicate.

The path to Austin's continuous progress has been significantly different from the Long Beach success story. My tenure in Austin began under a very different set of circumstances than what Carl Cohn or Chris Steinhauser encountered in Long Beach (Cuban, 2010, pp. 57–60). When I stepped off the plane in August 1999 to become the seventh Austin superintendent in that decade, I was greeted by a newspaper headline announcing that my new district had been declared unacceptable by the Texas Education Agency due to our bad dropout data submitted to the state. The national bond rating companies had placed us on the "negative watch," and the district had been indicted for test data manipulation. I also found out that, in the middle of this high-technology capital, AISD's information and financial systems were outdated and dysfunctional. I entered a district that had suffered through a decade of chaos and stagnation; experienced high teacher turnover and low employee morale; enjoyed no public trust; and had few systems in place for instruction, information services, or finances. Unlike in Long Beach, we had to begin from scratch, rebuilding the district.

REBUILDING TO SUCCEED

In this way, the Austin experience may be similar to that of many turnaround districts nationally. AISD's performance on numerous fronts had become so dismal that nearly everyone was ready for dramatic change. You know the old saying, "To get out of a hole, the first thing to do is stop digging." To get out of our hole, the first thing we did in Austin was boldly identify our challenges and our failures as a district. There was little ambiguity about how bad the situation was, so even though parents and the community may have lost faith in the school district, they were ready to support real change that made sense. There was a sense of urgency, and that urgency gave us an opening to change things.

Despite its difficulties, Austin had retained a large portion of its middle-class students because many of these students did quite well. The challenge was that Austin's low-income student population was growing dramatically, and these students' performance was dramatically lower than that of more affluent students. When I arrived the district's growth had been holding fairly steady for several years, and the low-income population made up slightly less than half the student population. Over the next ten years student enrollment grew significantly, from seventy-five thousand to eighty-three thousand students, with the largest portion of the growth from lower-income families, many of whom were recent immigrants. By the end of my superintendency in 2009, children in poverty made up nearly two-thirds of the student population. The percentage of English language learners grew from 10 percent in 1999 to 29 percent in my last year. We needed dramatic change to meet the needs of all students in the district.

As the Long Beach case illustrates, you can't build Rome in a day, and a school district can't be turned around in a day. At the same time, parents and students can't wait decades for you to make their schools better. Every student goes through the first eighteen years of his or her life only once. You have to get it right for that individual student as you work to make it right for all students.

To do that, we needed to make continuous progress in a stable environment. If you look at the National Assessment of Educational Progress/Trial Urban District Assessment (NAEP/TUDA) results for Austin, Boston, and Charlotte-Mecklenburg in North Carolina, you see that stability in district leadership has been an asset. I served as superintendent for ten years in Austin. Long Beach, incredibly, is having a leadership continuum of two decades. You need that time to scaffold changes, to build the understanding and engagement of your teachers and your students' families, to stay within and then increase the district's capacity to transform itself, and to put systems in place that will support continuous improvement in the classroom.

PLANNING FOR SUSTAINABILITY

So we embarked on a ten-year process that, in retrospect, looks completely orderly and planned, but in reality amounted to continually figuring out the most logical next step in building AISD into a high-performing district.

Our first step, after defining and prioritizing our major challenges, was to identify and to recruit talent and partners to help us solve the large systemic problems confronting our district. In contrast to the Long Beach approach, it would not have worked to build exclusively from within. AISD in 1999 did not have a strong enough cadre of talented educators ready to lead the change from within. The district had seen many gifted leaders flee to other school districts due to poor leadership in the 1990s. So for several key leadership positions I brought in experts on accountability, technology, human resources, and finance. Our school and academic leaders were, in large part, homegrown, but we created a partnership between these leaders and the Institute for Learning (IFL) at the University of Pittsburgh to completely revamp our approach to teaching and learning and to make it consistent across the district.

Given the fact that our district was indicted for data manipulation and made serious errors in reporting to the state, setting up a new accountability department to scrupulously oversee the accuracy and use of data was essential to rebuild public trust. Our school board agreed to raise taxes three cents immediately in August 1999 so we could put in place trustworthy technology systems that would support the business operations of the district and would bring instructional resources to our schools and classrooms. These were the relatively easy reforms. I knew our greatest challenge would be to reform teaching and learning in our more than five thousand classrooms.

Even more serious as we transitioned to the twenty-first century were the declining academic performance of many of our schools and the large achievement gaps between groups of students. Without stable leadership, this district had no proven system to support increasing student achievement for all students. As I've often said, our district was all *e pluribus* and no *unum*. Our schools were strutting off in different directions because they had had no consistent district leadership for so long and there was a strong culture of individualism. This is one of the major contextual factors, to which Cohn referred in his introductory piece, that distinguishes Austin from Long Beach, where there was a willingness to buy into comprehensive reform strategies and accept district-led initiatives.

The second step was to rebuild our academic system. As the cornerstone, we established the state's Texas Essential Knowledge and Skills (TEKS) standards as our content standards. These standards became our first nonnegotiable—the *unum*. We established the same high standards for all our classrooms. We tied the standards to a set of Instructional Planning Guides (IPGs) that our curriculum leaders, working with our master teachers, had developed. IPGs apply to every subject area and include resources and strategies for our most advanced students as well as for struggling students. This was a radical change in the delivery of instruction for Austin.

Another nonnegotiable was a core belief in an effort-based education system. We teamed with the IFL to devise a professional development program for all our administrators and teachers so that we would have a common language of teaching and learning across the district. Over the course of three years, AISD went from being a Tower of Edu-Babel to a coherent instructional system in which educators were all speaking the same language.

Next, we were becoming data driven, using data to guide instruction and to focus interventions on targeted student needs. This led us to our third step, looking for new systemic solutions to chronic student academic problems. Similar to the Long Beach experience, we were able to start small with some initiatives to address our most egregious problems and to learn from those small steps how to address challenges across elementary campuses, we created a Blueprint Schools initiative that required new campus leadership, significant turnover in faculty to bring in more experienced teachers, and a highly uniform curriculum tied to continuous analysis of student progress. Within three years, these four elementary schools came off the low-performing list and were recognized by the state for their improvement. From this experience, much as in Long Beach, we exported the key lessons we had learned on data-driven teaching to other elementary schools and eventually to our entire district.

With the Blueprint Schools initiative, we combined homegrown talent with outside expertise. I chose a proven campus leader, who had demonstrated success in both an affluent West Side school and in an economically disadvantaged East Side school, to lead this district turnaround effort. She put in place comprehensive systems and tools for improving operations, instruction, and data analysis to put in place our new standards-based and efforts-based methodology. These powerful and productive school-based systems and strategies were then adopted district-wide as a "bottom-up" reform, with support of "top-down" district leadership, when she was promoted to join the central office instructional team as one of two associate superintendents of Austin's seventy-eight elementary schools.

In contrast, to recognize and then change the largely anachronistic cultures of our comprehensive high schools, we required an outside evaluation to help us see what was right in front of our noses: the inability of our high schools to prepare a large number of our students for college. We therefore contracted with the Southern Regional Education Board's High Schools That Work program to give us an in-depth analysis of the state of our high schools that pulled no punches. As a result, our blemishes and shortcomings were laid out for all to see. This provided the impetus for a district-wide process of high school redesign, with support from the Bill & Melinda Gates Foundation and help from the Stanford University School Redesign Network, First Things First, the New Tech foundation, High Schools That Work, Educators for Social Responsibility, the Asia Society, and West Ed. Our communities are very much attached to their particular high school traditions. We could not have begun to transform our high schools without this external assessment and the external models we adapted for use in Austin (see Cuban, 2010, pp. 85–118).

Once you get new systems and practices in place, how do you know you are making real progress? Since the 1990s, Texas has had a fairly thorough accountability system, which it reorganized for greater rigor in 2003 and is in the process of ramping up again. This provides one measure of monitoring progress. When I came to AISD, we were one of the lowest performers among the large urban Texas districts. By 2009 we were one of the highest performers. But how do you gauge your progress in a larger context—in the national and international arenas?

As a fourth step, we wanted to measure the results of our reforms against the gold standard. People become skeptical of district growth on state tests only. Beginning in 2005, at my urging, the AISD board agreed voluntarily to join the NAEP/TUDA program. We had no idea how AISD would measure up, but we knew that if we ranked low among the urban districts nationally, we would need to set new targets. And if we ranked high, we would receive important external validation to bolster our own sense of progress. In the recently released 2009 mathematics results for grades 4 and 8, Austin students scored at or above the national averages. In grade 8 mathematics, Austin was one of only two TUDA, a special assessment designed to explore the feasibility of using NAEP to report public school students' performance at the district level, districts to demonstrate statistically significant progress over 2007 results; our subgroups ranked at or near the top in performance; and, remarkably, 39 percent of Austin students scored at the proficient level as compared to 33 percent nationally (National Assessment Governing Board, 2009). Building such independent confirmations of a district's productivity is one area in which I believe Long Beach should take the next step, as Austin did in joining the NAEP/TUDA program.

With systems in place and with transformation under way at all levels, the final step in this ten-year journey was to build an internal leadership succession model and to create incentive mechanisms that would sustain the pace of continuous improvement. First, this meant developing and retaining outstanding teachers and principals across the district. To do this we established a leadership academy to train assistant principals throughout the school year so they will be ready to step into school leadership roles when those open up. We not only worked with them on their understanding of systems and the skill sets they would need to operate a campus but also helped them build their capacity as teaching and learning leaders with expertise in the academic and assessment systems being implemented district-wide. And second, unlike Long Beach, AISD has built a strategic compensation and performance pay system for teachers and principals that includes significant financial incentives for increasing student performance. We developed and implemented this in partnership with our teachers organizations and have piloted it in a small set of schools, increasing that number each year. This is one of the most sophisticated systems for compensating successful educators in the country, and it is already reaping results by providing needed incentives for retaining our best educators, especially on our neediest campuses (Lussier & Forgione, 2010).

As Cohn says, transforming an urban school district is both simple and complex. Our path—defining challenges, putting working systems in place, creating new solutions for chronic problems, measuring ourselves against the best, and developing ongoing leadership and incentive systems to sustain change—may not work for all school districts. But it represents a progression that teachers and the public can understand and believe in. That is the key to sustaining change over the long haul.

REFERENCES

Cuban, L. (2010). *As good as it gets: What school reform brought to Austin.* Cambridge, MA: Harvard University Press.

Henig, J. R. (2009). Mayoral control: What we can and cannot learn from other cities. In J. P. Viterotti (Ed.), *When mayors take charge: School governance in the city* (pp. 19–45). Washington DC: Brookings Institution Press.

Loveless, T. (2009, January). *How well are American students learning?* (2008 Brown Center Report on American Education No. 10). Washington DC: Brookings Institution.

Lussier, D., & Forgione, P. D., Jr. (2010). Supporting and rewarding accomplished teaching: Insights from Austin, Texas. *Theory into Practice, 49*(3), 233–242.

National Assessment Governing Board (2009, Fall). *National Assessment of Educational Progress/Trial Urban District Assessment results for 2005, 2007 and 2009 in mathematics, reading and science for grades 4 and 8.* Washington DC: U.S. Department of Education.

Phillips, G. (2008, October). *NAEP-TIMSS linking study.* Washington DC: American Institute of Research.

Texas Education Agency (TEA). (2008, Fall). *Texas Assessment of Knowledge and Skills (TAKS) results: 2003–2008.* Austin, TX.

CHAPTER 11

Exiting the Superintendency

Laura Kelley

Four months into my fourth year of teaching, I heard an ominous voice, "Ms. Kelley, please report to the principal's office." After some mumbled apologies and explanations about being short staffed, my principal informed me I would no longer be teaching first grade. In just forty-eight hours, I would be a third-grade teacher on another floor in another wing of the building, with a completely different schedule. My career as a first-grade teacher in Washington, DC, Public Schools was over, with little time to prepare my exit.

Explaining the transition to a roomful of teary six-year-olds, I reassured them their next teacher would care about them just as much as I did. I encouraged them to continue reading and creating their own books. We hugged and had some quiet time and I answered questions about what would happen next. "Who will be our teacher?" "Why are you leaving us?" "Can we still visit you and call you?"

Determined to make this transition as momentous as the end of every other school year, I went to the store and bought twenty-five votive candles and began writing cards to every student. I wished them well and reviewed how far they had come in our time together, reminding them of their learning goals for the year. At the end of my last day, we had a candle-lighting ceremony and each lit our candles from the large center pillar, telling each other what we learned together and what we hoped the future would bring. "I hope my next teacher shakes my hand every morning like Ms. Kelley." "I hope I can read *Frog and Toad* by the end of the year." "I hope my next teacher isn't mean."

We simply did the best we could in a situation in which we felt little control but were resolute in making the most of the transition. I left them with many questions. I could see the fear and worry in some of their eyes and wondered, "Will all my hard work be wasted?"

All superintendencies, like every school year, must come to an end—although some come to a more abrupt end than others. What makes a superintendent's exit such a challenge is the loss experienced with any ending, compounded by the needs and feelings of tens (and sometimes hundreds) of thousands of children and adults as they transition from one leader's vision and ways of leading to another leadership approach. Like entry, a superintendent's exit from a district can help set a tone for embracing change, rebelling against it, or abstaining and passively withdrawing or even exiting a system altogether.

The demands of the urban superintendency are staggering, and there is virtually no way to please everyone at once. The position's personal and professional risks abound, and with the increased responsibility and salary come an exponential increase in exposure to criticism. Perhaps the most critical review of a superintendent's legacy and tenure will come as she leaves a district. In looking back, it is only natural for a superintendent and her stakeholders, including board members, community members, principals and district staff, teachers, and students to weigh the value of her leadership in the city. A tumultuous exit can taint the good work of several years of reform. By designing a conscientious exit, a superintendent can set the stage for new leadership to flourish.

Over thirty superintendents and as many as seventy-five board members, teachers, principals, central office personnel, and union leaders shared their perspectives about the process of a superintendent's exit. The pros and cons of announced versus unannounced, abrupt versus planned, mutual versus one-sided departures were discussed in depth. Based on the experiences of these various urban school leaders, our best advice in regard to exit is presented here.

THE RIGHT LEADER, IN THE RIGHT PLACE, AT THE RIGHT TIME

Quality search consultants will advise you that you "need a good fit" to have a successful superintendency because superintendents are hired for various reasons and roles. You might get hired to be a turnaround specialist, taking apart what hasn't and doesn't work and putting in place new structures to benefit all students. You could be hired for your perceived ability to sustain initiatives and maintain steady improvement. Other districts might recruit you to rebuild systems that years of corruption, neglect, or unstable leadership have decimated. Regardless of the reasons, a district might start looking for a new leader at any point along the way to take it to the next level of work or finish what you have started, resulting in turnover and transition.

As mentioned in the chapter on entry, the average tenure of urban superintendents is just three-and-a-half years, while half of those serving on boards of education report a tenure of four years or less (CGCS, 2008). All of the superintendents we interviewed agreed that this is not really enough time to implement lasting change. A synthesis of evidence across clinical studies found that longevity of tenure has a positive effect on academic achievement (Marzano, 2007). Most superintendents agree that at least five to seven years are needed to establish systemic improvement and make reform more permanent. Most of the case studies in this book defy the average, with six of the eight superintendents staying for four or more years in at least one of their superintendencies. Chris Steinhauser in Long Beach and Beverly Hall in Atlanta, with nine and twelve years, respectively, certainly pull the average up. Part of what makes these two superintendents unique is that they have managed to adapt over time, morphing into what their districts needed throughout their leadership. Still, boards of education and district staff may begin to wonder what, and who, will come next.

KNOW WHEN TO FOLD 'EM

The decision to leave when popular and beloved (if there is such a state in the superintendency) or stay and push for further reform is difficult at best. Explained a four-time superintendent,

> I've always said that the problem with most superintendents is that they don't know when to leave. They overstay their welcome. I always tried to leave when they still wanted me to stay. Knowing when to leave is a big part of the exit process, if you can have that luxury.

The message is clear: this work never ends. You never "finish" in this job of superintendent. Much like in teaching, the reality is that anybody who thinks he's ever going to finish is fooling himself, because he's never going to be completely done. There's always more he needs to do. However, knowing when to walk away may be savvy, but it's something many urban superintendents are criticized for in the press. "Careerists" and "uncommitted" are words sometimes used to describe leaders who leave of their own volition.

> A third-time superintendent is known affectionately as *the Builder*. In his fast-growing district he built on average ten schools a year. Cutting ribbons, greeting eager families, and working hand-in-hand with his city's mayor became his specialty. When the district's growth spurt ended and an impending budget crisis loomed ahead, he reevaluated his tenure. Turning to his trusted assistant who had stayed by his side through his three superintendencies, he asked, "I've been here for five great years. But will I enjoy the same latitude if I have to cut instead of expand? Is it time to get out while the gettin' is good?"

Superintendents, policymakers, and board members alike think the position has become too political. As the chief instructional leaders of districts, superintendents should be hired for their ability to improve educational outcomes for students. However, many superintendents will say they are more likely to be held accountable for financial or management problems. "Keep in mind," reminded a forty-year veteran African American female superintendent, "Most superintendents don't get fired for instructional issues. They get fired for political issues."

Staying ahead of the politics is a strategy many urban superintendents, who tend to have a following in an intense media spotlight, use to allow other district leaders to concentrate on the business of teaching and learning. Those who don't feel the winds of change or see the warning signs of diminishing support are often surprised by abrupt departures when either political or community support crumbles or leadership skills no longer match district needs. Veteran superintendents, however, advise their colleagues to keep their pulse on district, board, and community desires, warning "the board that hires is not the board that fires you." Notes one practiced superintendent, "I'm amazed how some superintendents say they didn't see it coming. Maybe they mistook the light at the end of the tunnel for being an out rather than a train coming at them."

LOVE'S LABOUR'S LOST

One of the most neglected aspects of exit is the domain of emotions. The emotional realities of loss are quite real, for the superintendent and the district. Whether you choose to leave or your board chooses for you, the emotional toll exit takes on the superintendent or the district is akin to the stages of grief. Anger, denial, depression, bargaining, and acceptance are all typical reactions to loss. In the case of Beverly Hall in Atlanta Public Schools, chins quiver and eyes glance down whenever discussion of "Who and what come next?" begins. Hargreaves (2009) talks about the ego involved in leadership succession, describing how few superintendents might want to step out of the limelight—even the critical spotlight—to give up their position and authority.

Superintendents have a responsibility to the districts they lead, even if they are leaving on unpleasant or contentious terms. It's balancing the multiple responsibilities you have to your district, your family, and yourself that elicits challenging and often conflicting emotions about exiting. The public and private critique and consideration can be just as divergent. Recalls one superintendent,

> It's interesting when people get hurt. Their reactions are mixed. Some of them say, "Well you know, we're really going to miss you and sorry you have to leave." Other people become pretty nasty and say, "You just used us, and you're a carpetbagger."

Other people might view your exit as a great opportunity for you but feelings of loss are still left behind.

WHEN TO ANNOUNCE?

"*Watch how you say good-bye, because you never know when you will have to say hello again.*"

This advice a mother shares with her daughter serves any superintendent well. You should always leave a district with the care you take to enter it. Some superintendents suggest leaving as soon as you announce to spare you and your staff the heartache and emotions of impending grief. Others advise announcing your exit well in advance of your actual departure to allow the district to prepare itself for transition. The pitfall of the early announcement, however, is the "lame duck syndrome," whereby it is both easier to implement changes because the danger of losing political support is less of a concern and more difficult to take action if district leadership is concerned about maintaining stability before a successor implements new reform. A longtime superintendent who announced his retirement eighteen months in advance describes his experience during his last year:

> I announced my leaving to allow the district to do the succession planning that needed to take place, which I knew would take a certain amount of time, but it took longer than I would have preferred. It made my last year tougher because when you announce you're leaving, you become increasingly invisible inside the organization. People pay less attention to you because they're looking through you to the next person, because they know you're not going to be there for long. Why should they invest more in you? Their long-term interest is who's coming next, not who's leaving.

Another district leader said the following:

> I saw leaving as an opportunity to put some things in place that I couldn't fix while I was staying because I didn't have to worry about marshalling my assets at that point and saving them. It helped the next person, too, to have fewer reforms to push.

INTERNAL OR EXTERNAL SUCCESSION?

To combat the disruption that invariably accompanies change, some districts opt to promote from within, selecting succeeding superintendents who are familiar with and have been a part of the momentum that predates exit. In Richmond Public Schools in Virginia, Yvonne Brandon was the next deputy to have been promoted to the superintendency, just as Deborah Jewell-Sherman was before her. The consistency of vision and execution brings stability to what was a once flagging school system, and Brandon's work of deepening the impact of the reforms, such as Charting the Course, that she helped implement was welcomed by district staff. Fear of an outsider coming in to change the way the system had learned to operate paralyzed many, leaving them in a "wait-and-see" mode. Now, Brandon not only is building upon the success she and Jewell-Sherman began but also is busily sharing district achievements, concentrating on a public relations campaign that few others could sell so well.

Although stability and change are not mutually exclusive, some school boards seek revolutionary outside leaders who will enter a district and cause the very disruption Richmond has tried to avoid. Rudy Crew was hired in New York City, and then again in Miami, in part to dismantle the corruption and lack of focus that existed in both cities for decades. Both positions return us to the idea of the right fit. Both Crew and the respective school boards had to ask themselves, "Is this a place I want to work? Do my skills fit what they need?" Crew was hired to come in and do exactly what he accomplished: disassemble large bureaucracies riddled with dishonest politics, reset the systems to improve instruction, and rebuild districts with new foundations for seeking achievement. His shaking up of systems, along with his firm beliefs about what is best for all children, inevitably rubbed some members of the community and school boards the wrong way. His abrupt departures may have been for the same reason he was hired: he dramatically upset the status quo.

PROACTIVE INSTEAD OF REACTIVE

Succession planning is a concept little practiced in the field of education. Leadership stability expert Hargreaves (2009, p. 10) sums it up best when he says, "Everything in K–12 education is instant, short-term, quick fix. As such, little attention is paid to long-term planning and even less to leadership succession or stability." The shift from replacement planning to succession planning requires a district to move from finding a backup to fill the superintendent box on an organizational chart to a more proactive stance of grooming talent for the future.

Whether a superintendent leaves suddenly to pursue another opportunity, she retires early, or the board opts to fire her in a hurry, her exit will often take the school district by surprise.

Warming Up the Bench: The Case for Distributed Leadership

Leadership works best when it is shared throughout a system and interconnected, rather than concentrated within a few individuals (or even one person). As Hargreaves (2009) suggests, however, this kind of distributed leadership paradigm can only really exist when the superintendent is confident and secure. One such superintendent makes a practice of hiring people who have different skill sets and bring something he doesn't to the leadership table:

> My feeling is you always groom people to be able to take your place. I'm always looking for people who could replace me. I always encourage you to hire people who are smarter than you because they add value to an organization.

Carl Cohn and Chris Steinhauser's approach to bench development has been in place for almost twenty years, and thus far it is serving Long Beach

Unified School District (LBUSD) well. The philosophy of preparing future leaders *before* they are needed is an unrealized dream of many urban districts. Recent budget cuts have forced many central office employees to return to school-level positions while retaining their central office responsibilities, expanding the depth of skills across LBUSD staff. If any one of these well-developed leaders leaves the district, there are other qualified leaders to step up or fill in, sustaining the momentum of district improvement.

Our best advice is to hire people who are committed not only to you and your vision as superintendent but also to the district. Understanding that the district is bigger than any one person is critical—for the superintendent, board, and district staff. "I think it's sometimes healthy for superintendents to miss meetings and have some of their people step up," explains a five-year superintendent. "One, it lets the board appreciate you a lot more as a superintendent. Second, it gives other people leadership. No organization should have one leader. I'm a leader of leaders, but there are other leaders who could step up."

The Need for Succession Planning: Leaving a Legacy

Former superintendent and president of the Center for Reform of School Systems Donald McAdams (2007) touts the importance of succession planning, claiming that the superintendent "is honor bound to act in the best interest of the school district, and it is in the district's best interest to be spared the lost momentum of a temporary office holder or an abrupt change of direction." As one superintendent describes her thoughts on the issue,

> I've invested a lot of time and energy into my work here. The least I can do is try to leave it so it at least has a chance of continuing. If I leave in such a dramatic fashion that that's not possible, then it's going to undo everything I've worked so hard to make happen. Wrapping it up and tying up loose ends is important.

According to the District Management Council (2008), succession planning should present an opportunity, not a crisis, to develop a cadre of leaders who can execute a district's goals. Few events are more disruptive to a school district than the turnover of superintendents, particularly when district priorities shift with new leadership. Almost unfailingly, any time a district hires a new superintendent, reform tends to "start over," with the new leader bringing her ideas and plans, eager to put her name on reform.

Seasoned superintendents understand this tendency to begin anew. As one experienced superintendent reflects on the realization that legacies go beyond one's name,

> I always viewed that my legacy would be in the people I left behind, not in the programs I created as a superintendent, which would be quickly undone by the next person. What you put into place programmatically is not often going to last much past you, but what you leave in the hearts of people will last for a long time.

Although the job is difficult and the pressures sometimes too great to bear, how and when you decide to leave your superintendency may determine the fate of your students, your reform work, and your future career as a district leader. What legacy will you leave in the hearts and minds of your communities?

REFERENCES

Council of the Great City Schools (CGCS). (2008). Urban school superintendents: Characteristics, tenure, and salary: Sixth survey and report. *Urban Indicator*. Retrieved April 5, 2010, from www.cgcs.org/Pubs/Urban_Indicator_08–09.pdf.

District Management Council. (2008). Succession planning for urban school districts: An introduction. *The District Management Council: Strategic advice and implementation support*. Retrieved April 30, 2010, from www.dmcouncil.org/library/management-briefs/35-succession-planning-for-public-school-districts-an-introduction.

Hargreaves, A. (2009, December 1). Leadership succession and sustainable improvement: promoting stability by distributing duties, networking across district lines and professional coaching of administrator newcomers. *Free Library*. Retrieved May 1, 2010, from www.aasa.org/SchoolAdministratorArticle.aspx?id=10134.

Marzano, R. J. (2007, March 1). The primacy of superintendent leadership: The authors' new research finds a strong connection between the work of the district CEO and student achievement. *Free Library*. Retrieved April 30, 2010, from www.aasa.org/SchoolAdministratorArticle.aspx?id=7074.

McAdams, D. R. (2007, January). Planning for your own succession. *School Administrator*. www.aasa.org/SchoolAdministratorArticle.aspx?id=7334.

EPILOGUE

Demography Is Not Destiny!

Deborah Jewell-Sherman

Long ago for some, and certainly by the 1983 release of *A Nation at Risk,* committed practitioners on the front line and determined researchers in the academy acknowledged two critical facts about the pervasive and insidious achievement gaps among subgroups of this country's youth: first, that the subpar education and the concomitant abysmal achievement levels of too many urban youth imperiled the continued preeminence of the United States on the global stage; and second, that transformational leadership was required to radically change the teaching and learning landscape so that demography would not continue to be destiny for generations of inner-city students, especially African Americans and Latinos.

The rise of individual leaders who smashed their "glass ceilings" and the subsequent successes they demonstrated had been singular, relatively unique occurrences. Groundbreaking individuals, such as Floretta McKenzie in Washington, DC, Richard Greene in New York City, Connie Clayton in Philadelphia, and Ramon Cortines in San Francisco, blazed new pathways for others to follow as they assumed the leadership of the nation's major cities, often as the first people of their genders or ethnicities to do so. Most followed a traditional career trajectory to the superintendency, and within their districts they effectively used their deep community ties as ballasts to sustain some measure of instructional coherence in spite of the divergent agendas that competing stakeholders continuously fostered. Their work within multifocused and misaligned school districts and with municipalities and governance structures that appeared impervious to change made the work of improving teaching and learning difficult at best and not the central goal it needed to be. Too frequently, superintendents of their era had to spend the preponderance of their time on the managerial and political dimensions of leading their urban districts, with the instructional agenda often viewed not as the central element of the work but rather as a by-product of focusing on the priorities of the adults and businesses who worked for and within the school community.

Disillusioned with the state of affairs and determined to increase the number and caliber of well-prepared, committed leaders, visionaries from the worlds of practice, research, and policy convened at the Harvard Graduate School of Education (HGSE), where they communed, collaborated, and designed the Urban Superintendents Program (USP). Implicit in its core mission and central to the preparation of its leaders was the belief that good teaching was the birthright of every child, in every classroom, in every school, and in every district across the country. Further, and certainly most radical for the time, the framers of this leadership program decided on and institutionalized a commitment to seeking stellar leadership outside the traditional boundaries of gender, race, privilege, and connections. Rather, they determined that women, people of color, and young, emerging leaders could be "infused with the notion that they were being groomed to reform the world." They believed that such educators—so frequently overlooked, discounted, and dismissed—could and would become accomplished assets rather than anomalies as they prepared to be superintendents, and in so doing transform America's urban educational core.

Twenty years after its inception, USP, in concert with mentors and partners across the nation, has produced twenty cohorts that have formed a means of advancement that is decidedly different in its composition from the proverbial "good old boys' networks" of the past. USP has instead been the springboard for legions of educational leaders who have each completed rigorous coursework, an internship embedded at the superintendent level, and a dissertation aimed at melding the discipline of research with the realities of practice. These transformational leaders are deeply dissatisfied with the current state of affairs in the public education sector. Yet in large, mid-size, and small districts—whether under the mantle of elected or mayor-appointed school boards—innovative and committed leaders have used their strong USP preparation to challenge the internal and external status quo and lead cadres of fellow educators in the pursuit of excellence as defined by significant improvement in teaching, in learning, and, especially, in the achievement of the students under their watch. In so doing, they have created new networks based on the aspirations and achievement of students, which are central to the critical work of reform.

Although other organizational structures have emerged and are showing varied levels of successful implementation, scale-up, and promise, USP leaders primarily have promulgated and vigilantly pursued change from within the districts they lead. Is the resistance one faces when transforming obsolete structures and systems frustrating? Frequently. And is the pace of changing the hearts, minds, and actions of recalcitrant special interest groups demoralizing at times? Definitely. Yet, is the work of leading the learning of teachers, staff, and communities to enhance the educational and life outcomes for students worthy of the sacrifice and effort? Absolutely! The undergirding pillars of the USP framework—equity, collaboration, policy and best practices, and accountability and responsibility—have prepared and empowered a continuing stream of leaders to stay within the existing system and fortified them to radically transform from within the educational policies and practices that are underserving America's children. When these leaders are asked why they have stayed on the battlefield and sought to bring about radical changes from within school districts, they clearly convey that it is because this is where the preponderance of the nation's urban youth, by some accounts as much as 97 percent, are being and will be educated.

For these leaders, simply giving vent to their deep anger at the inequities they've witnessed firsthand and leaving the urban core to its own demise is tantamount to giving up and walking away from the majority of urban students. So whether in Philadelphia, Austin, Baltimore, Albuquerque, San Francisco, Seattle, or numerous cities in between, USP-prepared leaders are adamant that change must and will occur, and equally emphatic that under their watch, different outcomes must and will ensue. These leaders view the superintendency as pivotal to improving school districts in America's cities, and their fight and commitment are to bring about exponential, radical, and sustainable improvements for the many, not the few.

Clearly there is not just one way to prepare twenty-first-century leaders to meet the challenge of bringing about equity in opportunity and excellence in outcomes for the students in urban schools. The work is so difficult, complex, and multifaceted that it will take the combined efforts of those within and outside of the public education sector to bring about the change in outcomes all seek. What makes USP worthy of analysis and emulation is its large number of successful participants, who include over one hundred graduates in leadership positions across the country and in complementary education fields; the diversity in gender and ethnicity these graduates portray; and the sheer scope of influence USP's graduates have had and are having on the sector.

In an era when so many quest for substantial reform of America's public schooling, and as HGSE embarks on a new educational leadership degree (EDLD) program, that will seek to build on the legacy and expand the impact of the graduate school, it is most appropriate to examine how USP, steeped in both the richness of the HGSE tradition of scholarship and the complexity and ambiguities of the world of practice, prepared so many to be more than singletons or "outliers." In addition, it will prove illuminating and useful to highlight those elements that may help all leadership programs that continue in its wake ensure they are able to prepare legions of successful leaders. For it will be such "outliers" who will daily leverage their preparation and pursue equity and excellence in teaching and learning as the norm for all the learners under their span of influence and leadership, who will multiply the networks and opportunities needed to meet the needs of the "whole child," and who ultimately will be instrumental in bringing about the change we all espouse. They will be joining other educational leaders who have demonstrated extraordinary levels of success, as indicated by the impact they have made on the sector and as measured by the exponential improvements in beliefs, practices, systems, and outcomes for today's students.

But how does an individual leader, let alone cadres of such leaders, develop the knowledge, abilities, courage, resilience, determination, and other skills, continuously improved and used in tandem, to achieve success on systemic levels? What are the elements that preparatory programs must incorporate to take ordinary beings—aspiring leaders certainly imbued with high levels of intellect, commitment, and compassion—and instill in them the ability to accomplish extraordinary things on behalf of America's urban children in their care, and in so doing fulfill the deepest hopes and dreams of these children's families?

All too frequently in the realm of so-called "enlightened" twentieth-century research, policy, and practice, those viewed as aspiring leaders have been culled from one gender, selected networks, and upper socio-economic tracks. Leaders not fitting this standard profile who have surmounted the considerable obstacles in their paths to success have been attributed with unnatural, innate abilities; deemed to possess far-reaching ambition; and viewed as driven by an all-consuming, superhuman effort—thus demonstrating that they merit what they've achieved. Were this potential pool, similar to W.E.B. DuBois's "talented tenth," the only source from which to secure and provide the transformational leaders needed for the education sector, the limitations on what is possible would be eerily finite, and from my perspective the future for change in public schools would indeed be bleak.

In Malcolm Gladwell's book *Outliers* (2008), he explores how individual leaders from very different spheres have been able to demonstrate stellar levels of success. Although some view success as the outcome of meritocracy, Gladwell notes that opportunity is a strong variable determining who will excel in their chosen fields. He further cites the culture and legacy of individual leaders as powerful predictors of success. To prevent demography from being destiny for those who lead, as well as for those whom they eventually lead, Gladwell stresses that there must be an equally powerful intervention. USP, in an effort to be that powerful intervention, was designed to significantly increase the number of outliers by expanding the pool of highly qualified superintendents and by giving these aspiring leaders the opportunity to learn to be experts. Therefore, I believe that Gladwell's analysis and his framework for what it takes for individuals to become exceptionally successful can be used to highlight and examine critical aspects of the program.

Most relevant to the preparation of urban superintendents are Gladwell's beliefs that outliers who become exceptionally successful individuals (1) have been placed in environments in which their talents are nourished; (2) have had to work very diligently to become experts; and (3) have gained from the synergistic benefits derived from cohort learning and working collaboratively with individuals who complement their skills and assist them in reaching their mutual goals. The USP addresses these beliefs in two significant ways, which I describe as "the chosen" and "the time."

THE CHOSEN

Gladwell describes the "Matthew Effect," where the rich get richer and the poor get poorer, as the process through which those perceived as being most talented and having the greatest promise are cultivated for greatness. Through the process of "selection, streaming and differentiated experiences" (Gladwell, 2008, p. 25), those perceived as exceptional are given advantages that promulgate success. The USP journey simulates the process of "accumulative advantage" bestowed on others by familial, cultural, societal, and economic privilege by providing opportunities in the following ways:

1. Selection—USP focuses on increasing the number of women, people of color, and individuals on differentiated career pathways, thus giving a head start to those most frequently excluded from leadership opportunities. From the onset, USP has viewed this diverse pool as having the critical abilities in abundance to be successful when given the opportunity to compete and lead.

2. Streaming—USP separates each year's students into a distinct cohort that exists within and among all of the doctoral students. Through scale-ups and simulations, leaders learn to interact as members of teams as they envision leading change in the sector. Throughout the USP journey, leaders come to understand that they have the tremendous opportunity, obligation, and responsibility both to collaborate as they intervene and to lead the learning in their districts by promoting new beliefs, opportunities, instruction, supports, and accountability systems that will have a positive impact on America's youth, especially those most disadvantaged.
3. Differentiated experiences—USP ensures that its cohorts take the most rigorous HGSE courses and modules, which offer training in leadership building blocks, with emphasis on instructional leadership. This work is undergirded by a yearlong Professional Seminar; coaching in visioning, speaking, and adult development; and a mentor-mentee relationship with an urban superintendent through a six-month internship. With a clear focus on practice, policy, and research, students complete the program with strong practical knowledge, so that they have the savvy to be effective change agents.

THE TIME

Gladwell defines the "10,000-Hour Rule,"(2008, p. 40) another aspect of opportunity, as the extraordinary amount of time that exceptionally successful people spend developing and enhancing their skills and abilities. He contends that no true outlier can be successful without putting in the time to become excellent at what she endeavors to do. In like fashion, USP has given each of its aspiring leaders the opportunities to learn *how* to be an expert in a number of ways.

The first opportunity is admittance. Harvard University was not within the lexicon or realm of possibilities discussed with most USP students during their formative years. To the contrary, many of the men and women who have sought this opportunity were the first in their families to have graduated from college. As such, the pursuit of doctoral studies at one of the most prestigious universities in the world was not within the set of expressed expectations for most USP students. When USP cast the net of opportunity in waters not usually charted, men and especially women and people of color dared dream that they, too, could navigate and learn along Appian Way on HGSE's main campus and leave with the requisite wisdom about leadership and organizational change, the certitude about the needs of the public education sector, and the moral courage to lead while continuing to learn.

The second opportunity is the financial support that has made the costs of leaving one's mid-career position to become a student bearable, even for those with families and children. The third opportunity is the collaboration and networking among HGSE faculty, professors from other graduate schools within and outside the university, nationally recognized superintendents, and sector leaders—in concert with the USP directors—so that student leaders cans explore and amalgamate their rich and relevant research when embarking on systemic reform as superintendents. The fourth opportunity is the elongated school year and the Professional Seminar, in which students continuously demonstrate a burgeoning synthesis of their prior experiences with new learning in the areas of practice, research, and policy through simulated solutions to real-world education sector challenges.

The fifth opportunity is the internship. This intense, six-month experience provides each student with mentorship by a superintendent leading a complex, challenging urban district. Students frequently intern within some of the nation's largest urban districts. All students are afforded a three-pronged experience that gives them a unique learning perch from which to learn about, test, and demonstrate leadership at scale. At first, interns shadow the superintendent, viewing the work of leading and transforming an entire urban district from the vantage point of the district leader. For six to eight weeks, interns are with their mentor superintendents through almost every interaction. There are multiple opportunities for the intern to debrief with the mentor superintendent about decisions involving instructional programs, political strategies, policies, management, and other leadership dimensions. From such unlimited access interns gain not only the experience of observing superintendents as they guide learning but also insights into the thinking that accompanies the decisions superintendents must make, ranging from the critical to the mundane. This gives the intern a firsthand perspective on the varied levers a superintendent uses to bring about change, as well as an understanding of the complexities inherent in system-level leadership. The final phase is the change project, which has system-level impact and is mutually determined by the superintendent and intern, and which the intern leads.

Through their previous experiences, these five opportunities, and subsequent leadership positions they hold prior to assuming superintendencies, USP participants meet or exceed the ten thousand hours Gladwell cites as a prerequisite for the level of success that qualifies one to be considered an "outlier."

CLOSING

Visionary leaders believe that "only those who can see the invisible can do the impossible." Many perceive the transformation of America's urban school districts as nigh unto unachievable; yet USP has prepared its graduates to tackle this impossibility on a daily basis. In teaching leaders to see urban districts as they must be, USP has prepared superintendents to shift the balance of power away from those with interests at variance with what students need, deserve, and must have to be successful. Participants have learned how to demand respect for child-centered agendas as they portray and articulate vivid aspirations, negotiate with those in positions of power, network with multiple stakeholders, envision bold and scaffolded strategic planning, and demonstrate moral courage.

In addition, USP has challenged participants to be leaders who will fight for those students who daily endure the crucibles of miseducation, poverty, and hopelessness. USP leaders do so by thwarting those within and outside of their districts who too frequently condemn urban youth to failure by depicting their futures within the confines of low expectations; by painting their horizons with strokes of benign neglect; and by castigating them, their parents, and their communities for all that they are not. Instead, USP has instilled in its leaders the "will to win." In the fight to transform the learning landscape for urban youth so that demography no longer determines destiny, they seek to win by outsmarting, outworking, strategic planning, and networking, and, if necessary, through intimidating. These leaders don't view improving educational outcomes as intellectual exercises for their district data points; rather, outcomes are deeply etched with the faces of thousands of students.

It has been said that educational leaders, like teachers, affect eternity, and that they can never tell where their influence will end. Certainly those who envisioned USP, such as Robert S. Peterkin and Patricia Graham, more than twenty years ago believed this to be true. Those involved in future preparatory programs must similarly recognize that their larger mission is to ensure that leaders are well prepared to improve educational outcomes for America's children. The legacy of USP will continue to be the work done by its graduates as they endeavor to shape a better future for the youth, families, and communities that make up this nation's urban core. In assuming the mantles of leadership, USP leaders will continue to work with every entity in the public education sector to defy demography and to chart a different destiny for *all* the students under their watch.

REFERENCE

Gladwell, M. (2008). *Outliers: The story of success.* New York: Little, Brown.

ABOUT THE AUTHORS AND SUBJECTS OF THE CASE STUDIES

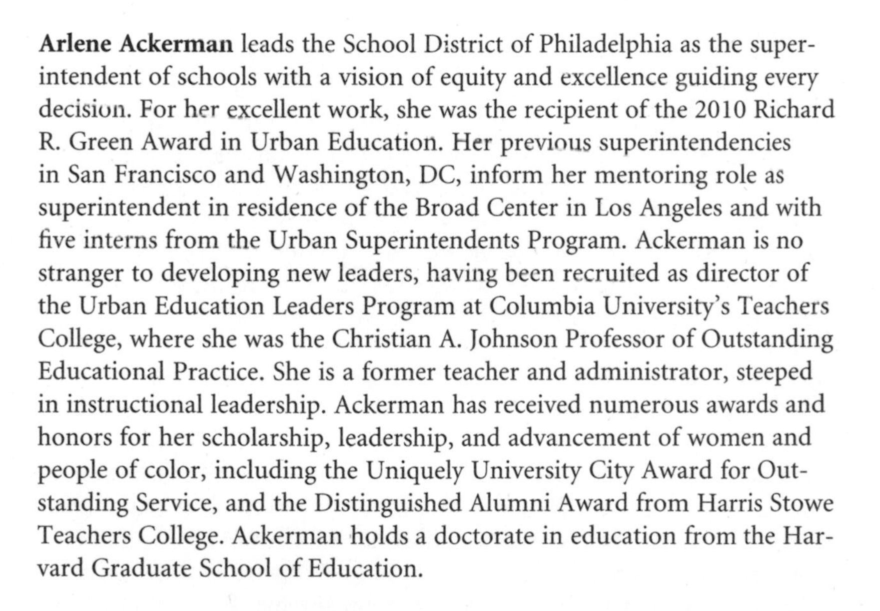

Arlene Ackerman leads the School District of Philadelphia as the superintendent of schools with a vision of equity and excellence guiding every decision. For her excellent work, she was the recipient of the 2010 Richard R. Green Award in Urban Education. Her previous superintendencies in San Francisco and Washington, DC, inform her mentoring role as superintendent in residence of the Broad Center in Los Angeles and with five interns from the Urban Superintendents Program. Ackerman is no stranger to developing new leaders, having been recruited as director of the Urban Education Leaders Program at Columbia University's Teachers College, where she was the Christian A. Johnson Professor of Outstanding Educational Practice. She is a former teacher and administrator, steeped in instructional leadership. Ackerman has received numerous awards and honors for her scholarship, leadership, and advancement of women and people of color, including the Uniquely University City Award for Outstanding Service, and the Distinguished Alumni Award from Harris Stowe Teachers College. Ackerman holds a doctorate in education from the Harvard Graduate School of Education.

Andrés Alonso "defines himself by his fervent commitment to students and families," as a former teacher of special education, as deputy chancellor of the New York City Department of Education, or as CEO of Baltimore City Public Schools. The *Baltimore City Paper* and the Greater Baltimore Committee, among other civic groups, have recognized Alonso's boldness of reform and notable results with awards for his public service and innovative leadership.

From his Fair Student Funding initiative to "Transformation Schools" in Baltimore, Alonso steadfastly believes that turnaround takes place in the classroom. The former attorney has been instrumental in disengaging the school district from its twenty-five-year-old special education consent decree, and the city now boasts increased services for students in need of accommodations. Alonso holds a doctorate in education and a juris doctorate, both from Harvard University.

Leslie Boozer has combined her business and education backgrounds in pursuit of her passion, to provide every child with a high-quality education. Prior to transitioning into teaching, Boozer worked as a business litigation attorney, specializing in contract disputes, negotiation, and employment litigation. Realizing a strong desire to improve the educational outcomes of children, Boozer became a high school teacher in the Los Angeles Unified School District. Most recently she served as an intern to the superintendent of schools of the Long Beach Unified School District, where she led a district task force charged with evaluating and improving the education of English language learners. Boozer is currently at Harvard, where she is working toward a doctorate in education in the Urban Superintendents Program. She holds a juris doctorate degree from the University of Cincinnati College of Law and a master's degree from the Harvard Graduate School of Education. Boozer continues to work closely with practitioners, having served as a consultant to a school district in Mississippi, as a research assistant for the Executive Leadership Program for Educators (ExEL), as an adviser for the university's teacher education program, and as the instructional coordinator and facilitator for the Harvard Institute for School Leadership.

Michele Brooks serves as assistant superintendent of family and community engagement for the Boston Public Schools. She brings over twenty years of advocacy and instructional experience to the city's school system and has previously served as a mayoral appointee on the Boston Schools Committee. As the founding director of the Boston Parent Organizing Network, Brooks coordinated the establishment of a network of community-based organizations and parent and educational advocacy groups focused on engaging parents in the improvement of Boston's public schools. Brooks holds a master's degree in education from the Harvard Graduate School of Education. Both in Boston and as a consultant to other school districts with the firm Transformative Solutions, Brooks is passionate about helping grant every parent's wish that schools "provide my child with a broad range of opportunities and experiences to gain the knowledge and skills to be successful in life."

Meria Joel Carstarphen is known as a superintendent ready to make changes and prepare children to succeed in a global economy. As the superintendent of the Austin Independent School District in Texas, she is already credited with inspiring the school district to take responsibility for its successes and failures. Prior to taking the helm in Austin, she served as the superintendent of St. Paul, Minnesota, and in senior leadership and accountability positions in Washington, DC; Kingsport, Tennessee; and Columbus, Ohio. In recognition for her dedication to closing the achievement gap and improving the educational outcomes of children, Carstarphen was honored in 2009 as one of Scholastic's ten Top Educators Under 40. Having studied extensively abroad, Carstarphen's instructional experience includes teaching Spanish and documentary photography at the middle school level, as well as elementary educational work in Spain and Venezuela. She earned a doctorate in administration, planning, and social policy with a concentration in the urban superintendency from the Harvard Graduate School of Education.

Carl A. Cohn's distinguished career in education has spanned over thirty years, during which he has worked in a variety of educational capacities, including as teacher, counselor, professor, superintendent, and federal court monitor. He is the former superintendent of the Long Beach Unified School District (LBUSD) and the San Diego Unified School District. Under his guidance, LBUSD became a model for high academic standards and accountability. For his commitment to fostering leadership and improving student achievement, he won the McGraw Prize in 2002, and LBUSD won the Broad Prize for Urban Education in 2003. After retiring from the superintendency, Cohn continues to influence educational leadership in California as a member of the Claremont Graduate University faculty. Cohn holds a doctorate in education from the University of California, Los Angeles. Further using his expertise, Cohn works as a faculty advisor for both the Broad Superintendents Academy and the Harvard Urban Superintendents Program.

Kristy Cooper is a doctoral candidate at the Harvard Graduate School of Education, where her research examines the social, organizational, and instructional contexts of schools and classrooms. Kristy has served on the editorial board of the Harvard Educational Review and is a coauthor of the 2009 book *Inside Urban Charter Schools: Promising Practices and Strategies in Five High-Performing Schools*. Prior to attending Harvard, Kristy taught elementary school in Los Angeles for six years and earned her national board certification as a middle-childhood generalist.

Rudolph F. "Rudy" Crew is currently a professor of clinical education at the University of Southern California and the president of Global Partnership Schools. He has developed a reputation for closing the achievement gap between low-income and minority students and their peers, and as superintendent of schools in Miami-Dade County in Florida, where he led the school district as a three-time finalist for the Broad Prize for Urban Education. He was also superintendent of schools in Sacramento, California, Tacoma, Washington, and chancellor of the New York City Department of Education. Crew authored the book *Only Connect: The Way to Save Our Schools* (2007), and the American Association of School Administrators (AASA) awarded Crew National Superintendent of the Year in 2008. A dedicated instructional leader, Crew has served as director of district reform initiatives at the Stupski Foundation and as executive director of the Institute for K–12 Leadership at the University of Washington. Nationally known for guiding some of the nation's largest school districts, he has received many awards, including the NAACP Educational Leadership Award, the Arthur Ashe Leadership Award, the Spirit of Excellence Award from Minority Development & Empowerment, Inc., and the Florida Association of Partners in Education Superintendent's Award. Crew holds a doctorate in education from the University of Massachusetts Amherst.

Amalia Cudeiro is superintendent of the Bellevue School District in Washington. Formerly a senior partner at Targeted Leadership Consulting, Cudeiro was also previously the deputy superintendent for the Boston Public Schools, and principal at both the Santa Monica Unified School District and the Baldwin Park Unified School District in California. Born in Cuba and educated in Spain through high school, Cudeiro completed all of her university work in the United States and possesses the strengths of being fully bilingual and biliterate, with special sensitivity and experience in issues of valuing diversity and bilingual education. During her tenure in the Boston Public Schools, Cudeiro was instrumental in the development of the school district's Principal Evaluation and Accountability Process. Further, in collaboration with the Center for Leadership Development, she engaged in the creation and implementation of a professional development program for current principals and a principal preparation program to hire and train new leaders. Cudeiro has a doctorate in education, from the Urban Superintendents Program at the Harvard Graduate School of Education.

Drew Echelson began work in education as a City Year corps member at the Lewis Middle School in Roxbury, Massachusetts. He later taught first, third, and fourth grade in Hartford, Connecticut. Echelson pursued graduate work at Harvard, where he completed his Ed.M. in School Leadership, Principal Strand. During that time he served as the principal intern at the Richard J. Murphy K–8 School, where he was hired as the director of instruction and concentrated his efforts on new and resident teacher development and support. He was later appointed as principal of the Tucker School, in Milton, Massachusetts, before beginning doctoral studies in the Harvard Urban Superintendents Program. Echelson completed his undergraduate work at the University of Connecticut in sociology and African-American studies.

Aaliyah El-Amin began her commitment to education with Teach for America in Atlanta, Georgia. Subsequently, El-Amin served as instructional facilitator for her Atlanta elementary school, where she supported the teaching staff in their instructional planning and delivery, managed the school's leadership team, and administered the professional development program for teachers. She has also served as the executive director of Teach for America–Charlotte, where she tripled the region's funding base in three years while managing over one hundred teachers in twenty-five schools. El-Amin holds a master's degree in early childhood education from Georgia State University, educational leadership/principal certification from the University of Georgia, and currently is a doctoral student at the Harvard Graduate School of Education.

Richard F. Elmore is the Gregory R. Anrig Professor of Educational Leadership and the director of the Consortium for Policy Research in Education at the Harvard Graduate School of Education. Elmore's research focuses on the effects of federal, state, and local education policy on schools and classrooms. He is currently faculty cochair of the Doctorate in Educational Leadership (Ed.L.D.) program at HGSE. With a belief that "we learn by doing the work, not by telling other people to do the work," Elmore continues to stay involved in practice by facilitating the Connecticut Superintendents Network and the Cambridge (Massachusetts) Principals Network. He has coauthored and edited several books on education, including *Instructional Rounds in Education: A Network Approach to Improving Teaching and Learning* (2009); *Managing School Districts for High Performance: Cases in Public Education Leadership* (2007); and *School Reform from the Inside Out: Policy, Practice, and Performance* (2004). Elmore has a doctorate in education from the Harvard Graduate School of Education.

Pascal D. Forgione Jr. is currently the Distinguished Presidential Scholar and executive director of the Center for K–12 Assessment and Performance Management at Educational Testing Services in Austin, Texas.

Before retiring as superintendent of the Austin Independent School District, he led the system to spearhead many innovative programs designed to improve academic achievement by successfully upholding high standards and quality assessments. From 1996 until 1999 Forgione was U.S. commissioner of education statistics with the National Center for Education Statistics, and from 1991 to 1996 he served as Delaware's state superintendent for public instruction. In addition, Forgione has held positions with the Connecticut State Department of Education, the National Center for Research in Vocational Education at the Ohio State University, the Syracuse Research Corporation, and the Maryland State Department of Education. Forgione has a doctorate in administration and policy analysis from Stanford University, a master's in urban history from Stanford, a master's in educational administration from Loyola College, and a bachelor's in theology and philosophy from St. Mary's Seminary and University.

Maria Goodloe-Johnson has a clear motto as the superintendent of Seattle Public Schools—"Every student achieving, everyone accountable." Prior to taking the lead in Seattle, Goodloe-Johnson was the superintendent of Charleston County School District in South Carolina and had served in multiple capacities, including as assistant superintendent, in Corpus Christi Independent School District in Texas. She began her career as a high school special education teacher and coach in Colorado. With a passion for developing future leaders, she currently serves on the Broad Advisory Board and has been a mentor for the Urban Superintendents Program. She also participates in the Aspen Urban Superintendents Network and the Aspen Institute-New Schools Entrepreneurial Leaders for Public Education program. For her great work, she has won many honors and awards, including being a 2008 fellow in the prestigious Entrepreneurial Leaders for Public Education program. Goodloe-Johnson holds a doctorate in education from the University of Colorado at Denver.

Beverly Hall is the superintendent of Atlanta Public Schools, where she has worked for the past eleven years. Her leadership in dramatically turning around the district has resulted in such recognition as the Richard R. Green Award in Urban Education from the Council of the Great City Schools in 2006 and the AASA 2009 National Superintendent of the Year. Prior to her tenure in Atlanta, Hall was superintendent in Newark, New Jersey, where she was the first person to lead the city's schools after the state takeover in 1995. Spending most of her early career as a teacher, principal, and administrator in the New York City Public Schools, she has a lifetime of experience in developing the comprehensive reform needed to turn around Atlanta, named by many as the "model of urban school reform" under Hall's leadership. Hall holds a doctorate in education from Fordham University.

James P. Honan is a senior lecturer at the Harvard Graduate School of Education. With a background working in financial management of nonprofit organizations, he teaches courses on organizational performance measurement and management, as well as higher education administration. At Harvard he is the educational co-chair of the Institute for Educational Management (IEM) and a faculty member in a number of executive education programs for educational leaders and nonprofit administrators. Honan has served as a consultant on strategic planning, resource allocation, and performance measurement and management to numerous colleges, universities, schools, and nonprofit organizations, both nationally and internationally. Honan holds a doctorate in education from the Harvard Graduate School of Education.

Paul D. Houston served as executive director of the American Association of School Administrators from 1994 to 2008, quickly establishing himself as one of the leading spokespersons for American public education through his extensive U.S. and international speaking engagements, published articles, and media interviews. Prior to joining AASA, Houston was superintendent of schools in three uniquely different public education systems: Princeton, New Jersey; Tucson, Arizona; and Riverside, California. His K–12 education experience also includes serving as an assistant superintendent in Birmingham, Alabama, and as a teacher and building administrator in North Carolina and New Jersey. His work in education has brought him numerous awards and accolades, including being honored by the Council of the Great City Schools for his leadership in urban education when he received the Richard R. Green Award in Urban Education. An undeniable voice in urban education, Houston has published more than two hundred articles in professional journals and has authored or coauthored multiple books, including *The Spiritual Dimension of Leadership: Eight Key Principles to Leading More Effectively* (2006) with Stephen L. Sokolow, *The Board-Savvy Superintendent* (2002), and *Exploding the Myths* (1993). Houston holds a doctorate in education from the Harvard Graduate School of Education.

Janice Jackson was most recently a lecturer in educational leadership and organizations at the Harvard Graduate School of Education and the senior associate on the Wallace Foundation–funded Executive Leadership Program for Educators. The former deputy superintendent of the Boston Public Schools and deputy assistant secretary for elementary and secondary education for the U.S. Department of Education consulted with district and state leadership teams to bring high-quality teaching and learning practices to scale. Prior to coming to Harvard she was an assistant professor at Boston College with a joint appointment in the Department of Teacher Education/Special Education, Curriculum & Instruction and the Department of Educational Administration and Higher Education. Jackson believes "to the child, the deepest reverence is due." Jackson holds a doctorate in education from the Urban Superintendents Program at the Harvard Graduate School of Education.

Deborah Jewell-Sherman is a graduate of the Harvard Graduate School of Education's Urban Superintendents Program and has built a reputation over the past decade as one of the most successful urban district superintendents in the country. Prior to joining the Harvard Graduate School of Education's faculty, Dr. Jewell-Sherman assumed the superintendency of the Richmond (VA) Public Schools in 2002 and signed a performance contract that stipulated she would improve student performance by 100 percent in one year or she could be terminated for cause. She exceeded the terms of her contract and amassed a track record of successes that culminated in her being named Virginia Superintendent of the Year 2009 by the Virginia Association of School Superintendents (VASS). During her six-year appointment as superintendent, 95 percent of Richmond's lowest-performing schools achieved full accreditation under Virginia's Standards of Learning assessments. Additionally, the district improved from 18 percent to 91.7 percent of all schools meeting this standard as measured by the state department of education (2008). Currently, Dr. Jewell-Sherman serves as the director of the Urban Superintendents Program, a key faculty member for HGSE's new Doctor of Education Leadership Degree Program, and as co-principal investigator for an initiative between HGSE and the University of Johannesburg in South Africa.

Christine M. Johns is the superintendent of the second-largest district in Michigan. In four years as superintendent, she has improved student achievement, secured in excess of $13 million in grant funds, and passed a $112 million bond issue. She has been deputy superintendent for curriculum and instruction in Baltimore County Public Schools in Maryland; assistant superintendent for instructional services in Pasadena, California; and an elementary school principal, instructional specialist, and teacher in Prince George's County, Maryland. Throughout her career she has increased student achievement for all children and has a consistent track record of developing partnerships and community engagement. She holds a doctorate in education in administration, planning, and social policy from Harvard University and the Urban Superintendents Program, as well as a master of science degree from Johns Hopkins University; she was a Broad Fellow in the Urban Superintendents Academy.

Carol Johnson is the superintendent of the Boston Public Schools. Johnson has a wealth of experience in public education as a teacher, principal, and administrator. She previously served as superintendent of Memphis City Schools, during which time she was recognized as the Tennessee Superintendent of the Year. Johnson has also served as superintendent of Minneapolis Public Schools, where she was also named Minnesota Superintendent of the Year, and as the superintendent of St. Louis Park Public Schools in Minnesota. Johnson is the recipient of numerous awards and honors, including the Joseph E. Hill Superintendent of the Year Award (2008). Committed to national policy change, Johnson serves as chair-elect of the board of directors for the Council of the Great City Schools, and on the Spencer Foundation Board, the Harvard University Urban Superintendents Program Advisory Board, and the College Board. Johnson holds a doctorate in education from the University of Minnesota.

Susan Moore Johnson is the Jerome T. Murphy Professor of Education at the Harvard Graduate School of Education, where she studies and teaches about teacher policy, organizational change, unions, and administrative practice. A former high school teacher and administrator, she has a continuing research interest in the work of teachers and the reform of schools. Johnson and a group of advanced doctoral students are currently engaged in a multiyear research study, the Project on the Next Generation of Teachers, which continues to examine how best to recruit, support, and retain a strong teaching force. Johnson is an author and editor of several books, including *Managing School Districts for High Performance: Cases in Public Education Leadership* (2007); *Finders and Keepers: Helping New Teachers Survive and Thrive in Our Schools* (with the Project on the Next Generation of Teachers, 2004); *Leading to Change: The Challenge of the New Superintendency* (1996); *Teachers at Work: Achieving Success in Our Schools* (1990), and *Teacher Unions in Schools* (1984). Johnson holds a doctorate in education from the Harvard Graduate School of Education.

Laura Kelley has committed to serving some of our country's most vulnerable students and populations as a social worker and urban educator. She taught elementary school in District of Columbia Public Schools and worked in Boston as a social worker. As an instructional coach in the Baltimore City and Boston public school districts, Kelley has focused her attention on helping teachers improve the educational experiences of children in the classroom. In addition, she has worked as an adjunct instructor in literacy at Trinity University and as director of professional development for a private, nonprofit literacy organization in Washington, DC. She works and studies with Harvard's Urban Superintendents Program, supporting aspiring superintendents in their learning of systemic school leadership as she hones her own leadership skill set as intern to the superintendent of Rochester City School District Jean-Claude Brizard. She is pursuing her doctoral degree at Harvard and holds a master's in education in administration, planning, and social policy from Harvard University and a master's in clinical social work from Boston University.

Larry Leverett is oft referred to by the descriptor he coined about distributing leadership and his dedication to parity: "equity warrior." He is currently the executive director of the Panasonic Foundation, a corporate foundation with a mission to help public school systems with high percentages of children in poverty improve learning for all students so that they may use their minds well and become productive, responsible citizens. Leverett served as superintendent of schools in Greenwich, Connecticut, and Plainfield, New Jersey. His career in education has also included urban and suburban experiences as a classroom teacher, elementary principal, assistant superintendent, school board member, and assistant state commissioner of education. Leverett serves on advisory committees for the George Lucas Educational Foundation, Educators for Social Responsibility, the Urban Superintendents Program Advisory Board, and the Laura Bush Foundation for School Libraries; he also heads the New Jersey Superintendents Network to improve leadership's understanding of the instructional core. Leverett holds a doctorate in education from Columbia University's Teachers College.

Karen L. Mapp is a lecturer at the Harvard Graduate School of Education (HGSE), where she teaches and conducts research in the areas of educational leadership and educational partnerships among schools, families, and community members. Before coming to HGSE, Mapp was the interim deputy superintendent of family and community engagement for the Boston Public Schools (BPS). While at BPS, she continued to fulfill her duties as president of the Institute for Responsive Education (IRE), an organization that conducts research on and advocates for effective school, family, and community partnerships to support the educational development of children. She is the author of several articles, including "Making the Connection Between Families and Schools," published by the *Harvard Education Letter* (1997), and "Having Their Say: Parents Describe How and Why They Are Engaged in Their Children's Learning" in the *School Community Journal* (2002). She also coauthored with Anne Henderson *A New Wave of Evidence: The Impact of School, Family, and Community Connections on Student Achievement* (2002) and is an author of *Beyond* *the Bake Sale: The Essential Guide to Family/School Partnerships* (2007). Mapp holds a doctorate in education from the Harvard Graduate School of Education.

Brian G. Osborne is superintendent of schools in South Orange and Maplewood, New Jersey, taking the helm after a four-year period as chief of staff for teaching and learning in the New York City Department of Education. Prior to leading in New York he served in Plainfield, New Jersey, directing the district's accountability initiative, training school leaders in data-driven instructional decision making, and evaluating impact on student achievement. Osborne began his career in education as an elementary school teacher, and he cofounded a public high school in the South Bronx. Under his leadership in South Orange and Maplewood, the district is intensely focused on improving teaching and learning for every child, in every classroom, every day. Osborne holds a master's in education and is pursuing a doctorate in the Urban Superintendents Program from the Harvard Graduate School of Education.

Robert S. Peterkin is the Professor of Practice Emeritus and former Francis Keppel Professor on Educational Policy and Administration and director of the Harvard Graduate School of Education's Urban Superintendents Program, where he served from 1991 to 2010. Prior to his work at Harvard, Peterkin was the superintendent of schools in Milwaukee, Wisconsin, and Cambridge, Massachusetts. His early career as a special education teacher and principal before working in several central office positions in the Boston Public Schools informed his commitment to serving all students at high levels, including those traditionally "at the margins." Peterkin is a national expert on desegregation cases and for seven years acted as the court-appointed monitor for a school district federal court consent decree. His continuing leadership in education includes heading transition teams for numerous entering superintendents and advising the New Jersey Superintendents Network, dedicated to transforming public schools by focusing on the instructional core. Peterkin holds a doctorate in education from the University of Massachusetts Amherst. He received the Chancellor's Medal from the University of Massachusetts Amherst in 2002 and the Effie H. Jones Humanitarian Award from AASA, which honors educational equity and excellence, in 2006.

Maree Sneed is a partner in the Washington, DC, law firm of Hogan & Hartson, where she specializes in education law. She is a former teacher and administrator with school systems in Maryland and Oklahoma and has been involved in litigating on behalf of school districts in both state and federal courts. Most recently she was counsel of record in two Supreme Court cases, *Schaffer* v. *Weast* and *Parents Involved in Community Schools* v. *Seattle School District No. 1*. She has counseled school districts on the development of policies and plans for English language learners and on racial and sexual harassment, and she has assisted school districts in developing court-ordered and voluntary student assignment plans—as well as magnet plans and policies—including those that comply with the requirements of the federal Magnet Schools Assistance Project. Sneed was on the faculty of the Harvard Graduate School of Education for ten years. She was a board member for Teach for America, Washington, DC, and a board member and secretary of the National School Boards Foundation. Sneed holds a juris doctorate from Georgetown University Law Center, a doctorate in education from the George Washington University, and a master's in education from the University of Oklahoma.

Joshua P. Starr is the superintendent of the Stamford Public Schools in Connecticut. He has been the director of school performance and accountability for the New York City Department of Education, where he helped design a comprehensive approach to measuring school performance. He has served as deputy senior instructional manager in the New York City Department of Education; the executive director of operations for Freeport School District in New York; and the director of accountability for the Plainfield Public Schools in New Jersey. He began his career in education as a special education teacher in Brooklyn, NY. Starr holds a doctorate in education from the Urban Superintendents Program at the Harvard Graduate School of Education.

Christopher "Chris" Steinhauser is the superintendent of the Long Beach Unified School District in California. Over the past nine years of his leadership, the school district has been a four-time Broad Prize for Urban Education finalist, winning the award in 2003. He has earned a well-deserved national reputation for improving student achievement and regularly collaborates with school districts around the country. A twenty-eight-year veteran educator, Steinhauser has served as a teacher, principal, and central office administrator. For his work in closing the achievement gap and increasing college readiness, Steinhauser has received numerous awards and honors, including the Harvard Club's Excellence in Education Award and the College Board's Joe Allen Exemplar Award, and he has been a finalist for the Richard R. Green Award in Urban Education. Steinhauser has a master's in education from California State University, Long Beach.

Rebecca A. Thessin is an assistant professor of educational administration at The George Washington University Graduate School of Education and Human Development. While training new school leaders at George Washington, she consults with school districts and conducts research. Her research focuses primarily on effective professional development for teachers and administrators, the use of data to improve instruction, school improvement, and urban district leadership. Prior to her current position, she served as the director of school improvement and professional development in Stamford, Connecticut, where she led the district's implementation of an improvement process for professional learning communities and formed a professional development council to author a professional learning plan for Stamford. She first became committed to improving teaching and learning from the school and district levels while coordinating professional development for principals as the aide to the deputy superintendent in the Boston Public Schools and then serving as an administrator at a Boston high school. Thessin began her career in urban education as a high school teacher in Connecticut, Massachusetts, and West Virginia. She holds a doctorate in the urban superintendency from the Harvard Graduate School of Education.

Holly Weeks is adjunct lecturer in management leadership and development science at the Harvard Kennedy School and visiting Professional Seminar instructor in communication and the vision speech at the Harvard Graduate School of Education. She teaches, writes, and consults on communications issues through Holly Weeks Communications. Her publications, broadcasts, and blogs range from *Failure to Communicate: How Conversations Go Wrong and What You Can Do to Right Them* (2008) to articles for the *Harvard Business Review* and *O, the Oprah Magazine,* to pieces for ESPN Radio and CBS News Sunday. She was an associate in communications in the Harvard Business School MBA Program and Distinguished Instructor in management communication, negotiation, and conflict resolution at the Radcliffe Institute of Harvard University. She has a master's degree in English literature from the University of Edinburgh and a bachelor's degree cum laude in English and American language and literature from Harvard College.

WHAT'S ON THE CD AND HOW TO USE IT

The CD included in this book has been developed to support the work of instructors and facilitators in effectively using the teaching cases included in *Every Child, Every Classroom, Every Day.* To accompany each case, the CD offers both teaching notes and exhibits intended to assist instructors in setting the stage for active learning and engagement in the major facets of the work of urban school leaders. Although there are an endless number of lesson objectives and teaching activities that could be developed to support the cases included in this book, the teaching notes and exhibits included can assist instructors in *initiating* such learning conversations on the work of urban leaders. In effectively using the case method of teaching, instructors and participants then share collective responsibility in shaping the resultant outcome.

Within each section of teaching notes, professional development facilitators, instructors in the graduate classroom, and urban leaders engaging their own leadership teams in discussions of theory and practice will find suggested activities and reflective questions to use in framing conversations focused on aspects of the USP Leadership Framework—equity, collaboration, accountability, and policy and best practices. Specifically, each teaching notes section includes

- Lesson objectives on which to focus a case conversation
- Guiding questions to use in class or as the case is read
- A forty-five- to sixty-minute teaching activity
- Questions for reflection to connect the case to the participants' real-life experiences in schools and districts

The exhibits included on the CD, which have been referenced in the teaching cases, offer the reader and the case facilitator additional clarity on the work of urban leaders and the outcomes of this work in each of the districts portrayed. Charts, tables, and sample documents have been provided with this intent. To accompany Chapter Four, for instance, the exhibits offer both demographic and achievement data for the Seattle public schools as well as illustrations of the PELP Coherence Framework, Seattle's strategic plan, and the district scorecard.

Instructors and facilitators may consider asking participants to use the tools provided on the CD as they read a case and prepare to engage in a case discussion. Alternatively, a facilitator may elect to use the guiding and reflective questions as part of the collective case discussion, and the exhibits could be viewed and analyzed by the participant group as a whole. Facilitators are also encouraged to review the introduction located on the CD itself to gain greater understanding of the case method of teaching and how the teaching notes might be used to support this type of collaborative learning.

In assembling this CD, we intended to provide tools for facilitators to use in employing the case method of teaching as they unpack the four core values of the USP Leadership Framework. We did not, however, intend to dictate the learning conversation, and encourage instructors to learn collectively with participants in analyzing the actions and decisions taken by the urban superintendents portrayed in this book.

SYSTEM REQUIREMENTS

PC with Microsoft Windows 2003 or later
Mac with Apple OS version 10.1 or later

USING THE CD WITH WINDOWS

To view the items located on the CD, follow these steps:

1. Insert the CD into your computer's CD-ROM drive.
2. A window appears with the following options:

    Contents: Allows you to view the files included on the CD.

    Software: Allows you to install useful software from the CD.

    Links: Displays a hyperlinked page of Web sites.

    Author: Displays a page with information about the author(s).

    Contact Us: Displays a page with information on contacting the publisher or author.

    Help: Displays a page with information on using the CD.

    Exit: Closes the interface window.

If you do not have autorun enabled, or if the autorun window does not appear, follow these steps to access the CD:

1. Click Start → Run.
2. In the dialog box that appears, type d:\start.exe, where d is the letter of your CD-ROM drive. This brings up the autorun window described in the preceding set of steps.

3. Choose the desired option from the menu. (See Step 2 in the preceding list for a description of these options.)

IN CASE OF TROUBLE

If you experience difficulty using the CD, please follow these steps:

1. Make sure your hardware and systems configurations conform to the systems requirements noted under "System Requirements" above.
2. Review the installation procedure for your type of hardware and operating system. It is possible to reinstall the software if necessary.

To speak with someone in Product Technical Support, call 800-762-2974 or 317-572-3994 Monday through Friday from 8:30 A.M. to 5:00 P.M. EST. You can also contact Product Technical Support and get support information through our Web site at www.wiley.com/techsupport.

Before calling or writing, please have the following information available:

- Type of computer and operating system.
- Any error messages displayed.
- Complete description of the problem.

It is best if you are sitting at your computer when making the call.

Published by Jossey-Bass
A Wiley Imprint

PART #: 978-K-PART-1948-6
Packaged with ISBN-13: 978-0-470-6-5176-6

INDEX

Page references followed by *fig* indicate an illustrated figure

C

D

E

F

G

R

S

T